Aspects of Love in John Gower'
Confessio Amantis

Medieval History and Culture
Volume 25

STUDIES IN MEDIEVAL HISTORY AND CULTURE

Edited by
Francis G. Gentry
Professor of German
Pennsylvania State University

A ROUTLEDGE SERIES

Studies in Medieval History and Culture
Francis G. Gentry, *General Editor*

1. "And Then the End Will Come"
   Early Latin Christian Interpretations of the Opening of the Seven Seals
   Douglas W. Lumsden

2. Topographies of Gender in Middle High German Arthurian Romance
   Alexandra Sterling-Hellenbrand

3. Christian, Saracen and Genre in Medieval French Literature
   Imagination and Cultural Interaction in the French Middle Ages
   Lynn Tarte Ramey

4. Word Outward
   Medieval Perspectives on the Entry into Language
   Corey J. Marvin

5. Justice and the Social Context of Early Middle High German Literature
   Robert G. Sullivan

6. Marriage Fictions in Old French Secular Narratives, 1170–1250
   A Critical Re-evaluation of the Courtly Love Debate
   Keith A. Nicklaus

7. Where Troubadours Were Bishops
   The Occitania of Folc of Marseille (1150–1231)
   N. M. Schulman

8. John Cassian and the Reading of Egyptian Monastic Culture
   Steven D. Driver

9. Choosing Not to Marry
   Women and Autonomy in the Katherine Group
   Julie Hassel

10. Feminine Figurae
    Representations of Gender in Religious Texts by Medieval German Women Writers
    Rebecca L. R. Garber

11. Bodies of Pain
    Suffering in the Works of Hartmann von Aue
    Scott E. Pincikowski

12. The Literal Sense and the Gospel of John in Late Medieval Commentary and Literature
    Mark Hazard

13. The Reproductive Unconscious in Late Medieval and Early Modern England
    Jennifer Wynne Hellwarth

14. Mystical Language of Sense in the Later Middle Ages
    Gordon Rudy

15. Fair and Varied Forms
    Visual Textuality in Medieval Illustrated Manuscripts
    Mary C. Olson

16. Queens in the Cult of the French Renaissance Monarchy
    Public Law, Royal Ceremonial, and Political Discourse in the History of Regency Government, 1484–1610
    Elizabeth A. McCartney

17. The Contested Theological Authority of Thomas Aquinas
    The Controversies between Hervaeus Natalis and Durandus of St. Pourçain
    Elizabeth Lowe

18. Body and Sacred Place in Medieval Europe, 1100–1389
    Dawn Marie Hayes

19. Women of the Humiliati
    A Lay Religious Order in Medieval Civic Life
    Sally Mayall Brasher

20. Consuming Passions
    The Uses of Cannibalism in Late Medieval and Early Modern Europe
    Merrall Llewelyn Price

21. Literary Hybrids
    Cross-dressing, Shapeshifting, and Indeterminacy in Medieval and Modern French Narrative
    Erika E. Hess

22. The King's Two Maps
    Cartography and Culture in Thirteenth-Century England
    Daniel Birkholz

23. Pestilence in Medieval and Early Modern English Literature
    Bryon Lee Grigsby

24. Race and Ethnicity in Anglo-Saxon Literature
    Stephen J. Harris

Aspects of Love in John Gower's
Confessio Amantis

Ellen Shaw Bakalian

Taylor & Francis Group
NEW YORK AND LONDON

Published in 2004 by
Routledge
605 Third Avenue, New York, NY 10017
4 Park Square, Milton Park, Abingdon, Oxon OX14 4RN

Routledge is an imprint of the Taylor & Francis Group, an informa business

Copyright © 2004 by Taylor & Francis Books, Inc.

All rights reserved. No part of this book may be reprinted or reproduced or utilized in any form or by any electronic, mechanical, or other means, now known or hereafter invented, including photocopying and recording, or in any information storage or retrieval system, without permission in writing from the publisher.

Notice:
Product or corporate names may be trademarks or registered trademarks and are used only for identification and explanation without intent to infringe.

First issued in papperback 2013

ISBN 13: 978-0-415-86144-1 (pbk)
ISBN 13: 978-0-415-96976-5 (hbk)

Library of Congress Cataloging-in-Publication Data
Bakalian, Ellen Shaw.
  Aspects of love in John Gower's Confessio amantis / by Ellen Shaw Bakalian.
    p. cm. — (Studies in medieval history and culture ; v. 25)
  Includes bibliographical references (p.) and index
  ISBN 0-415-96976-X (hardcover : alk. paper)
    1. Gower, John, 1325?–1408. Confessio amantis. 2. Tales, Medieval—History and criticism. 3. Love in literature. I. Title. II. Series.
PR1984.C63B34 2003
821'.1—dc21   2003015930

Series Editor Foreword

Far from providing just a musty whiff of yesteryear, research in Medieval Studies enters the new century as fresh and vigorous as never before. Scholars representing all disciplines and generations are consistently producing works of research of the highest caliber, utilizing new approaches and methodologies. Volumes in the Medieval History and Culture series will include studies on individual works and authors of Latin and vernacular literatures, historical personalities and events, theological and philosophical issues, and new critical approaches to medieval literature and culture.

Momentous changes have occurred in Medieval Studies in the past thirty years in teaching as well as in scholarship. Thus the goal of the Medieval History and Culture series is to enhance research in the field by providing an outlet for monographs by scholars in the early stages of their careers on all topics related to the broad scope of Medieval Studies, while at the same time pointing to and highlighting new directions that will shape and define scholarly discourse in the future.

Francis G. Gentry

For my parents, Grace and Karekin, whose encouragement and love I have always relied upon; for Professor Robert R. Raymo, whose enthusiasm and invaluable help has sustained me; for my two young daughters, Margaret and Charlotte, who bring me fresh joy each morning; and especially for my "swete herte" Jeff, whose indulgence and love enabled me to write this book, in its dissertation form.

In memory of my "worldes blysse," Jeffrey R. Smith
(4/19/65-9/11/01)
"To lytel while our blysse lasteth!" (BD 209-11)

Contents

ACKNOWLEDGMENTS   xiii
ABBREVIATIONS   xv
INTRODUCTION   xvii

CHAPTER ONE
The Struggle between Nature and Reason in Gower's *Confessio Amantis*   3

    The Tale of Rosemund   12
    The Tale of Thisbe   20
    Conclusion   31

CHAPTER TWO
Marriage and the Four Wives   33

    The Tale of Penelope   35
    The Tale of Alceone   45
    The Tale of Alcestis   52
    The Tale of Lucrece   57
    Conclusion   73

CHAPTER THREE
The Love Relationships of the Forsaken Women   77

    The Tale of Deianira   80
    The Tale of Medea   85
    The Tale of Dido   100
    The Tale of Phyllis   105

    The Tale of Ariadne   113
    Conclusion   120

CHAPTER FOUR
Lovesickness in the *Confessio Amantis*   123

Conclusion   153

NOTES   161
BIBLIOGRAPHY   189
INDEX   197

Acknowledgments

I WOULD LIKE TO ACKNOWLEDGE AND THANK PAUL FOSTER JOHNSON, DISSERTATIONS Editor at Routledge, for contacting me about revising my dissertation. I would also like to thank Francis G. Gentry for reading my work and giving me the green light at Routledge. It was a pleasure to find myself back in the library, writing about Gower and Aspects of Love, even though my mind often dwelled on memories of my marriage, which was shattered on September 11, 2001. I too well know how it feels to have one's "herte blede" (TC I.504), and I know that I suffer most grievously from lovesickness.

I discovered John Gower's poetry as a doctoral candidate at New York University. When I first read the *Confessio Amantis* I found myself drawn to Gower's Tales of Love. I will always remember my dissertation advisor's enthusiastic response when I tentatively told him I was going to write on Gower—there was no turning back after that meeting. If ever there was a wonderful teacher, a very learned scholar who inspires others, it is Robert R. Raymo, whom I am pleased to call my good friend.

My husband Jeff was enthusiastic about my work, and we enjoyed talking about Gower's Tales of Love on our walks home from the NYU library. It is with great sadness that I see this work published without Jeff by my side; it is yet another "blody teris" in my heart (TC III.1445).

Abbreviations

Gower

CA	*Confessio Amantis*
MO	*Mirour de l'omme*
VC	*Vox Clamantis*
Tr	*Traitié pour essampler les amantz marietz*

Chaucer

BD	*Book of the Duchess*
HF	*The House of Fame*
PF	*Parliament of Fowls*
KnT	*Knight's Tale*
TC	*Troilus and Criseyde*
GP	*General Prologue*
MkT	*Monk's Tale*
MerT	*Merchant's Tale*
MLT	*Man of Law's Tale*
FranT	*Franklin's Tale*
LGW	*Legend of Good Women*

Ovid

RA	*Remedia Amoris*
AA	*Ars Amatoria*
Am.	*Amores*
Met.	*Metamorphoses*
Her.	*Heroides*
Fasti	*Fasti*

Other Texts

RR	*Roman de la Rose*
DP	*De Planctu Naturae*
ST	*Summa Theologiæ*
Aen.	*Aeneas*
PT	*Piramus et Tisbe*, Matthew of Vendôme
Troy	*Historia Destructionis Troiae*, Guido delle Colonne
Viaticum	*Viaticum*, Constantine the African
Peter *Viaticum B*	Questions on the *Viaticum, B*, Peter of Spain
Gerard *Glosses*	Glosses on the *Viaticum*, Gerard of Berry
Johannes *Liber*	The *Liber de heros morbo*, Johannes Afflacius

Introduction

MODIFYING NATURE, KEEPING ONE'S NATURAL INSTINCTS UNDER REASON'S control, and learning to love properly is a duty which Genius tries to teach Amans in John Gower's *Confessio Amantis* (1390–1392).[1] The traditional conflict between man's *kinde* or nature and his reason is a common theme in medieval literature, and it is the thread which runs through the tales of love Gower tells in the *Confessio*. Gower uses the word *kinde* to denote sexual love, the natural law of mankind and animals, "the forces and instincts controlling the physical world."[2] Gower never denies mankind's sexuality, but he continually stresses that reason, not *kinde* or passion, must rule man and woman in love matters. Without reason guiding man, society and the civilized life Gower so wanted to preserve would slowly unravel. To Gower, marriage offers man the perfect reconciliation between the dueling forces of nature or *kinde* and reason, and throughout the tales in the *Confessio* he proposes "honeste love," a reciprocal love which "dar schewen the visage / In alle places openly," as the remedy to what ails man and society (CA IV.1478–79). This book explores how Gower uses the aspects of love in the *Confessio*—the notions of *kinde* and reason in the sphere of love; "honeste love" in marriage; passionate and excessive love; and lovesickness—to emphasize and to illustrate his beliefs that reason must rule man in all things, including his natural instincts to love.

Gower writes in the tradition of those poets who view reason as a restraining force in society, and he writes about the struggle between Nature and Reason in the *Confessio*, as I outline in chapter one. Gower drew upon Alan de Lille's *De Planctu Naturæ* and *Anticlaudianus*, and Guillaume de Lorris and Jean de Meun's *Roman de la Rose*, writers who are influenced by Boethius' *Consolation of Philosophy* and Bernard Silvestris' *De mundi universitate (Cosmographia)*. I examine Alan's *De Planctu Naturæ* and Guillaume and Jean's *Roman de la Rose*, two works which influenced Gower in his effort to write a poem which goes "the middel weie" between *kinde* and reason (CA Prol.17). In this chapter I also examine the Tale of Albinus and Rosemund and the Tale of Pyramus and Thisbe to discover how the Confessor Genius uses these tales to teach Amans to temper his passionate nature with reasonable behavior. My argument is supported with passages from Gower's *Mirour de l'Omme* (1376–79),[3] *Vox Clamantis* (1378–83),[4] and *Traitié pour essampler les amantz marietz* (1397).[5] In the Tale of Albinus and Rosemund,[6] the married lovers are guilty of the sin of Pride, the first Deadly Sin. Gower explores this vice and its Daughter sin of Vain Glory in a tale in which a marriage rapidly unravels. With this tale Gower illustrates how a prideful man destroys the perfect harmony and love within his world. The second tale examined in this chapter, the Tale of Pyramus and Thisbe, is one of intense and emotional pathos.[7] In this tale of double suicide, Gower emphasizes the lovers' irrational failure to rely upon their reason, and I reiterate Gower's position that both men and women are held accountable for their actions.

Chapter two considers what I term the Marriage Tales of the Four Wives: Penelope, Lucrece, Alcestis, and Alceone. The Four Wives are the esteemed married ladies who march in the Company of Lovers past the semi-conscious Amans at the poem's end. The Four Wives tales are found in Ovid and in Geoffrey Chaucer,[8] but Gower treats them differently for his purpose is to illustrate "honeste love" in marriage. I compare Gower's treatment of the marriages of the Four Wives to his presentation of marriage in general in the *Mirour*, *Vox*, and *Traitié*, whenever possible; no scholarly research examines this aspect in Gower.[9] Each of the Four Wives and their husbands enjoy a mutual and reciprocal love, and in their marriages reason tempers sexual passion; hence their worlds exude peace and harmony. The high regard with which Gower presents the Four Wives corroborates his strong belief that marriage is the legitimate means for man to control his passions, and live properly in God's eyes.

Chapter three examines the love relationships of the Forsaken Women—Deianira, Medea, Dido, Phyllis, and Ariadne—another group of women who walk by Amans in the Company of Lovers. The Forsaken Women all make foolish love choices, and are led by passion to disregard reason and indulge in sexual liaisons, most without the benefit of a legitimate marriage bond, and they are thus abandoned by men who are unfaithful. I group the Forsaken Women together in order to examine and compare their love decisions to the Four Wives, and to Gower's sources. Genius uses the tales of the Forsaken Women and their love relationships to remind Amans that mankind should uphold the law of *kinde* and anyone who satisfies his or her sexual desires without the sanctity of marriage is guilty of sin. Over the years Gower's Tale of Jason and Medea has been singled out as one of his very best.[10] Scholarship on Deianira, Phyllis, and Ariadne tends to focus on Gower's sources and on Chaucer, not Gower, and much of my work is therefore new.[11] The tales examined in this chapter feature men and women who are ruled by *kinde* or passion, and who consequently live in a world mired in discordia, revenge, destruction, and death.

Chapter four takes the aspect of lovesickness, a disease treated as a serious illness by medical practitioners in the Middle Ages, and examines how Gower uses it in the frame of the *Confessio*. Lovesickness is a disruptive force that causes man to act irrationally and to abandon his reason. The penitent Amans is a lovesick man whose symptoms are conventional, but his cure, an admonition to leave Love by the Goddess Venus herself, is unique. Amans' unbalanced love and the lovesick behavior which ensues runs directly counter to the poet's belief in an ordered universe, in which man is ruled by reason, not passion, and love leads to marriage. Recently Mary Wack published a book on lovesickness in the Middle Ages, focusing upon the medieval medical texts with which Gower was more than likely familiar.[12] I compare the medieval medical commentator's definitions of and cures for lovesickness with those defined in the *Confessio*, while noting the similarities between how lovesickness is portrayed in Gower, Chaucer, and Ovid.[13]

Scholars such as Derek Pearsall and Linda Barney Burke have asserted that Gower is sympathetic to women; and indeed, the *Confessio* lacks the anti-feminist tone found in contemporary literature, including Gower's own works, the *Mirour* and the *Vox*.[14] Although I agree that Gower treats women in a sympathetic light, I argue that Gower is a humane poet, giving fair treatment to either gender. Gower places great emphasis on how each man and woman rules him or herself, believing that discordia or concordia in the world at large results from each man or woman's personal behavior, from the king down to the peasant. In Book VII of the *Confessio*, Gower strives to teach young King Richard II how to rule England properly, writing that if the king tempers his own behavior with reason and moderation, the kingdom as a whole will benefit, resulting in an England engulfed in harmony. In the love tales of the *Confessio*, Gower puts forth his belief in a man ordered by reason, a microcosm which thus influences the macrocosm of the world. I focus upon Gower's underlying theme of "honeste love" in marriage as the means to achieve this harmonious world.[15]

Most scholarship on the women characters from antiquity tends to focus on their roles as victims at the hands of men. In the *Confessio*, however, I believe Gower utilizes the Four Wives and the Forsaken Women to illustrate his belief that women and men are responsible for their actions in love and thus to God. It is, again, in the microcosm of these *exempla* that Genius teaches Amans how to love and thus live properly. By writing on both the tales of the Four Wives and the Forsaken Women I highlight the differences in their relationships, and note that each woman receives her due reward for her actions in love, as I trace the underlying thread of "honeste love" that Gower advocates in the *Confessio*. The poet's concern with *discordia* in the world along with his illustrations of the destruction of peace and harmony are wrapped in his desire for love to succeed. He believes that man and woman are equally accountable for their actions in love and thus life, and the tales in the *Confessio* emphasize this responsibility. In Gower the successful partnerships and marriages in the *Confessio* each have a woman who speaks and acts, and a man who pledges and keeps his vow of fidelity. These are the lovers who will succeed for the love they share is balanced and "wel at ese" (CA IV.1476).

Aspects of Love in John Gower's
Confessio Amantis

Chapter One

The Struggle between Nature and Reason in Gower's *Confessio Amantis*

THE MEDIEVAL PLATONISM THAT DEVELOPED AT CHARTRES DURING THE renaissance of the twelfth century gave shape to the idea that the goddess Nature ruled on earth as God's subordinate.¹ The efforts of the early writers, notably Bernard Silvestris and Alan of Lille, whose seminal works conceived the medieval goddess Nature, place her within "the context of the Christian faith," which lead to some of "the most distinctive characteristics of the allegorical goddess."² In their writings—Bernard's *De Mundi Universitate* (*Cosmographia*) (1145–1156),³ and Alan's *De Planctu naturæ* (1160–1165)⁴ and *Anticlaudianus* (1181–1184)—these Christian poets sought to defend God and the Christian faith against pagan philosophy. In her role as God's vice-regent on earth, Nature became a teacher and a guide of truth for mankind. In Bernard and in Alan of Lille Nature assumes the central position from which she expresses her conviction that man is capable of using his reason to guide him through an understanding of the moral order of the natural world.⁵ Bernard's *De Mundi Universitate* (*Cosmographia*) paved the way for subsequent poets to explore the relationship between mankind and nature, including Alan, Jean de Meun, Chaucer, and Gower.⁶ I begin by examining the notions of *kinde* or nature and reason in the *De Planctu* and Guillaume de Lorris and Jean de Meun's *Roman de la Rose* (1237; 1275–1280), works upon which Gower drew, before turning to two tales in the *Confessio*, the Tale of Rosemund and the Tale of Thisbe.

Two allegorial figures, the Goddess Natura and the priest Genius, were established by Alan, and frequently adopted and adapted by poets throughout the Middle Ages. Alan's goddess Natura appears in both the *De Planctu* and in the *Anticlaudianus*.⁷ Alan of Lille also established the medieval characterization of Genius, a figure which became associated with a tutelary deity,⁸ and appears most notably in the *Roman*, and the *Confessio*. In the *De Planctu* Nature's priest, Genius, excommunicates mankind for engaging in the unnatural vice of sodomy

3

and ignoring the voice of reason inherent within him. In the *Confessio* Gower does not personify Nature, but he fashions Venus' priest, Genius, from Alan's Nature.[9] The struggle inherent within man to control *kinde*—the passionate nature he shares with animals—is something which medieval philosophical tradition defined as natural law. The sources upon which the scholastics relied for their knowledge of natural law were Cicero, St. Paul, and, later, Aristotle, among others.[10] The Roman jurist Ulpian defined natural law as the common instinct of animals, and this law is the one accepted during the twelfth and thirteenth centuries.[11] Natural law, then, is the same as natural instincts, something which controls both man and animals. By personifying Nature, Bernard and Alan of Lille changed the way medieval writers wrote about nature, and perhaps how readers thought about nature.

Plato's *Timaeus*, and Calcidius' commentary upon it, were two central texts in the discussion of nature,[12] which Alan of Lille drew upon for the *De Planctu*.[13] St. Thomas Aquinas followed Plato to formulate that all humans have the capacity to do good, and their natural inclination leads them to goodness. In the *Summa Theologiæ*, Aquinas discusses the question of natural law. He states that there are three precepts:

> There is in man, first, a tendency towards the good of the nature he has in common with all substances; each has an appetite to preserve its own natural being. . . . Secondly, there is in man a bent towards things which accord with his nature considered more specifically, that is in terms of what he has in common with other animals; correspondingly those matters are said to be of natural law which nature teaches all animals, for instance the coupling of male and female, and the bringing up of the young, and so forth. Thirdly, there is in man an appetite for the good of his nature as rational, and this is proper to him, for instance, that he should know truths about God and about living in society. (ST Q.92.2.2)[14]

Aquinas' belief that moral obligation imposed by reason inclines a man to do good, and the idea that man's natural power gives him ability to distinguish between good and evil, became common principles in the Middle Ages. Gratian and the Decretists defined natural law as "that which is contained in the Scriptures and which teaches man to do to others what he would have others do to himself."[15] Before Christ, the early philosophers practiced virtue according to reason, but the Gospel reforms the natural law into moral precepts according to Christ's teachings. Man has the capacity to do good, but he is susceptible to temptations. This is the battlefield for medieval poetry such as the *De Planctu*, the *Roman*, and Gower's *Mirour*, *Vox* and the *Confessio*.

Nature and Reason in Alan of Lille's *De Planctu Naturæ*

In the *De Planctu* Nature gives man the power of reason in the hope that Reason will guide him to love properly,[16] but man disappoints that hope. Mankind sins against Nature by disregarding reason and engaging in homosexual activities and other sexual dalliances which Genius views as directly against Nature's teachings. Nature and Reason share a close kinship in Alan's poem, and Genius, Nature's priest, is inextricably bound to both characters; they are practically inseparable.[17] When Alan's Dreamer first sees Nature, he is in a trance and does not recognize the beautiful maiden who descends from the clouds and approaches him.[18] The maiden is a mystical, mysterious figure to the Dreamer, but all the elements which gather about her and celebrate her arrival on earth know her (DP 109). Nature is an idealized goddess, and man's failure to recognize her is itself a symptom of the very disease that prevents him understanding his own capabilities. The goddess sheds tears for man's sexual transgressions and his disobedience to her laws of regeneration.

Nature scolds the Dreamer because of his inability to recognize her. She lectures him for his "blindness of ignorance" and "weakness," saying his "reason [is in] exile . . . your mind robbed of an intimate knowledge" of me (DP 116). Nature reminds man it was she who gave him the ability to reason, his "distinctive powers," and "the power of recollection" (DP 118), but Reason will ever be in "continual hostility" with its contrary and enemy, Sensuousness (DP 119). The two powers struggle for control of man: Reason invites Sensuousness "to come to the source of virtue so that he may rise," but Sensuousness corrupts man and "changes him into a beast" (DP 119). Nature tells the Dreamer she arranged the antagonism between sensuality and reason at Reason's advice "so that if Reason could in this debate turn Sensuousness into an object of ridicule, the first reward of victory would not be without subsequent ones" (DP 119). The battle between Nature and Reason, then, has been pre-arranged by Reason herself. It is up to man to choose the victor.

Man is supposed to defeat lust and gain his proper reward, but rather than defeating it, in the *De Planctu*, man fully surrenders to fruitless perversions, contrary to Nature's teachings, including sodomy. Nature complains that she gave man "many graces and privileges" and in return she receives ill-payment (DP 134). Alan of Lille briefly considers Trojan and Ovidian tales to illustrate his point of man's heedless surrender to sensuality: Nature provided Helen of Troy with great beauty, but she used it to commit adultery with Paris; Myrrha, another beauty, slept with her unknowing father; and Medea, unnatural mother, killed her sons. It is because of these transgressions and misuse of her gifts that Nature has come to earth to decide man's fate. At the poem's denouement, mankind is excommunicated by Nature's priest for his ingratitude to Nature for her gifts, including the gift of reason, which has been misused. Despite Nature's anger with mankind, she urges him towards proper loving, advocating marriage as the best way to express the procreative law.[19]

Lawful marriage between man and woman is stressed in the *De Planctu*. Alan of Lille describes how God has ordered the world, with marriage at its core:

> When the artisan of the universe had clothed all things in the outward aspect befitting their natures and had wed them to one another in the relationship of lawful marriage, it was His will that by a mutually related circle of birth and death, transitory things should be given stability by instability, endlessness by endings, eternity by temporariness and that the series of things should ever be knit by successive renewals of birth. He decreed that by the lawful path of derivation by propagation, like things, sealed with the stamp of manifest resemblance, should be produced from like (DP 145).

Alan's Nature lectures man on moderation, urging him to starve the flesh and thus his sensuality:

> Let a meal of food, that is ordinary, plain and rarely taken, grind down the proud complaining flesh, . . . Thus tenacious Cupid will take a rest. Let the reins on Cupid within you be tightened and the sting of the flesh will grow faint and dull: the flesh will thus become the handmaiden of the spirit (DP 194).

Near the end of the poem, the Dreamer sees Hymenaeus, the god of marriage. On Hymenaeus' clothing are the pictures of a marriage ceremony:

> the faithfulness proceeding from the sacrament of matrimony, the peaceful unity of married life, the inseparable bond of marriage, the indissoluble union of the wedded parties (DP 197).

Chastity, the virgin maiden, follows the god. On her clothing are pictures of women renowned for their chastity, Lucrece and Penelope, two of the *Confessio*'s honored Four Wives. Temperance appears, followed by Generosity and Humility. All weep for man's transgressions, for he has disregarded the marriage bonds which would have ensured for him a peaceful union. Much to Nature's distress, man is unfaithful to the sacrament of marriage, for lust and adultery were unleashed in the world, when Nature retired to heaven. Nature blames Venus for loosening lust upon the world because she committed adultery with Antigenius, yet Nature refuses to accept any responsibility for mismanaging her deputy Venus, or for neglecting her duties on Earth.[20] Venus thus becomes an example of "how the elephantine leprosy of lust" ruins many (DP 165). Nature urges mankind to express sexual love within the confines of lawful marriage by using his reason, Nature's supreme gift to man.

Gower espouses this same belief in the *Confessio* by stressing the importance of marriage in the love tales he tells Amans; similarly, in the *De Planctu*, the law of Nature dictates that sexual passion be led by reason and expressed only within the bonds of marriage, between husband and wife. Alan's Nature deems this expression of passion proper for it helps her do her duty to replenish the earth. This early work views nature's law as something that operates with the assistance of reason; indeed, reason is one of the most important gifts Nature has given mankind, and reason must work to control his natural behavior, his passions. In Gower man is equipped with both natural impulses and reason, and in both Alan of Lille and in Gower, Nature and Reason work together. Gower offers marriage as the best defense against wanton desire, and as the most pleasurable relationship for mankind throughout the *Confessio*.

Nature and Reason in the *Roman de la Rose*

The conflict between Reason and Nature encompasses the narrative action in the *Roman*. On one side the Lover Amant has Reason, who continually advises him to turn his back on love, while sexual passion's advocate, Nature, who urges him to achieve what he desires, is on the other. Reason instructs Amant to love lawfully and wisely, but he ignores her advice, turning instead to a host of characters who offer him advice on how to win his beloved, the Rose. In the *Roman*, particularly that portion of it written by Jean de Meun, Nature and Reason battle each other for control of the Lover. In the *Roman* Nature and Reason are separate entities,[21] and unlike Alan's Nature in the *De Planctu*, Jean's Nature has nothing to do with Reason. In fact, Jean's Nature even announces that she did not give man his reasoning capabilities:

> Man's understanding I well recognize
> As something not provided him by me;
> My jurisdiction does not stretch to that.
> I'm neither wise nor powerful enough
> To make a creature so intelligent.
> Whate'er I make is mortal; I create
> Nothing that lasts throughout eternity.
> (RR 19051–58)[22]

Jean's Nature refuses to accept any responsibility for man's reasoning capabilities, her enemy in the quest for the Rose: she is a sexual force, not a rational power. This is a significant departure from Alan, and the differences between the character of Nature in the two poems are the result of Jean de Meun's "careful and deliberate modification of the figure handed down to him by Alan of Lille and other writers."[23]

While Alan's Nature and Gower's Genius both sanction procreation within the bonds of the marital state, Jean's Nature in the *Roman* admits no boundaries to her law of sexual expression: Nature's interest lies in sexual passion only. In the *Roman* the Lover embraces passion and continuously fights with Reason, disregarding her advice, and contemptuously ridiculing her in the last few lines of the poem. Marriage is never referred to in the *Roman*. Despite the enormous influence of the *Roman* on medieval poets, Gower draws an independent and moderate conclusion from it, advocating sexual passion only in a lawful marriage of mutual love. Gower, like Alan, expects mankind to control his passions with his reason, whereas Jean's Nature promotes sexual satisfaction at any cost. Man's duty to populate God's earth is not emphasized in Gower; interestingly enough, however, Gower promotes a sensuous, sexual love for his married couples, and he does not shy away from displays of marital affection or from using words which conjure up passionate lovemaking.[24] Alan's Nature and Gower's Genius more closely resemble Jean's Reason than his Nature. Jean's Reason represents a rational view of love, and she urges the Lover to turn his back on his sexual urges which distort the goodness of procreation. The Lover, of course, completely ignores Reason's advice.

In the *Roman*, Reason first appears in the fragment written by Guillaume de Lorris; she turns up again and in more depth in Jean de Meun's completion of the poem. Reason "objects to loving . . . on the Augustinian grounds that it is a love misdirected in its end and hence cupidinous; the [primary] objection . . .[in both sections of the poem] is the rationalist's complaint that such a foolish and mad passion is unreasonable and lacking in *mesure*."[25] Gower objects to mad passion in the *Confessio* too: lovers who act without *mesure* subsequently fail at their love quests. Throughout Gower's poem, Genius stresses the difference between proper loving, "honeste love" that has marriage as its end, and selfish or cupidinous love, as seen in Amans' passion for his lady. The fact that she does not respond to Amans' advances, preferring to snub him whenever possible, typifies his ill-placed, selfish passion, a love without *mesure*. In Gower reason "always connotes 'measure' and restraint."[26]

In the *Roman* Reason's role is to convince Amant to abandon his quest for the Rose. She lectures him about his decisions to come to the park named Delight and to befriend Idleness, two acts she considers senseless. The Lover cries as Reason continues to scold him. She calls him a sot, and urges him to "Into oblivion consign that god / Who has so weakened, tortured, conquered you" (RR 3008–09). Reason contends that "Nothing but foolishness is this disease / Called love; 'twere better it were folly named" (RR 3024–25). In Guillaume's *Roman*, Reason is fully Love's enemy. She says that Idleness fast becomes a lover's friend, and once in love, men will not undertake a profitable

The Struggle between Nature and Reason in Gower's Confessio Amantis

task; if he is a clerk, he leaves his learning (RR 3028–29). No matter how laboriously a man exert himself in Love's cause, he will inevitably lose, for joy in love

> Comes but by chance and lives but a short time,
> Only to fade away.
> (RR 3031–32)

Reason never counsels the Lover to embrace Love; indeed, Guillaume's Reason has a hard-hearted, no nonsense hatred of love, and she advises Amant to cease listening to his heart. Abandon love:

> Now firmly seize the bits between your teeth;
> Resist the guidance of your stubborn heart,
> Against whose will you'll have to use some force.
> You will be ditched if passion keep the reins.
> (RR 3044–47)

Like any person in love, Amant becomes angry at Reason, the intruding third party. His retort resembles Amans' complaint to Genius in Book VIII of the *Confessio*, in which Genius, the third party, offers advice which Amans does not think applicable to his situation. In the *Roman*, Reason, being reasonable, sees that her lecture will not help this lover and so she leaves; she does not appear again until Jean de Meun begins his section of the *Roman*. When Reason returns she greets the despairing Amant with a rather sarcastic question:

> Fair friend . . .
> How goes the battle? Are you ready now
> To leave off loving? Have you had enough?
> (RR 4225–27)

There is a sassiness in Jean de Meun which is not found in Gower, who nonetheless is influenced by these two poets.

In the *Roman* and in the *Confessio* both lovers seek as much knowledge as possible about the god/goddess of Love and his/her power. Amans begs Genius to tell him all he knew of love:

> With al min herte I you beseche,
> That ye me wolde enforme and teche
> What ther is more of youre aprise
> In love als wel as otherwise,
> So that I mai me clene schryve.
> (CA IV.3699–3703)

In the *Roman* Reason promises to give the Lover better knowledge of the one who brewed

> Such agonizing drink for you that now
> You're quite disfigured.
> (RR 4250–55)

Jean's Reason knows that if she is to rescue the Lover from the grips of Love she needs to educate him,[27] and she resorts to using the "long string of oxymorons borrowed *en masse*" from Alan's *De Planctu*, who borrowed some of them from Ovid.[28] Love is freezing hot, pleasurable pain, and a "happy hell and saddened Paradise" (RR 4296). Familiar phrases all. Gower also makes use of these phrases in Book V of the *Vox*, when he writes of the dangers that feminine beauty can pose to knights:

> Love is sickly health, troubled rest, pious sin, warlike peace, . . . weeping laughter, [and] laughing lamentation (VC 5.2.50ff).

These phrases reiterate that Love is incomprehensible: how can Reason make any sense of something that is described as freezing hot? Love is not so easily categorized, and it defies reason, uniting pain with pleasure. In the *Roman* Reason recommends flight as the best strategy for escaping Love's pangs and torments:

> No better potion can you drink than flight;
> No elsewise can you happiness enjoy.
> Follow Love, and he will you pursue:
> Avoid him, and away from you he'll flee.
> (RR 4312–18)

Recommending flight does not seem to be a very reasonable strategy, but Reason is unable to make sense of love, and avoidance is the advice she offers. Amant, however, will not follow Reason's advice and abandon Love. In the *Vox* Gower also recommends flight from Love: "Lest you be conquered like a lion, you must flee like a hare" (VC 5.3.210.) Alan's Nature also advocates a retreat from Love: "You can by yourself, however, restrain this madness, if you but flee; no more powerful antidote is available" (DP 153).

In the *Roman* Amant's passionate desire is detrimental for it is not a natural love, obeyed by all men and beasts. Reason tells the Lover his desire is one without the limits of reason, a

> Far madder love . . . ,
> Which you'd best leave if you care for your good.
> (RR 5792–94)

This is a key passage in the poem, and its notion that a middle ground must be found between passionate sex and reasonable love echoes in the *Confessio*. Gower's Amans has also embraced a "mad love" and he must learn to abandon it. In the *Confessio*, Gower presents the middle argument between *De Planctu* and the *Roman*:

> I wolde go the middel weie
> And wryte a bok betwen the tweie,
> Somwhat of lust, somwhat of lore,
> That of the lasse or of the more
> Som man mai lyke of that I wryte.
> (CA Prol.17–21)

For the good of the realm, Gower prefers that all sexual activity be guided by reason and "be expressed in the marriage bed."[29] Alan of Lille and Gower both agree that sexual relations between people other than man and wife are unnatural and do not benefit the realm, but Alan's work presents it as a law of Nature, while Gower sees it as a law of Reason. Nowhere in the *Confessio* does Gower say that only lawfully married couples can have sexual relations, but in Gower those who ignore the voice of reason in love matters suffer the consequences, as I will demonstrate with the tales of Albinus and Rosemund, and Pyramus and Thisbe.

The influence of the *De Planctu* and the *Roman* upon Gower is most apparent in the *Confessio*, a poem in which he attempts to guide Lovers to love reasonably.[30] Genius shares similarities with both Nature in the *De Planctu* and Reason in the *Roman*, as I have illustrated. Gower skillfully changes the character Genius to fit his needs—as he so often does with the tales, by either eliminating elements or embellishing them—in order to focus upon the moral he wishes to illuminate. Gower "is deeply concerned with moral psychology."[31] As Venus' priest who nonetheless promotes married love, Genius' dual nature parallels the struggle within all mankind, between his passionate and his reasonable natures. By creating a confessor who recommends marriage—what he considers proper loving—over sexual delight—what the priest's deity Venus advocates—Gower has reconciled the two traditional voices into one. That the voice is unreliable puts the onus on mankind to defeat passion and choose proper loving. It is the same hope that Alan of Lille has for man in the *De Planctu*. In his mediating role, Genius relates "all his narratives to a framework of moral, political, and cosmological ideas which express a deep commitment to hierarchy,"[32] a hierarchy in which man must obey his God-given innate ability to reason. It is possible for man to learn to moderate his *kinde*, and Genius' tales make it clear that the modifying part is the difficult part, especially for someone like Amans who is so deeply lovesick. Learning to modify one's behavior is difficult, yet recovering his reason is one of the first steps which an immoderate lover such as Amans needs to take. Genius reminds Amans that God gives man

> reson forth withal,
> Wherof that he nature schal
> Upon the causes modefie.
> (CA VII.5377–79)

Reason modifies nature—Gower believes this is necessary for the proper rule of mankind and thus the world.

Lovers who foolishly disregard reason stumble upon disaster again and again in the *Confessio*. As Gower writes in the *Traitié*, man's soul aspires to the good, but his body is drawn to *kinde* and the act of engendering (Tr I.1–3). It is a constant struggle between passions and reason.[33] In the *Mirour* Gower writes that Saint Augustine and Saint Jerome preached continence over marriage (MO 17917–53), but in the *Confessio* Gower advocates matrimony, not chastity, and the tales he tells fully advance marriage as the means with which man can harness his sexual desires and thus obey reason. In the Tale of Rosemund, and the Tale of Thisbe, Genius teaches Amans what can happen when passionate love is unmoderated by reason.

The Tale of Rosemund

Finding proper love is a skill which must be learned, and once found, it must be properly nurtured. Albinus and Rosemund have found love despite the fact that their marriage is a marriage of war, but unfortunately neither husband nor wife nurtures the love, and the tale is "a genuine love tragedy."[34] Genius tells the tale to teach Amans to avoid the sin of "avantance," of boasting, and especially boasting of oneself, a branch of the Deadly Sin of Pride:

> The vice cleped Avantance
> With Pride hath take his aqueintance,
> So that his oghne pris he lasseth,
> When he such mesure overpasseth
> That he his oghne Herald is.
> That ferst was wel is thanne mis,
> That was thankworth is thanne blame,
> And thus the worschipe of his name
> Thurgh pride of his avantarie
> He torneth into vilenie.
> (CA I.2399–2408)

Genius tells Amans that Love competes with and hates this vice above all others (CA I.2450–58). Gower's source for this tale is more than likely Godfrey of

Viterbo (ca.1125–1192),[35] who told the tale in the *Pantheon sive Memoria Saeculorum*.[36] Gower changes the tale quite purposefully to suit his desire to illustrate the sin of boasting in love.[37] Albinus, who sins against Love by boasting, suffers a great loss—his beloved wife, his kingdom, and his life.

The tale recounts the battle of the Lombards against the Gepts in northern Italy. Albinus, a man "of gret chivalerie," the "myhti kyng" of the Lombards, slays Rosemund's father Gurmond, leader of the Gepts, in a battle (CA I.2462, 2467). How Albinus slew Gurmond is important to the sin of self-boasting upon which the story is based, for he did it in a very unchivalrous manner:

> Albinus slowh him in the feld,
> Ther halp him nowther swerd ne scheld,
> That he ne smot his hed of thanne,
> Wherof he tok awey the Panne.
> (CA I.2469–72)

Gower is not usually ironic in tone and thus it is notable that he calls Albinus chivalrous yet writes that he killed Gurmond, an unarmed man, without any regard to the code of conduct that someone like Chaucer's Knight abides so closely. Albinus should have made Gurmond his prisoner; killing him as he did is shameful murder. Albinus not only chops off the defenseless king's head, he decides to make a cup out of the skull "To kepe and drawe into memoire" his victorious battle with the Gepts (CA I.2475).

Rosemund is described as "A fair, a freissh, a lusti on"—a real beauty in Gower's verse (CA I.2483). Gower rarely describes feminine beauty; indeed, in his lexicon, the poet seldom describes any character's physical being,[38] and Rosemund is one of the few female characters whose physical and emotional being is praised in the *Confessio*. The victor in battle often wins a bride, and Albinus weds Gurmond's daughter. Genius, however, is careful to define their marriage as something more than a spoils of war, something much more tender; indeed, he describes their love in rare terms. Albinus' heart fell on Rosemund and they wed immediately:

> His herte fell to hire anon,
> And such a love on hire he caste,
> That he hire weddeth ate laste;
> And after that long time in reste
> With hire he duelte, and to the beste
> Thei love ech other wonder wel.
> (CA I.2484–2489)

Although their marriage is a product of war, the couple lives together peacefully—"in reste"—and "love ech other wonder wel" (CA I.2487–89). Their marriage is remarkable only in the peaceful terms that Gower uses to describe it. Gower then introduces a precarious strain by employing Fortune and her ever-spinning wheel; notably it is Venus who turns the wheel:[39]

> Bot sche which kepth the blinde whel,
> Venus, whan thei be most above,
> In al the hoteste of here love,
> Hire whiel sche torneth, and thei felle.
> (CA I.2490–93)

By using the medieval commonplace of the wheel, it is clear that Albinus' fall is imminent. The king is unable to remain humble, and it is this human flaw, the sin of pride and vain glory, which topples him. Albinus is poised at the top of Fortune's Wheel. He is described as a wealthy king

> Of pes, of worschipe and of helthe,
> And felte him on no side grieved,
> As he that hath his world achieved.
> (CA I.2495–97)

For love of Rosemund, Albinus plans a "feste . . . / . . . that was for his wyves sake" (CA I.2499–2500). It is a very festive affair, complete with great horses, "assaied / For joustinge and for tornement" wearing "perled" and "Embroudred" blankets and trappings (CA I.2508–11). Lords and ladies in attendance wore their "beste arrai" to watch the jousting tournament, and afterwards, everyone gathered in the king's hall for dinner (CA I.2512). It is the kind of occasion not usually described by Gower but one frequently found in medieval romance tales. Talk turns to "Al . . . of armes and of love" at this splendid affair, and the king is overwhelmed by the merry and lavish affair he has arranged for his wife:

> The king himself began to glade
> Withinne his herte and tok a pride.
> (CA I.2532–23)

So full of his ability to host and command such a grand feast and tournament, Albinus swells with pride and arrogance, and cruelly yet unwittingly he destroys his happy marriage. Albinus' skill in arms—which in reality is not skillful but unchivalrous behavior—enabled him to win Rosemund as his wife, but what he seems to forget is that the army he defeated and the king he mercilessly killed was Rosemund's father. Albinus shows "absolutely no consideration" or husbandly regard for his wife's feelings, "valuing his own pride above her dignity" and love.[40]

The Latin marginalia that appears alongside this portion of the text states that "proudful boasting alone has provided the tinder of this entire misfortune" (CA I.2501).[41] In the *Mirour*, Gower writes on the sin of Vainglory, a sister to Boasting, and daughter to Pride:

> ... worldly Vainglory takes much pleasure in vain honors, praise, renown, wealth, power, circumstance, knowledge, fair speech, beauty, strength, valor, rich garb, fair adornment, castles, high towers, and the power of commanding people; she believes herself creator rather than creature. Ah, what folly, that she wants to fight even with God Himself! (MO 1249)

St. Thomas Aquinas quotes Cicero in a section in the *Summa Theologiæ* on vainglory:

> Cicero says, We must beware of coveting glory, for it robs us of freedom of spirit, in defense of which magnanimous men ought to strain every nerve. So vainglory is opposed to magnanimity (ST Q.132.2.3).

Aquinas writes of vainglorious men such as Albinus, who seek "unimportant things merely to take glory in them" (ST Q.132.2):

> But as regards what he thinks of himself, the vainglorious man is opposed to the magnanimous by excess, because he considers as important the glory which he seeks, and strives for it beyond his real worth (ST Q.132.2.2).

Albinus is indeed an excessive, vainglorious man.

Albinus seeks praise for acquiring his bride Rosemund in a war in which he killed her father, thus defeating her people. These are well-known facts, for which he has more than likely already garnered praise from his people. What the people probably do not know is something that we as readers do know: that Albinus murdered her father shamefully. He overreaches himself in seeking added glory which is beyond what he deserves. Gazing over the multitude of revelers, Albinus spies, "as if by accident,"[42] the cup made of Gurmond's head which was prominently on display in the hall. The cup, which represents his prowess and thus his conquering kingdom, is richly decorated

> ... with gold and riche Stones
> Beset and bounde for the nones,
> And stod upon a fot on heihte
> Of burned gold, and with gret sleihte
> Of werkmanschipe it was begrave
> Of such werk as it scholde have,
> And was policed ek so clene

That no signe of the Skulle is sene.
(CA I.2537–2544)

Albinus exchanges his cup for the skull cup and has it filled with wine which he presents to his wife, saying "Drink with thi fader, Dame" (CA I.2551).[43] Rosemund cannot see the skull beneath the polished gold and stones, and she drinks as her husband commands.[44] Albinus' pride swells, and he is unable to control himself. He announces to the throng of lords and ladies that the cup is made of "hire fader Skulle," and through his prowess he has won "his wyves love" (CA I.2557, 2562). There was "mochel Pride alofte" and the crowd of party-goers comment upon this wondrous announcement, but Rosemund alone

> . . . was softe,
> Thenkende on thilke unkynde Pride
> Of that hire lord so nyh hire side
> Avanteth him that he hath slain
> And piked out hire fader brain
> And of the Skulle had mad a Cuppe.
> (CA I.2564–2569)

Rosemund, silently holding the cup, suffers greatly (CA I.2570). Christopher Ricks notes that Gower's use of the word "softe" is always significantly potent;[45] in this case it invokes Rosemund's gentle nature, now deeply wounded. Gower draws great sympathy for Rosemund in this brief scene. In one moment Rosemund's joy in her marriage and in the love she shares with Albinus is crushed by a cruel and stunning blow to her heart. Holding the cup, perhaps half-filled with wine, she is overwhelmed by horror of holding her father's skull, and is filled with sadness for his death. Perhaps she looks with confusion at the man who sits "nyh hire side" (CA I.2566); his love for her was so great that the feast and tournament are in her honor. But she now sits silently, thinking on "unkynde Pride," for vainglory is the cause of Albinus' unnatural and heartless behavior; he shows no compassion for his wife's feelings. Gower describes the word "pride" as "unkynde"; it is unnatural to man's soul and Nature, and a sin against God. Pride is the greatest and the first sin, and Albinus and his wife will suffer horridly for it.

Once dinner is over, Rosemund pleads an illness and excuses herself from the feast. Rosemund's pride has been sorely wounded and wounded publicly. In private she complains bitterly to her maid Glodeside that Albinus made her drink from her father's skull "Among hem alle," and this insults her and her father's memory (CA I.2580). The love she had for her father has been ridiculed, as has the love and the pride she had for her country and countrymen. Furthermore, she has been reduced to a spoils from the war, and she may feel cheapened by her husband's boasts of how he won her love. Albinus has reduced his wife to the level of an object, but so swelled with pride is he that he does not realize what he has done;[46] it is another instance of a man ignoring reason. Together she and Glodeside plot revenge. Rosemund vows that she "schal noght be glad / Til that sche" sees her husband so troubled that he cannot boast anymore (CA I.2583–85). That Rosemund, an adoring and adored wife, can turn so suddenly into a woman vowing revenge is startling. Her wrath is understandable, but the depth of her anger and the speed with which she seeks hot revenge is sudden and excessive. Her immoderate desire to see her husband suffer as she has suffered is based "not on the ghastliness of the crime, but rather on the vice of *avantance*."[47] Although Albinus' crime is horrific, Rosemund lacks the pity she needs to forgive her husband of his errors and thus heal their marriage. In the *Mirour* Gower writes of Pity which stands against Homicide:

> Pity is the treacle or remedy that completely cures the heart of poisonous swelling so that there may be no abscess of old rancor, from which Anger drinks. On the contrary, through her mercy (of which she is wholly composed), she forgets every outrage committed against her, so that she no longer sees it; for she would not seek for all the world vengeance on any creature that is like her in nature (MO 13957).

Pity and humility would have sustained the harmony which existed in this marriage; had Rosemund been able to swallow her pride and practice either virtue she would have been able to repair the damage to their marriage and salvage their peaceful world.

Rosemund uses what is commonly known as the bed trick to persuade her maid's lover into killing Albinus. Glodeside had previously agreed to sleep with her lover Helmege that very night. The queen gets into Glodeside's bed, and Helmege makes love to her, thinking she is Glodeside. When Rosemund reveals herself to him, she says that if he does her pleasure, she and all her heritage will be at his command (CA I.2611–19). In an unforeseen twist of events, Helmege is filled with "wylde loves rage" for Rosemund, a rage "which noman him can governe," and he agrees to do whatever she commands: he slays Albinus. Helmege becomes the instrument of Rosemund's will, but he is under the considerable power of sexual passion, which cannot abide by reason (CA I.2620–23). Genius interjects a telling statement "And thus the whiel is al miswent" as Albinus' kingdom spins out of his controlling grasp (CA I.2624). The two traitors, Rosemund and Helmege, described as sharing "a certain felaschipe," flee the kingdom, taking "the tresor of the king" with them (CA I.2635, 2632–33).[48] Soon after they flee, they are poisoned at the command of a Duke who first gave them shelter, and then promptly orders their deaths, upon hearing of their evil deeds (CA I.2640–46).

A feminist perspective might view Gower's Rosemund as an ornament to a braggart king, or as representing the gendered position of a powerless female: she is married to Albinus according to the laws of war, her father is dead, his people have been vanquished by Albinus' army, and she is awarded to the victor as a prize.[49] We do not know anything about their courtship, to use the term broadly, nor her thoughts about marrying Albinus. Gower presents Albinus and Rosemund to us as a married couple, and we are told that Albinus honors and loves his wife so much so that he throws a banquet in her honor. Albinus deeply offends Rosemund at the banquet, yet she suffers quietly at his side, an obedient queen. Later, in private, Rosemund unleashes her anger, and becomes anything but a powerless female. She actively seeks to destroy her husband by tricking Helmege into bed with her, and then she uses her new power to convince Helmege to kill her husband. Rosemund, like many other women in the *Confessio*, speaks through her actions, and transgresses her gender to act upon her passions. Unfortunately, she acts without using her reason, and she destroys her marriage and her world.

Genius reminds Amans that these tragic events came of Pride:

> Good is therfore a man to hide
> His oghne pris, for if he speke,
> He mai lihtliche his thonk tobreke.
> (CA I.2648–2650)

Hiding one's prize and guarding one's own will is something Albinus cannot do. Genius first describes the sin of "Avantance" as the herald of Pride, and he warns Amans not to boast about himself in any manner:

> For what man thilke vice haunte,
> His pourpos schal fulofte faile.
> (CA I.2656–57)

The prowess of which Albinus boasts is in fact shameful behavior, unbecoming of the king's knightly status (CA I.2399–2403). The Latin sidenotes at I.2405 of the tale pointedly comment on the reason for Albinus' fall:

> The vanities of a boastful tongue diminish renown, which silence would have established as permanent in honor. A boaster does not perceive the praise of his merit; therefore he values himself publicly, in the words of the world.[50]

Once Albinus begins to boast, he is only moments away from losing everything. Fortune sees to it.[51] Albinus overreaches himself and is swept away by his pride in his own prowess and power. Gower writes in the *Mirour* of the sin of boasting:

> The fourth proud daughter [of Pride] boasts in everything she says; therefore her name is Boasting. He who loves this girl, both in telling the truth and in lying, often boasts in his speech of his great intelligence, of his power, of his valor, of his substance. He does nothing good that he conceals; rather, he tells of all his qualifications, whereby he boasts of his own honor; a herald would go no further in speaking of it (MO 1729).

Further he writes:

> The wise philosopher said, "Such as your heart is within, such your word will express." That is apparent with the proud man, who boasts in his exaggeration of his knowledge and of is lineage and of his wealth. For he tells everything of his virtues so that everyone may know it, so that he may have no equal among the neighbors in the city where he lives. As Solomon witnessed, often you see evil come upon him (MO 1813).

Evil befalls Albinus in short order. His mouth speaks the boastful words that live in his heart, and he spreads news of his own accomplishments. Albinus is unable to keep himself in check, a precept inherent in Gower's poetry. To live moderately and to take everything in moderation is one of axioms which the Goddess Nature in Alan's *De Planctu* also preaches.[52]

In the *Traitié* XI Gower summarizes the Tale in three verses. He adds a few pertinent details which are not found in the *Confessio*. We are told that although Albinus holds Rosemund dear, she does not return her husband's love because she is angry that her father is dead; furthermore, Gower states that God does not bless a marriage created from the spoils of war; no mention of this is in the *Confessio* (Tr XI.1.5; 2.10–12; 2.8–9). The Latin sidenotes refer to Rosemund's adultery, and while Albinus is called aggressive, no mention is made of his boasting (Tr XI.1).

This tale is one of the few in which we see, albeit for a very short time, a happy loving couple living together lawfully as man and wife. That Gower has taken the trouble to describe a solid loving marriage and then have it unravel is striking. All this reiterates the dangers and the strong tentacles of the sin of Pride. Gower has carefully drawn a marriage of mutual love between Albinus and Rosemund, which makes Albinus' sin of pride that much more serious; he had a good marriage and he threw it away through his unnatural, unreasonable behavior. As king, his foolish love actions resonate throughout his land, now a ruler-less empire, where dissension and disorder rule.

Genius ends the tale with a *sententia* for Amans, warning him that a man filled with Vain Glory will overreach himself, as Albinus' does:

> Of love gete him avantage,
> Anon he wext of his corage
> So overglad, that of his ende
> Him thenkth ther is no deth comende:
> For he hath thanne at alle tide
> Of love such a maner pride,
> Him thenkth his joie is endeles.
> (CA I.2711–17)

Humbleness is important in lover matters, as Genius explains to Amans:

> My Sone, tak good hiede
> So forto lede thi manhiede,
> That thou ne be noght lich a beste.
> Bot if thi lif schal ben honeste,
> Thou most humblesce take on honde.
> (CA I.3043–47)

Proud behavior in man is sinful in love matters, or anything else. In seeking revenge Rosemund is just as guilty of sinning against Love as is her husband. Together this couple is responsible for the unrest and turmoil which ensues from their boastful and revengeful actions. In her quiet thoughts, Rosemund calls her husband's boasting his "unkynde" behavior, and she is correct to do so for boasting is unnatural, a Deadly Sin against God, and in the *Confessio* it stands opposed to Love too. The precept that "unkynde" behavior in one man resonates throughout the world is reiterated in this tale and throughout Gower's work. It is a theme which will come up again and again in the poem: a man or woman who lives without heeding reason will destroy his own happiness, the happiness in his community and in the world surrounding them. In this tale Gower makes it clear that neither husband or wife is able to abide by reason's rule, and their inability to govern their actions in Love ruins the happiness they once shared and the kingdom they once ruled together.

The Tale of Thisbe

"Unkynde" or unnatural behavior is also a factor in the Tale of Thisbe. Gower borrows this tale from Ovid's *Metamorphoses*, and he probably relied upon the *Ovid moralisé*,[53] a fourteenth-century French adaptation and moralized commentary on the *Metamorphoses*, which included material from other Ovidian texts such as the *Heroides*, and other sources including Dares and Dictys, and Benoit's *Roman de Troie*. Boccaccio includes Thisbe in *De Claris Mulieribus* (1355–59),[54] and Chaucer tells her tale in the *Legend*.[55] The stories collected in the *Legend* honor women for their constancy in love, but Thisbe's name is not usually included among "standard medieval catalogues of exemplary female sufferers."[56] Chaucer includes Thisbe in a list of unhappy lovers on the wall in the Temple of Venus in the *Parliament of Fowls*, mentions her suicide in the Man of Law's Tale, and praises the lovers' ingenuity in the Merchant's Tale. As with many of the tales which both Gower and Chaucer told, it is difficult to determine who borrowed from whom.[57] Gower strips much of the Ovidian aspects of the poem, and thus his tale differs from the source and Chaucer's rendition, which followed Ovid. Another possible source is a twelfth century Latin school text, adapted from Ovid by the grammarian Matthew of Vendôme, who studied under Bernard, from approximately 1130–1140.[58] Matthew's text, the *Piramus et Tisbe*, retains Ovid's story as we find it in the *Metamorphoses*.[59]

Gower's Tale of Thisbe is told with a rare intensity.[60] It quickly gathers momentum and acquires a frantic pace which contributes to its overall depiction of a reckless love, the type of love which Gower does not reward. The secretive and passionate love between Pyramus and Thisbe limits their ability to advance their relationship reasonably towards an open and honest marriage. Gower's "lusti Bacheler" Pyramus is peerless, and there is no maiden so beautiful as his Thisbe (CA III.1343,1344,1347). They live next door to each other, but are separated by a wall:

> Among the whiche tuo ther were
> Above alle othre noble and grete,
> Dwellende tho withinne a Strete
> So nyh togedre, as it was sene,
> That ther was nothing hem betwene,
> Bot wow to wow and wall to wall.
> (CA III.1336–1341)

It is unclear whether they have ever met; in Chaucer, they know of each other only through their reputations—he, for his bravery, she for her beauty—rumors spread by women, the town gossips (LGW II.720). Despite the physical divider, Gower's Cupid has shaped it so

> That he his fyr on hem ne caste:
> Wherof her herte he overcaste
> To folwe thilke lore and suie
> Which nevere man yit miht eschuie;
> And that was love, as it is happed,
> Which hath here hertes so betrapped.
> (III.1353–58)

It is conventional, of course, to portray love as a force which cannot be overcome, but in this tale it is especially noteworthy, for with Cupid's fire now within them, Pyramus and Thisbe act furtively and furiously to satisfy their passionate desires. They decide to carve a hole in the wall "Thurgh which thei have her conseil take / At alle times, whan thei myhte" (III.1372–3). Genius is impressed with how the lovers have managed to communicate, and he praises what can be accomplished—"not so much to their own resourcefulness as to the power of love compelling them":[61]

> ... whan ther be tuo
> Of on acord, how so it go
> Bot if that thei som weie finde;
> For love is evere of such a kinde.
> And hath his folk so wel affaited,
> That howso that it be awaited,
> Ther mai noman the pourpos lette.
> (CA III.1363–69)

Gower's lovers are resourceful, and their ingenuity serves them well, but it is unclear as to why they have to resort to such secrecy.

Ovid states at the onset of his tale that Pyramus and Thisbe are forbidden to marry by their parents. Matthew follows Ovid, hinting at the undeniable lure of Love:

> They wish to be joined in marriage, but the harsh vigilance of their parents forbids the fulfillment of what they both want. What their parents can forbid, they forbid. Venus, unacquainted with denial, exercises a freer will. A forbidden love grows; it cannot be checked and it rejoices in opening up forbidden paths (PT 228).

In the *Legend* their fathers, two noblemen of great renown, both oppose the match:

> There myghte have ben bytwixe hem maryage,
> But that here fadres nolde it nat assente.
> (LGW II.729–30)

Two hundred years after Gower and Chaucer, Shakespeare tells this tale as a playlet in the *Midsummer's Night Dream*, and he, like Chaucer and Ovid, alludes to the familial barriers between the two lovers, but Gower does not say a word about rival families, forbidden fruit, or any other obstacles between Pyramus and Thisbe except the physical wall between their homes. Furthermore, Gower does not mention the word "marriage" here or at any other time in his tale, and this is noteworthy in a poet who stresses marriage throughout the *Confessio*.

In the *Metamorphoses*, Ovid portrays the pair as neighbors whose love grows from a friendship. In Ovid the lovers find a crack in the wall, and they secretly converse through it. Delany does not doubt that Ovid's image of the "crack" in the wall is a playful one which can be read as a symbol for female genitalia.[62] She points out that in the *De Planctu* Alan of Lille refers to Pyramus and Thisbe as he deplores the prevalence of homosexuality:[63]

> No longer does Pyramus cleave to Thisbe through a cleft in the wall: the little cleft of Venus has no charm for him (DP 71–72).

Gower does not utilize the sexual connotations found in Ovid or Chaucer. Instead, he focuses upon the urgency of the lovers' sexual passion. In the *Confessio* Pyramus and Thisbe's love affair begins innocently enough, for they seek a way to "winne a speche, / Here wofull peine forto lisse" (CA III.1360–1). Gower's lovers, who we are told are shaped for Love by Cupid, carve a hole in the wall so they can speak, but by choosing to use the word "lisse," a word which indicates "alleviation of suffering, relief, remedy for disease or pain, cure,"[64] Gower clearly indicates that they desire more than just conversation—a physical release in the form of sexual relations (CA III.1351–53). Immediately Gower has established that the lovers are in Love's grip and want to satisfy their erotic desires; the innocent tale gives way to something more sensual. There is no mention of a pledging of troth or a marriage, and this serves as a warning signal to the readers that Pyramus and Thisbe are under the command of *kinde* and not reason.

Speaking through a crack in the wall is a primitive way of communicating, and soon the lovers are dissatisfied with the arrangement. They are described as burning with the fire of love—Thisbe "loveth hote" Pyramus. They yearn to somehow find a way to be together privately without a wall between them (CA III.1375). In a reckless decision which proves to be their undoing, they plan to meet one night at "the tounes ende, / Wher was a welle under a Tree" (CA III.1380–81). It seems to be their only option. Gower does not explain why the lovers must meet in secrecy at night, and we can only imagine that they share an impatience to embrace. This passionate urgency is what drives them towards their self-destruction. Matthew's lovers also burn with an impatience that cannot be checked by reason: "Madness is balanced by madness, suffering by suffering, fire by fire, passion by passion" (PT 229). Intimating that sexual release is a cure for their sickness,[65] Matthew writes that "they hasten to heal themselves; by this ruse they hasten to enjoy their desires" (PT 230). In Ovid and Chaucer, a secret rendezvous is also planned, but Gower eliminates most of what he finds in Ovid.

To guard against anyone seeing her leave the town, Gower's Thisbe travels in disguise (CA III.1385). Her disguise is not damned here, but in the *Vox* Gower denounces ointments and false hairpieces as the accoutrements which wily women use to ensnare men:

> For the fashion in such a case is that a woman beautify her face, so that by means of ointments she may appear quite handsome. She skillfully marks her eyebrows and daubs her lips with rouge; with blended tints, she helps them to be more becoming (VC 5.6.390ff).

An atmosphere of menace builds as they each head out of the town's walls to their appointed meeting spot.[66] Gower emphasizes Thisbe's secrecy as she "Al prively the softe pas / Goth thurgh the large toun unknowe" (CA III.1386–87); surely she is rash to leave her parent's home at night, in disguise, to meet her lover. Thisbe acts freely, and is responsible for her own actions.

In Ovid's, Matthew's, Chaucer's, and Gower's versions, Thisbe is the first to arrive at the well. In Gower she sees a lion, and she flees, dropping her wimple "as fortune scholde falle" (CA III.1392–96). Thisbe watches the lion, described as in a wild rage, kill its prey and eat it; Gower turns the scene into a frightening one, and emphasizes Thisbe's helplessness as she cowers behind a bush (CA III.1398,1400;1413). The lion then finds Thisbe's wimple and bloodies it up, takes a drink from the well, and returns to the forest (CA III.1400–10).[67] Gower's short scene emphasizes the dangerous situation in which Thisbe has put herself; she is a foolish young woman alone in the wilderness. She is too frightened to move:

> Bot as a bridd which were in Mue
> Withinne a buissh sche kepte hire clos
> So stille that sche noght aros;
> Unto hirself and pleigneth ay.
> (CA III.1412–15)

Gower takes great pains to describe this scene "in great emotional and circumstantial detail,"[68] as he has carefully done throughout the tale. Thisbe remains in the bushes, afraid to see if the lion has left.

Ovid's Pyramus arrives at the meeting spot and sees the lion's footprints and Thisbe's bloody scarf. The animal tracks are a clever device, and both Matthew and Chaucer utilize it, but Gower does not. Chaucer's Pyramus arrives late—Chaucer writes "al to longe, allas, at hom was he!" (LGW II.824). In Gower Pyramus' tardiness contrasts with Thisbe's hastiness to meet him. By the moonlight Pyramus finds her bloodied wimple gnawed by the lion, and he believes his lady is dead (CA III.1406, 1419). He panics. Gower writes that never has a man heard such tidings or seen a sight which has afflicted a man's heart as what Pyramus sees (CA III.1420–25). Pyramus complains, moans and "Began his handes forto wringe" (CA III.1426). He is panic-stricken. Pyramus' fears are worse than reality, as Matthew's Narrator wisely notes: "No matter how many genuinely fearsome evils fear foretells, it threatens still worse imaginary ones; it is a bad prophet in doubtful circumstances" (PT 230). Without looking for her, Gower's Pyramus decides that she must be dead:

> ... sodeinly
> His swerd al nakid out he breide
> In his folhaste, and thus he seide:
> 'I am cause of this felonie,
> So it is resoun that I die,
> As sche is ded be cause of me.'
> (CA III.1428–1433)

Believing that his tardiness caused her death proves to be too much anguish for the young lover to bear. He uses the word "resoun" to describe why it is that he must die, but the effect of this is "ironical, since Pyramus has so plainly lost his reason," recalling Gower's "constant theme that loss of reason is the cause of sin."[69] In haste Pyramus places his sword's pommel on the ground, and he thrusts it "thurgh his herte . . . up to the bare hilte . . . and himself he spilte" (CA III.1443–1446). Genius makes it quite clear that Pyramus is acting in anger and in foolhaste, both in his hasty conclusion that Thisbe is dead, and in his suicide, and irrational lovers such as Pyramus and Thisbe suffer for their blind errors in the *Confessio*.[70] At every point in the tale, in fact, Gower emphasizes the lovers' irrational failure to rely upon their reason.

Coming out of the bushes, Thisbe sees her dead lover, and is overwhelmed: "hire herte schette," she is unable to speak, and she swoons. (CA III.1453, 1455). She awakens from her trance, and while looking upon her lover she catches her breath and calls to Venus and Cupid (CA III.1457–60). In an unusually long speech,[71] Thisbe demands to know what sin Pyramus committed to meet such a death, noting that he has been a loyal, youthful lover—an interesting point in light of the *Confessio*'s denouement:

> For he youre heste hath kept and served,
> And was yong and I bothe also:
> Helas, why do ye with ous so?
> Ye sette oure herte bothe afyre,
> And maden ous such thing desire
> Wherof that we no skile cowthe;
> Bot thus oure freisshe lusti yowthe
> Withoute joie is al despended
> Which thing mai nevere ben amended.
> (CA III.1470–1478)

Thisbe rails against the goddess, an action that is not usually rewarded in medieval literature.[72] She blames the gods for setting their hearts on fire, and for ruining the joy they shared and could have shared. She fails to take responsibility for his death, and this compounds her sins. Thisbe picks up the dead body and holds him, "now sche wepte and nou sche kiste," until at last (CA III.1483,1486):

> ... er sche it wiste,
> So gret a sorwe is to hire falle,
> Which overgoth hire wittes alle.
> (CA III.1486–88)

She places the "swerdes point" at her heart, and falls down upon it (CA III.1488,1490):

> And thus bothe on o swerd bledende
> Thei weren founde ded liggende.
> (CA III.1493–94)

Thisbe has lost her wits and, acting without reason, she kills herself. Blinded by love, the young couple are incapable of using their reason.[73]

Chaucer's Thisbe is also wild with grief: she tears her hair, weeps, and even "with his blod hireselve gan she peynte" (LGW II.875). She kisses "his frosty mouth so cold," and wonders aloud who killed him (LGW II.877). He awakens for a moment, a detail Chaucer (and Matthew) borrow from Ovid but Gower eliminates—and then she sees her bloodied wimple and his empty sword sheath. She is quiet for a moment as she realizes what has occurred, and then she calmly announces that she is strong enough to kill herself:

> 'I wol thee folwe ded, and I wol be
> Felawe and cause ek of thy deth,' quod she.
> (LGW II.894–95)

Chaucer follows Ovid, whose Thisbe comes to the realization that she is the cause of Pyramus' death and she takes full responsibility for it. Gower's heroine reacts quite differently, as noted above.

Genius warns Amans to beware of his own responsibility to conduct himself properly in Love matters, that he avoid rash behavior and keep his wits about him at all time, so that his thoughts and therefore his actions are not futile, as Pyramus' and Thisbe's. Gower's line—"kep that thou thi witt ne waste / Upon thi thoght in aventure"—is difficult to translate, but I believe he is referring to the couple's impetuous decisions (CA III.1498–9). Pyramus concludes quite suddenly that Thisbe is dead and that he is at fault (CA III.1428). He decides to kill himself before he thinks to look for her or call out her name. He and Thisbe both act impulsively. It is important that man meet his obligations and not pursue ridiculous adventures cooked in daydreams, as Amans does. Neither Pyramus nor Thisbe act responsibly, not in planning their adventure, nor in keeping their appointment, and their irrational haste to love is faulted.

In the *Confessio* Gower focuses on the natural impulses within man, so much so that "an awareness of these forces pervades every love-tale that Gower tells."[74] Gower never explains Pyramus and Thisbe's urgency to be together as anything other than an overwhelming passion. Matthew characterizes it as "unchecked lunacy [which] surpasses madness" (PT 228).[75] The urgency the lovers feel to consummate their love is not a rational need, and it is their inability to control their sexual passion which pushes them towards their gruesome deaths. Pyramus' and Thisbe's love is too passionate, and mad passion such as theirs does not heed reason; their foolish behavior is not rewarded in Gower's poetry.

In the Tale of Thisbe, the lovers rush to plan a way to share their erotic desires, without the benefit of a wedding. They plan to meet secretly at night, thereby exposing themselves to the dangers of the darkness—thieves, wild animals, or the basic impropriety of a young lady walking out of the town walls alone. The couple chooses *kinde*, passionate desire, over reason, their better judgment, and in so doing they ignore the voice of reason. Perhaps Gower does not mention any barriers to their love in order to emphasize the magnitude of their sin against Love, the sin of foolhaste which is a property of Wrath, a Deadly Sin. Hot-headedness never gets lovers anywhere in Gower, and in this tale there is no exception. Had the lovers been ruled by wisdom and met at daylight, or perhaps more to Gower's point, had they waited until their presumed union was sanctified by the church, a premise which underlies the *Confessio*, they may have been fortunate enough to be rewarded by Love. Promises of love are never exchanged by these young lovers, and no vows of marriage—not even secret ones—are pledged. In the *Legend* Pyramus and Thisbe pledge themselves to one another in a covenant which the Narrator sees fit to praise (LGW II. 778–90).[76] Chaucer alludes to this covenant in the death scene when Thisbe utters what Minnis characterizes as "arresting word-play:"[77]

> 'And though that nothing, save the deth only,
> Mighte thee fro me departe trewely,
> Thow shalt no more departe now fro me
> Than fro the deth, for I wol go with thee.'
> (LGW II.896–99)

Matthew also implies that there existed between the pagan lovers a bond of marriage. In his tale Thisbe's short death speech echoes with words from the Christian wedding ceremony: "Let no hand dare to sunder those whom death has joined together" (PT 232).

Thisbe walks through town wearing a disguise of some sort; perhaps her wimple partially covers her face (CA III.1385). She exerts herself by going abroad at night, a freedom that women in the Middle Ages are not permitted. Thisbe is aggressively seeking a lover, a husband, and in secretly meeting Pyramus as she does, she is assuming a male privilege, that of walking out of the town walls, without a chaperone or companion;[78] arguably it is Thisbe's first time walking freely as a man would do. Bold Thisbe displays a female masculinity. In her disguise, Thisbe transgresses her gender and "prove[s] . . . [herself to be] a strong and independent" character; her walk out to the well near the forest took some bravery (CA III.1391).[79] Disguise "often endows . . . [women characters] with the power to act in their own behalf and with an individualism unheard of for other female characters in medieval literature."[80] Killing herself, although both a rash and sinful action, is one of only two things Thisbe has done on her own behalf in the tale; she exerts herself forcefully, but it is for the last time.[81] Although Thisbe is not Pyramus' wife, she plays the role of obedient wife by following Pyramus into death; she even uses the same sword.[82] Jill Mann refers to Chaucer's Thisbe, but it is the same with Gower's heroine: in death the lovers become one being, "male courage and female courage become indistinguishable."[83]

No matter how admirable it may be for Gower's Thisbe to act as a strong and independent woman, she is not acting in accord with reason and the rules of her society, and this is against the precepts of Gower's *Confessio*. Moments before her suicide, Thisbe holds the dead Pyramus, and is described as if she were in a trance, operating without reason, unable to think clearly (CA III.1483–88). And that kind of ungoverned behavior is exactly the kind that his Confessor warns Amans against. Pyramus kills himself thinking he is the cause of Thisbe's death, while Thisbe refuses to acknowledge even the slightest amount of responsibility for Pyramus' death, and this point becomes Genius' first comment upon the tale:

> Now thou, mi Sone, hast herd this tale,
> Bewar that of thin oghne bale
> Thou be noght cause in thi folhaste,
> And kep that thou thi witt ne waste
> Upon thi thoght in aventure,
> Wherof thi lyves forfeture
> Mai falle.
> (CA III.1495–1501)

Accepting responsibility for one's actions in love and in life is a precept Genius hopes Amans will learn from this tragic tale. Gower eliminates the metamorphosis found in Ovid.[84]

Gower is a firm believer in man's reasoning capabilities, and he writes on this theme continuously. He recognizes that there is a constant struggle between man's *kinde* or natural impulses and his reason, but nonetheless he believes man must choose reason over passion at all costs. He is not a fatalist; he believes that man has the free will to choose his own destiny, and that is one of the reasons why he is incensed by irrational behavior. Too much passion leads to loss of reason; it is a precept St. Thomas Aquinas preaches in the *Summa Theologiæ*:

> [There are three ways] in which a man who is emotionally aroused fails to consider in particular what he knows in general, for emotion hinders such consideration. . . . The third way is by way of physical condition which somehow hampers reason so that one is unable to act freely, e.g. the way sleep or drunkenness physically disables one for rational accomplishments. This last can also occur by reason of emotional pressure which can be so intense that a man is completely deprived of the use of reason, for many men are completely carried out of their minds by excessive wrath or love. (ST Q.77.2.R2)

In Book III the vice examined is Wrath and her five daughters; "contek" or contention, is one of the daughters. The MED defines "contek" as "dissension , discord, conflict, strife," and cites Book III.2735 in the *Confessio* as an example. In this passage, Genius cautions Amans to have patience and mercy, especially if he hopes to be a lover:

> Thou schalt be soft in compaignie,
> Withoute Contek or Folhaste:
> For elles miht thou longe waste
> Thi time, er that thou have thi wille
> Of love.
> (CA III.2734–38)

In the *Mirour* Gower describes Contention:

> Contention, who spares no friend, wears her heart in the middle of her mouth. This the wise man says in his teaching. For whatever she bears in her heart, she lets out by the open door, so that to hear her is a judgment. Seneca also compares Contention to the furnace that is lighted, whose flame never dies out; for all the water of the Thames or even of the Gironde, if it were added, could not suffice—so strong it is (MO 4153).

The MED's second definition for contek is "the action of engaging in a physical encounter in combat, or in warfare," and the *Confessio*, Book III, is again cited. This passage begins the section on the vice of Wrath, of which two of the

Daughter sins are "Contek and Homicide, / That ben to drede on every side" (CA III.1093–94):

> Contek, so as the bokes sein,
> Folhast hath to his Chamberlein,
> Be whos conseil al unavised
> Is Pacience most despised,
> Til Homicide with hem meete.
> (CA III.1095–99)

Thus contek or dissension is linked with both foolhaste and homicide; two actions which are illustrated in the tales of Albinus and Rosemund and Pyramus and Thisbe. The Angry man, filled with Ill Temper, one of the Sin's daughters, is unable to think clearly. In the *Mirour* Gower writes

> ... anyone would be foolish not to see that it is well to avoid Ill Temper, through whom the virtues are always overthrown, through whom reason is destroyed and turns into madness, through whom in society good people are often troubled, through whom many a man in this life forgets himself and then his God, whereby in the end he will be destroyed (MO 4033).

A man needs Patience to stand against Ill Temper and Homicide:

> Patience ... has Mercy as her handmaiden, so she never has her hand stretched forth to take vengeance with the sword, and if she sees others do ill in this respect, she is much disturbed in her heart (MO 13897).

Rosemund is inflamed with Ill Temper and she displays no mercy for her husband's error; she is not at peace until she commits Homicide. In the Tale of Rosemund passions are roused by pride and revenge, reason is overthrown, and death and destruction follow. Pyramus and Thisbe both lack patience, too. Gower rebukes Pyramus and Thisbe for their rashness in love, for he never idealizes amorous abandonment in the *Confessio*. The frantic pace of the tale contributes to its overall message of furtive, secretive love, and emphasizes Pyramus' and Thisbe's love error. Love that is freely expressed between a man and a woman, and acknowledged by their families and neighbors, is the kind of love that Gower advocates. When reason is overthrown in the internal battle between will, reason and love, the vices win, as they do in these tales. Only Lovers who adopt reason and restraint in their lovemaking will be successful in love—this is the aspect of love continually emphasized in Gower's *Confessio*.

Conclusion

There is within the Aspects of Love an "incompatibility between the drives of nature and the demands of morality" which becomes "troublingly apparent" through the *Confessio*.[85] This incompatibility is often illustrated in the tales Genius tells, and what drives the poem towards its end. Nature can be in harmony with reason; nature can even prompt a man towards reason, as the ending of the *Confessio* so well illustrates. Gower reconciles these two forces in the tales that he tells, and he does so by continually recommending that man heed the voice of reason and therefore keep his natural impulses under control. Following this natural, sexual impulse while disregarding reason is what propels many lovers in the *Confessio* into situations which spin out beyond their control. In the Tale of Rosemund Genius examines Pride, the first Deadly Sin, and illustrates how Albinus foolishly throws away his happy marriage, his kingdom and his life by his unreasonable propensity to boast of his sexual and battlefield conquests. Gower focuses upon unrestrained passion in the Tale of Thisbe to portray how they recklessly disregard what is deemed proper by reason and society, in both planning a secret rendezvous and in their double suicide.

Following Alan of Lille and Jean de Meun, Gower explores the tension between *kinde* and reason in the tales of love that he tells. Marriage offers man the means to harmonize his natural reason with his natural instinct, and by telling tales of married and unmarried lovers, Genius tries to teach Amans how to reach this harmony in his own life. Gower espouses man's ability and his duty to govern his behavior and live and love properly throughout his three major works, the *Mirour*, the *Vox*, and the *Confessio*. In claiming that man should not be ruled by *kinde*, his passions, alone, Gower affirms his belief that man needs to rely upon his ability to reason, the faculty which distinguishes man from beast. Gower does not view Nature as "morally suspect," and he never condemns Nature's promptings, but he does insist that they can be in harmony with reason.[86] The two faculties, passion and reason, both work together and play against each other, and the tales within the *Confessio* illustrate that while it is a struggle for man to overcome his irrational desires and passions, it can be accomplished, as it is most significantly in the Marriage Tales of the Four Wives. Although mankind often succumbs to the pleasures of the flesh, he can control his passions with his reason. Gower illustrates both man's—and woman's—habit of succumbing to his desires in the Tales of the Forsaken Women, and in controlling them in the Tales of the Four Wives.

Chapter Two
Marriage and the Four Wives

A MONG THE COMPANY OF LOVERS WHO WALK BY THE UNCONSCIOUS
Amans in the final scenes of the *Confessio* are the "foure wyves" (CA
VIII.2615), women famous from Antiquity for their wifely chastity,
prudence and fidelity: Penelope, Alceone, Alcestis, and Lucrece. They walk
silently by the wounded lover as he hears their names "most comended" and
"Men" gave them

> reverence
> As thogh they hadden be goddesses,
> Of al this world or Emperesses.
> (CA VIII.2610–12)

Amans learns that the "foure wyves[']" tales of "alle goode / . . . Mariage[s]" have been recorded "in Cronique" by many poets (CA VIII.2615, 2617–18, 2620). The Four Wives and their Marriage Tales embody truth in marriage, a central theme of the *Confessio* which Gower stresses throughout the poem. Gower tells their tales—or the parts of them suited to his needs—and further honors each Wife by placing her in the pageant of revered lovers in Book VIII. Penelope guarded her virtue while waiting patiently for her husband to return from war; Alceone, sick with grief, bravely left her human form to follow her beloved husband into the next world; Alcestis literally died so her cherished husband would live; and Lucrece chose suicide in order to remove a dishonorable stain from her and her honored husband's name. Truth and "honeste" love in marriage—Gower's love-doctrine—is best expressed in the Marriage Tales of the Four Wives.

Gower relies upon Ovid's *Heroides*, *Metamorphoses*, *Fasti*, and *Ovid moralisé*, as well as the many commentaries available during the fourteenth century on these works, for his Marriage Tales of the Four Wives.¹ During the Middle Ages, Ovid's texts were very popular and there was a "considerable . . . effort to moralize Ovid." ² Gower is obviously very familiar with Ovid, but it is difficult to determine precisely which Ovidian source Gower used for what detail for he could have been familiar with many of the "mediaeval Ovid" works. In the Middle Ages, Ovid the Preceptor was viewed as "a champion of married love," and his *Ars amatoria* and *Remedia amoris* were the among the most popular texts.³ The *Ars* and the *Remedia* were highly glossed and edited by church men who sought to moralize Ovid and make his works acceptable.⁴ Genius uses Ovid's tales to point out Amans' sins against Love following the medieval "don't do this" method of teaching. This method of teaching sometimes makes the sin seems more attractive than the cure; however, the practice in the twelfth century and later was to describe the sin so man avoids it.⁵ Genius tells Amans how to succeed in love by pointing out what does not work, much like Ovid does in his pair of handbooks for lovers, the *Ars* and the *Remedia*, but the deep cynicism found in Ovid is missing from the *Confessio*.⁶

Gower's Marriage Tales of the Four Wives heighten and promote married love, as he does throughout the *Traitié*. Although I am focusing on the women in these Marriage Tales, historically the emphasis in the tales themselves is often on the male character. There is little doubt, for example, that Penelope's letter in Book IV of the *Confessio* is merely part of the much larger and more substantial Ulysses tale, told in five episodes throughout the poem. I believe illumination of Gower's women is needed, especially in relation to the importance that Gower attaches to marriage. A marriage of reciprocal love is Gower's cure for controlling a passionate nature, and the best way for man and woman to enjoy a life of mutual happiness. Gower sieves through his sources to give us unique portraits of four women who are the epitome of the perfect wife. His portraits of the Wives and their marriages, and his sympathetic rendering of their tales, reveals something of his sympathy towards women. I will examine and contrast the marriages and relationships to the *Traitié*, and to Ovid's and Chaucer's renderings. In the *Traitié*, he emphases truth-in-marriage:

> Of the three blessed estates it is the second which disposes itself to marriage in righteous love; and he who brings to ruin this order in wantonness has much to fear if he does not lead himself back. Therefore it is good that each one prepare himself to love with unblemished fidelity. He is not loving who misguides his love (Tr XVIII. 2.8–14).

In this passage Gower leaves room for the sinful man to right himself, while advocating fidelity.

Throughout the *Confessio* Gower stresses that marriage must be based on 'trouthe':

> Forthi scholde every good man knowe
> And thenke, hou that in mariage
> His trouthe plight lith in morgage,
> Which if he breke, it is falshode.
> (CA VII.4226–9)

The Four Wives and their husbands have pledged their "trouthe" to one another and they honorably keep their vows. Gower stresses the bonds each wife has made with her husband, which affords them a peaceful and happy marriage. In the *Mirour* Gower describes Matrimony, the third daughter of Chastity, who is "endowed with authority, dignity, holiness, honor" (MO 17137). These are some of the characteristics that the Four Wives embrace and embody in their Marriage Tales.

The Tale of Penelope

Gower writes about the Greek war leader Ulysses in five places throughout the *Confessio*, each episode serving to represent a different deadly sin. In Book IV of the *Confessio*, which focuses upon the Sin of Sloth, Genius tells Amans the Tale of Penelope and her letter to her long-absent lord and husband Ulysses. Penelope is honored for her steadfast love and loyalty by ancient and medieval poets, and in Book IV she is exalted by Gower as well. In the letter she chides Ulysses for his long absence from home, a story Genius tells to teach Amans about the sin of Sloth. The love depicted between Ulysses and Penelope in this episode and in the homecoming scene in Book VI is a deep and caring love, the kind of love which Gower characterizes as "honeste" love. They are well matched in wisdom and resourcefulness, and their marriage is marked by a sexual attraction and frank sensuality which is not typically illuminated in other renditions of the tale. Ulysses is sometimes characterized by a voracious sexual appetite—he sleeps with both Circe and Calypso—but in Gower Penelope seems to share this drive, too. Her loyalty to Ulysses, a man who clearly loves her but nonetheless is unfaithful to her, is perhaps naïve, but in the *Confessio* Gower side-steps the issue of infidelity and focuses instead on their mutual love. The love between this married couple illustrates how Gower depicts a married love "Wherof the love is al honeste" (CA IV.1484).

Gower borrows this tale from the first letter in Ovid's *Heroides*, a choice position in this collection of intensely private love letters written by women to their absent husbands or lovers. The letters detail moments of crisis in the love affairs, and the women's pleas to their wayward men are both rich with the language of longing and bold with accusations of transgressions. The women in the *Heroides* sit on the sidelines as their men pursue heroic destinies in which they do not have a part.[7] In the fourteenth century the *Heroides* was read as an ethical work commending chaste wives,[8] and Penelope was the "prime *exemplum* of lawful and chaste love" for Ovid-commentators.[9] From antiquity forward, she is known as the most truthful and steadfast of wives. Gower's other sources probably included Guido delle Colonne's *Historia destructionis Troiae* (1287) and Benoit de Sainte-Maure's *Roman de Troie* (1272–87), two accounts of the Trojan-Greek battle. Chaucer commends her in the Balade within the Prologue to the *Legend*, while noting that she nonetheless does not compare to the illustrious Alcestis, who appears in that poem holding Cupid's hand (LGW Prol. 249–253). Perhaps Chaucer meant to include Penelope's tale in the *Legend*, but it is not one of the nine extant legends.[10] Chaucer writes of "Penelopees trouthe and good Alceste" in Book V of the *Troilus* (TC V.1778), and mentions her with Alcestis in the Man of Law's Tale (MLT 75), the Franklin's Tale (FranT 1442–43), and the *Book of the Duchess* (BD 1080)—yet he never tells her tale.

Gower begins his tale with praise of Penelope, "Which was to ... [Ulysses] his trewe wif" (CA IV.153). The siege at Troy continues, and Ulysses and his army of men are among the worthy knights who have camped there a long time (CA IV.149–150). Genius tells us Penelope's exact words of the letter to Ulysses, whom she addresses as "'Mi worthi love and lord also'" (CA IV.157). In her letter she complains of his "lachesce," and begs him to come home (CA IV.154). The MED defines "lachesse" or "lachesce" as "tardiness [or] procrastination," and cites Genius' explanation of a slothful man in Book IV:[11]

> The ferste point of Slowthe I calle
> Lachesce, and is chief of alle,
> And hath this propreliche of kinde,
> To leven alle thing behinde.
> Of that he mihte do now hier
> He tarieth al the longe yer,
> And everemore he seith, 'Tomorwe."
> (CA IV. 3–9)

In the Latin headnote to Book IV, sloth is described as "nursemaid to the vices" (CA IV.1). Penelope begins her letter with a universal statement: that a woman left alone and unguarded will be wooed by men (CA IV.157–164). It is a clever way to attract her slothful husband's attention. Penelope has no shortage of would-be lovers: "welnyh every man ... my love secheth, / With gret preiere and me besecheth" (CA IV.168–70). Some tell her "That ye ben ded," or that ye ben besein / To love a newe and leve me"(CA IV.178–181). Despite her lonely and precarious situation, it is most interestingly that Gower's Penelope does not express anger or impatience in her letter; neither is she a shrew or a nag. The relatively calm tone of voice heard throughout the purposeful and methodical letter heightens Penelope's noble upbringing and worthy character. Many poets follow commentators who wrote about wives who screech and scream like jackdaws, but Gower disregards these conventions entirely; Penelope's voice is not even mentioned. Penelope carefully composes a letter which gently baits her husband's jealousy, a word Gower does not use in this tale, but which is nonetheless invoked. She is someone Gower's audience could admire both for her restraint and her wisdom; she is a woman ruled by reason.

In the Middle Ages, English menfolk were often away from home, either engaged in war, or on crusades. Ulysses' long stay at the Troy campaign and Penelope's lonely situation would perhaps be understandable to the women in Gower's audience. Like many women in London and the English countryside in the fourteenth century, Penelope managed the household alone.[12] Because of real life situations such as this, Gower's audience knew that Ulysses ought to have some concern over who is guarding not only his wife, but his estate, his title, and his kingdom. Penelope and their young son Telemachus are the surety to his kingdom; if she remarries, her new husband assumes Ulysses' title, that of king and ruler. Ann McMillan writes of Chaucer's *Legend*, but the point is equally valid for Gower's Penelope tale and Gower's London:

> In the world of Homer . . . , a man's choice of wife could literally be a matter of life and death. If he went away to war for a long time, she gained at least some measure of control over his property. Unchastity might lead to deceit, theft, murder, or to the passing of a man's property into the hands of bastards. A good wife was a man's most important investment, for which the culturally enforced ideal of chastity functioned as a sort of guarantee.[13]

One is tempted to wonder why Ulysses does not consider his good wife while he lingers in Troy and later dallies on the islands with Circe and Calypso.

Penelope writes that she has retained her spotless reputation—"Mai noman do my chekes rede"—but pointedly ends her letter by reminding her husband that slothful behavior tempts Fortune (CA IV.186–189). She closes the letter by appealing to her husband's sensuality, suggesting he "thenke hou that sche was al his," and once together again, he "wolde his love aquite, / To hire ayeinward" (CA IV.193,195). The second definition of the word "aquite" in the MED is "to reciprocate (love)."[14] Penelope displays her frisky side as she appeals to her husband's sexual desires; the couple, of course, has not shared a bed in many years. Penelope does not want a letter from her tardy husband—"he non other paper waste"—rather she urges him to come home immediately: "come himself in alle haste" (CA IV. 198,197). Ulysses is under the spell of Sloth, but Penelope has no sympathy for his plight. She expects him to "kepe and holde his trowthe / Withoute lette of eny Slowthe" (CA IV.199–200). Penelope entreats her husband to keep his pledge to honor his marriage vow, to come home and act the role of husband. Gower emphasizes this solemn vow which Penelope and

Ulysses have pledged to one another: she is beleaguered with would-be lovers, and her home is overrun with suitors, yet she has remained loyal and steadfast to her absent husband. She honors her vow of truth to Ulysses with her every action; therefore it is fitting that she is revered as a paragon of wifely virtue.

In the world of chivalry and warfare, the one in which Ulysses accumulates such fame, "trowthe" is also defined as steadfastness. Ulysses is guilty of neglecting not only his wife, but his kingdom and his people as well. It is permissible to guess that Gower is taking a stab at Richard II, who neglects his people by not producing an heir to the throne.[15] Like Richard II, Ulysses is slothful in love and in his duties to the people over whom he rules. Ulysses is also guilty of infidelity, a word whose opposite, fidelity, is implied in the word "trowthe," but interestingly enough, nowhere in the several episodes of the Ulysses tale that Gower recounts does the poet admonish the hero for his infidelity. Whether or not Penelope knows or cares that her husband has cheated on her is not mentioned in the letter tale in Book IV.

Penelope's letter reaches Ulysses at Troy "wher the grete Siege / Was leid" (CA IV.202–03). Ulysses is described as a man ruled by reason:

> . . . wisdom hath pourveied
> Of al that to reson belongeth,
> With gentil herte underfongeth.
> (CA IV.201–02)

He is "riht inly glad" to receive a letter from his "trewe wyf" (CA IV.208). While reading the letter Love seizes Ulysses' heart and he cannot stop thinking about her:

> Bot love his herte hath so thorghsesed
> With pure ymaginacioun,
> That for non occupacioun
> Which he can take on other side,
> He mai noght flitt his herte aside
> Fro that his wif him hadde enformed.
> (CA IV.210–16)

Like Amans, Troilus and countless other lovers struck by Cupid's arrow, Ulysses is consumed by Love. Once Love seizes the heart, a man's reason is overcome—"thei knowe noght / What reson is"—and he is filled with desire (CA VI.86–87). Gathering "al the wille of his corage," Ulysses defeats sloth and vows to "take the viage / Homward" as soon as the siege is over (CA IV.217–19). Sloth is not an easy Deadly Sin from which to recover, but it is a black stain upon Ulysses[16] that he neglects one of the most virtuous women in all literature. Many poets follow Homer and praise Ulysses for his wisdom, but Gower's Ulysses seems less worthy, less sapient, less heroic than his myth testifies. Nonetheless Ulysses conjures up Penelope's image, "Which he desireth most of alle" (CA IV. 223–24), he returns to her:

> He made non delaiement,
> Bot goth him home in alle hihe,
> Wher that he fond tofore his yhe
> His worthi wif in good astat.
> (CA IV.226–29)

By returning home, Ulysses defeats "Slowthe" (CA IV.231) using both Love and Reason: it is an unusual example of how a man's reason and his passion can work together to achieve the same ends! Genius reminds Amans that sloth "hindreth many a cause honeste," and in this case, it nearly ruined the "honeste love" shared by Penelope and Ulysses (CA IV.232).

In the *Heroides* Penelope questions her husband's sloth in a direct manner; Gower's Penelope is much more subtle. Gower's Penelope does not have the anger or the suspicion of Ovid's heroine. In Ovid Penelope assumes Ulysses has a new lady-love and out of jealousy, she taunts him ruefully: "Perhaps you describe me as simple, / and fit only for keeping your royal house" (Her 92–93). Her biting tone cuts through the centuries, and conjures up the anger of a woman scorned. Ovid does not tell his readers of the illicit affairs Ulysses enjoys with both Calypso and Circe; readers are left to recall those adventures from Homer. In Ovid's hands Penelope becomes a suspicious woman, while Gower concentrates upon the bond of truth and love between the couple, and his Penelope does not write angry words. Gower's Penelope knows when to be silent; this admirable characteristic adds to her patience and virtuous character.

Ovid's Penelope writes that father Icarius "begs / me to abandon my widow's bed. / He scolds me and says I am foolish to wait" (Her 97–99). Boldly defending her identity, Penelope says "I am Penelope and I / am Ulysses' wife (Her 100–101), thereby stating that she is, like Criseyde, her "owen wommman," able to stand independent, yet pleased to be his wife (TC II.750). This is an interesting statement which bolsters her reputation as strong and proud woman. Penelope is proud to be the wife of a king, and she does not want to relinquish that title for the one her father uses—widow. She hauntingly ends her letter by reminding her husband that when he left her in Ithaca, she was a young girl, but time marches on, and she is now "an old woman" (Her 142). Naming herself as old is a bad move. This is the letter of a woman who has not read Ovid's *Ars*, a book which urged women to always strive to maintain their youthful looks. Calling attention to one's age is directly contrary to Ovid's teachings. Gower excludes these details, but his medieval audience most likely knew Ovid's rendition.

Behind the scenes in Ovid's Penelope tale then is a Penelope who, as head of the household,

> alternates between male and female roles throughout the action: she plays the deserted wife, . . . forgiving wife, a range of characters who all, of course, are focused on the goal of restoring her status as wife. This strong determination, which disregards gender and societal constraints, is an important factor in the characterization of the abandoned wife as a hero.[17]

To apply this argument to Gower, as soon as Ulysses returns home in Book VI of the *Confessio*, Penelope drops her heroic stance to become the "forgiving wife," and she is thus no longer an important player in the Ulysses tales Gower tells. Gower does not show us her domestic and managerial skills, but they lurk in the background.

In Gower the mere thought of Penelope's womanliness—the "visage of Penelope"—is enough to heat up Ulysses' desire to see his wife. Penelope is usually described as a beautiful woman, but all Gower tells us is that her beauty, or at the least her "visage," propels her slothful husband into action. Perhaps Gower's lack of description enables him to focus upon the characteristics which raise her above all women, her prudence and loyalty. Throughout antiquity Penelope is celebrated as a faithful and a devoted wife who takes no lovers while her husband is away at Troy. Gower eliminates portions of the Penelope myth, such as the tapestry weaving, and focuses instead upon the passionate love shared by the couple. Although Ulysses is guilty of neglecting his wife, he does respond to Penelope's letter with merit, and it becomes clear that the couple share a good marriage. The rest of the Homeric tale—the ten years of wandering and the sexual dalliances with Circe and Calypso—is completely ignored by Gower in the letter episode.

In Book VI Gower, however, describes Ulysses' homecoming and we are told of his sexual escapades. During his sojourn on the islands, Penelope is far from Ulysses' mind. He seduces both Circe and Calypso through his mastery of sorcery (CA VI.1459). Ulysses, married man,

> He tok of hem so wel his part,
> That he begat Circes with childe.
> (CA VI.1460–61)

He then sets sail for Ithaca, leaving the "toswolle" Circe behind (CA VI.1467). When he finally returns home to Ithaca and to Penelope, his sin is unknown to her. Gower inserts sudden praise for Penelope and describes how she held off her suitors (without mentioning the tapestry):

> A betre wif ther mai non be,
> And yit ther ben ynowhe of goode.
> (CA VI.1472–73)

Ulysses boasts of his wife's goodness and loyalty, calling her "on of al the beste" (CA VI.1479,1481). Penelope is delighted to see her husband home:

> In al this world ne mihte be
> A gladdere womman than was sche.
> (CA VI.1489–90)

She welcomes her slothful husband home without chiding him. Several lines later we learn that the fame of Ulysses' return spreads "Thurghout the lond," and "mochel joie" is made of his homecoming (CA VI.1492,1496). The people are glad to see him, and his wife "was such as sche be schold"; presumably Penelope forgives her husband of his sin of sloth (CA VI.1506). Despite the fact that we know Ulysses has been unfaithful, the picture Gower presents is one of domestic joy. In Gower actions speak so much louder than words; Penelope never questions her husband's delay. She has been alone for over ten years, she has faced down suitor after suitor, she has carefully maintained control of the kingdom, and she has raised their son to manhood: her patience and fortitude are rewarded.

The differences between the characters of the wife and the husband are by this time quite apparent. By Book VI Ulysses has become an adulterer unworthy of the virtuous Penelope, and it is difficult to reconcile the two tales. Gower describes Ulysses leaving a pregnant Circe and sailing home towards Penelope in practically the same breath. Despite the emphasis Gower places upon truth in marriage in this tale and in others, and despite the praise heaped upon Penelope as a virtuous wife, Gower does not condemn Ulysses for his adulterous liaison with Circe in the *Confessio*. Ulysses is guilty of adultery, a sin which most certainly makes the wise king unworthy of such an exemplary queen, but Gower does not mention it. Reconciling Ulysses' adulterous affairs to his marriage to one of the best of all women is an old problem in the Ulysses tradition. As W. B. Stanford puts it, "How could a man who yielded to the amorous enticements of Circe (and Calypso) be regarded as a noble example of prudence and virtue?"[18] Later classical writers never quite solved this problem; neither does Gower. In Gower Ulysses is killed by his illegitimate son, but it is not because he is an adulterer—he is murdered because he has lost his ability to reason and correctly interpret the dream of his own death (CA VI.1484). Perhaps Ulysses' inability to reason is somehow tied to his sin of adultery; perhaps because he is overcome with passions run amok he no longer can interpret dreams.

In the *Traitié*, however, Ulysses dies as a direct result of his infidelity (Tr VI.3). Gower devotes one verse to the Tale of Ulysses and Penelope, and explains Ulysses' infidelity without exonerating him: King Ulysses, to please his body, was unfaithful to Penelope (Tr VI.3.15–16). Ulysses meets an untimely and rather sudden death, which is linked to his adulterous behavior in the Latin sidenote (Tr VI.3). The verse's refrain refers to the circular motion of life: the end of life's journey indicates or embodies the entire path from which it began (Tr VI.3.20–21). Unfaithful Ulysses thus receives his just due—death. In the *Mirour* Gower writes that three punishments await the man or woman guilty of adultery: mutilation, defamation, or sudden death (MO 9025). This is reiterated in the refrain of the *Traitié* VIII: "God will avenge the broken marriage" (Tr VIII.6). In the *Mirour*, adulterous husbands amass more of the poet's wrath than adulterous wives:

> But what shall we say of foolish husbands, who for their part have committed the evil of adultery and have betrayed their faith? Surely, in my opinion, they do much worse in their turn than women. For a husband has at his side his wife as his subject and servant, who is always ready to do his will; so it is not necessary that he be taken by love for other women (MO 8977).

Ulysses doubly defiles Penelope's marriage bed by two adulterous affairs, one with Circe, the other with Calypso. He does not apologize for the affairs, and neither does he confess or make amends to his wife. Their marriage is indeed brought to ruin, and so is he, through his bastard son's murderous hand, according to the *Traitié*. Gower writes: "Therefore whoever corrupts marriage shall be brought ruin unless he has the grace to make amends" (MO 9073). In the letter tale in the *Confessio*, however, Gower glosses over the parts of the Ulysses/Penelope myth which do not fit his pro-marriage agenda. In praising Penelope as a good wife, Gower echoes the sentiments of medieval writers who considered her to be the epitome of virtue.[19]

Gower's poetry can be disappointing in its silence, but it is a common feature of his oeuvre. We are simply not privy to Penelope's thoughts, and we cannot assume she knows of Ulysses' adulterous affairs.[20] In reading Gower we want to know Penelope's reaction to her husband's infidelity; likewise, we want to know what Alcestis says to Ametus on his deathbed, and we want to know what Lucrece is thinking when she realizes Arrons is about to rape her, but Gower does not tell us: "what sche mette, / God wot" (CA VII.4966–68). Yeager argues well that

> despite these tantalizing silences, the fact is that we seldom feel out of touch with the inner workings of Gower's characters. We can derive their thoughts

from their actions quite satisfactorily—and it is important that we see this as a method Gower employed to present or portray—not as a failure to acknowledge—introspection.[21]

Regardless of whether Penelope knew Ulysses committed adultery, her behavior is how we must perceive her: she is a paragon of wifely virtue in all her actions.

Gower recounts another portion of the Ulysses and Penelope tale in Book IV, lines 1815–1900 of the *Confessio*. Genius tells Amans the episode in which King Nauplus persuades Ulysses to join the Greek forces at Troy. From this tale we gather a bit more information about the sensual love shared by Ulysses and Penelope. Nauplus asks Ulysses to join the Troy campaign, but Ulysses, who "loveth hote" his wife Penelope, would rather stay at home with her (CA IV.1820, 1823). Their love is characterized here as not only a deep emotional regard, but as frank sensuality.[22] To avoid war, Ulysses schemes to "best beguile" Nauplus, so he can "duelle stille / At home and welde his love at wille" (CA IV.1824,1825–27). The MED translates the verb "to weld" as "to control," have "authority, command"; also, "to make proper use of something."[23] Ulysses enjoys the sexual pleasure he and Penelope share, and they seemingly make love often. He is a slave to wantonness, preferring to frolic in bed with his wife Penelope than join the army at Troy. This detail, that Ulysses burns with desire for Penelope, is an intimate glance into a marriage in which sex plays a prominent role. There exists a healthy dose of sexual attraction between the married couple which is utmost in Ulysses' mind. His passion outweighs his call to duty and to reason, handily winning the struggle between reason and *kinde*, and he feigns insanity to avoid joining the campaign. Nauplus, however, sees through Ulysses' trick and is appalled by his cowardly and ungallant behavior. He taunts him for preferring his wife's company to his fellow knights' (CA IV.1861–68). Nauplus sternly warns Ulysses that double shame awaits him, that his reputation will be hindered if word gets out that he "sette[s]" his "lustes . . . above" his knighthood (CA IV.1875–79). Ulysses, whose heart is "fyred / Upon his wif," hears Nauplus' words and is ashamed of his behavior (CA IV.1882,1885). The "sotie / Of love" hindered Ulysses' ability to reason, but with Nauplus' help, Ulysses regains his reason and goes off to battle (CA IV.1887–88). Genius reminds Amans that Love's power is great, and does not discriminate between wise man and fool (CA VI.84):

The wise Salomon was nome,
And stronge Sampson was overcome,
The knihtli David him ne mihte
Rescoue.
(CA VI.93–96)

One can see where the Renaissance and modern poets got the notion to magnify "the erotic element in Ulysses' character into a dominate passion"[24]—it runs through Ovid, and Gower picks it up and amplifies it.

Marriage is a bond which Gower holds in high esteem, but man's reason and his duty to follow it carries an equally strong contract in Gower's repertoire. While it is most honorable that Ulysses as a lover wants to remain at home with his beloved wife rather than join the Greek troops, this decision could ruin his reputation as a worthy knight. In the headnote to book five, chapter four of the *Vox*, Gower writes of "lustful love for women," saying it can "dominate a knight, . . . [and] veritably extinguish . . . all chivalrous virtue in him" (VC 5.4):

> When a wise knight falls [under a woman's spell], his fame forsakes him, as though he were fatuous and foolish. When carnal love holds the mind ensnared, an intelligent man's reason becomes irrational. When the brightness of human intelligence is clouded over by the shadow of the flesh, and the spirit of reason withdraws into the flesh, man's reason stands utterly scorned. It is a slave to the flesh, and scarcely retains the post of handmaiden (VC 5.4.230ff).

Had Nauplus' scheme failed, according to the *Vox* passage above, Ulysses would have become a shell of his former self, scarcely a handmaiden, a man scorned for his foolishness, his reason slave to his flesh. Ulysses, however, recovers his reason, and joins the Greeks. Blind love ensnares all men, but men who curb their passionate natures and follow reason will receive the "world's praises" for their chivalrous behavior (CA IV.1).

Despite the difficulties the various Ulysses and Penelope myths present, the manner in which Gower presents this husband and wife is remarkable for his attention to the love they share. Penelope's virtuous behavior is unmatched, and her husband's deep love for her is apparent in his reaction to her letter. That Penelope manages to call her husband home without blaming him or questioning his tardiness exemplifies her nature as the paragon of virtue among women, and a chaste and lawful lover, the first of the revered Four Wives. Their homecoming scene is a joyous occasion of a married couple embracing and preparing to enjoy one of the fruits of marriage sanctioned by Gower, sexual enjoyment. In this Ulysses episode, Genius gives us a bit more information about married love. In marriage, couples can satiate their sexual appetites "At home and welde [their] . . . love at wille" (CA IV.1827). It is not the thrust of Gower's message, but it illuminates one of the glories of married love: marriage offers couples sanctioned sexual fulfillment.

The Tale of Alceone

Genius tells Amans the Tale of Alceone in Book IV of the *Confessio*; it is another tale that focuses on the sin of sloth. Genius says that some slothful men prefer sleep to lovemaking, something Amans is aghast to hear. When it comes to love, Amans is not lazy: "To love forto ben excused / That I no Sompnolence have used" (CA IV.2769–70). He works hard to try to obtain his lady's interest and win her pleasure. He twitters about her, always at her "comaunde":

> To rede and here of Troilus,
> Riht as sche wole or so or thus,
> I am al redi to consente.
> (CA IV.2794–97)

Amans would rather love than sleep, but he admits to suffering from sleeplessness, one of the many symptoms of lovesickness.[25] Amans tells Genius he is tormented in his sleep by dreams "drecched to the fulle / Of love" (CA IV.2896–97). In his dreams "Danger [the lady's guardian] is left behinde" and consequently Amans receives much joy, but when he awakens, "al torned into sorwe" for none of the dream is true (CA IV.2903–04,2908). In an effort to cure him of his lovesickness, Genius recounts a tale from "olde daies gon" (CA IV.2926).

This is the Tale of Alceone, which Gower found in Ovid's *Metamorphoses*.[26] Only in Gower does the metamorphosed Alceone dote on her husband, and Gower adds many tender touches to illustrate the conjugal happiness this couple shares and which are not found elsewhere in other versions of the tale. In Chaucer's rendition of the tale in the *Book of the Duchess*, the deep love Gower conveys is missing. Chaucer eliminates Ceix's leave-taking of Alceone, a lovely scene in Gower, and he foregoes the metamorphosis at the end of the tale. Chaucer's Alceone dies from grief as soon as she learns her husband is dead; thereby the couple is not reunited or rewarded by the gods with another life. Gower, however, uses the two metamorphoses to "display ... [a] humane, moral and sentimental redirection of purpose," something he does with other Ovidian narratives as well.[27] Even as seabirds Alceone and Ceix share a bond of love.[28] Gower concentrates on Alceone and her dream, but the centerpiece of the tale is the very fine marriage the two lovers share, a mutual affection that sustains them through their metamorphoses into seabirds.

Gower wastes little time in letting the reader know that Ceix and Alceone share a loving marriage, something he adopts from Ovid. Gower uses simple but beautiful words to describe the love the king has for his wife Alceone:

> Which as hire oghne hertes lif
> Him loveth.
> (CA IV.2930–31)

The king's brother has been turned into a "Goshauk," a transformation that leaves Ceix with a great sadness (CA IV.2935). Like many medieval Christians in the fourteenth century, Ceix plans to go on a pilgrimage to do sacrifice and pray to the gods so his brother will be restored to human form (CA IV.2938,2941,2943). From this information we learn that King Ceix is a man of great compassion. He loves his wife, yet he feels so much commiseration for his brother that he is determined to travel "Into a strange regioun" to pray for his restoration (CA IV.2939). Ceix's decision to help his brother is a kindly, brotherly act, and if Alceone has objections, we do not know about them. In Ovid, Alceone does not want her husband to travel without her; in Gower, her thoughts are unspoken. In the *Book of the Duchess*, Chaucer does not mention a brother, and we are not told why Ceix "wol wenden over see" (BD 67). Unlike Ulysses, Gower's Ceix is not a slothful man. His brother needs help, and although he weeps to leave his wife, he carries out his plan of action.

In the *Mirour*, Gower writes about the third daughter of Chastity, Matrimony:

> Against vile Adultery, Chastity has her third daughter, who is called Matrimony. The canon and the civil laws says that she is good and gentle in four points with which she is endowed: authority, dignity, holiness, honor. These four points are gathered together in her, so that her virtue is honored by good people and much loved according to the view of the gospel (MO 17137).

In marriage, husband and wife should obey the laws of Matrimony. Matrimony is endowed with "authority, dignity, holiness, and honor," and the husband, of course, is the undisputed head of these four points. Gower illustrates this precept in the brief moment when we are told Ceix decides to go on a pilgrimage. Alceone accepts her husband's decision, and Ceix simply goes. I bring out this point because in Ovid's version of the tale Alceone does not want her husband to go, especially to go alone, and she complains long and loud. Gower does not follow Ovid's misogynistic strain here; indeed, the women in the *Confessio* are not shrews. In Ovid Alceone's accusatory tone hints at a selfishness that is nowhere to be found in Gower:

> Where is that care for me, that used to come before everything else? Can you now depart, without a qualm, leaving Alcyone behind? Are you now resolved to journey far away? (Met. XI.394–431)[29]

Ovid's Alcyone is terrified of "the dismal ocean," and her husband refuses to bring her with him because he believes the journey will be a difficult one (Met. XI.393–431).

Gower honors Alceone, as he does Penelope, as prudent wives who embrace Matrimony's four points, "authority, dignity, holiness and honor," and who keep the marital vow to obey their husbands.[30] Throughout the tales of the Four Wives, Gower emphasizes the word "wyf" as if it alone signifies virtue and chastity. To Gower, "wyf" is a badge to wear honorably, and although it technically means "married woman," Chaucer uses it to indicate that White in the *Book of the Duchess* is as virtuous and good a wife as any of the Four Wives.[31] Neither Alceone or Penelope are Christian women, but Gower is able to use these models of wifely virtue to illustrate his Christian beliefs, which are echoed in the *Mirour*. Often in Gower the pagan, Ovidian doctrine fits quite nicely into his sometimes overtly Christian love-doctrine of "honeste" and prudent love.

Gower's Alceone goes down to the docks to see her husband off on his sea voyage:

> And forto don him felaschipe
> His wif unto the See him broghte.
> (CA IV.2950–51)

"Felaschipe" indicates friendship, it indicates company, it indicates care and affection. Ceix wants his wife to be with him until the last moment. They are good friends and firmly in love. She asks him "With al hire herte" when she will see him again, and he takes his leave, promising to return in "tuo Monthe day" (CA IV.2952,2955). The pain of their imminent separation already weighs heavily upon Alceone's heart. Gower makes the leave-taking very brief, but in it he gives us enough information to know the couple will dearly miss each other's company. It is a tender adieu, and a private moment:

> He tok his leve, and forth he seileth
> Wepende, and sche hirself beweileth,
> And torneth hom.
> (CA IV.2957–59)

Although the words are few, Gower's description of this heartbreaking moment lacks nothing. One can imagine the lovers weeping, he at the ship's rail, she on her walk home. Gower conveys human emotion brilliantly in this realistic and intelligible farewell scene. His husband and wife shed tears at their separation, as lovers often do. Chaucer does not illustrate this leave-taking at all; indeed, Chaucer is notably brief in this tale, whereas Gower is not. In Chaucer we are told that Ceix went across the sea, and five lines later, we learn he has drowned.

Two months pass, yet Alceone has heard "no tydinge" from her beloved husband. She "beseche[es]" the goddess Juno with prayers "To wite and knowe hou" her husband fares (CA IV.2964,2969). Juno sends "Yris hir Messagere / To Slepes hous" asking him to "make an ende" and tell Alceone "hou it was" (CA IV.2972–74,2976). In Ovid, there is a marvelous scene in which Ceix's ship is caught in the throes of a heavy storm at sea. The ship sinks and all the men, including Ceix, drown. Ceix is described as slipping under the ocean waves with the word "Alceone" on his lips. In Chaucer, we are told a tempest broke the ship's mast and

> made it falle,
> and clefte her ship, and dreinte hem alle.
> (BD 71–72)

Gower's audience, however, has no idea what has happened to the king. He skips the shipwreck scene, which serves to heighten the suspense of the tale. Following Ovid, in both Gower's and Chaucer's versions of the tale, Juno sends her messenger Iris to journey to the "Slepes hous," a splendid place where dreams are like cobwebs stretched from one corner of the room to the next. Gower's masterful command of description is particularly illustrated in this passage:

> The god of Slep hath mad his hous,
> Which of entaille is merveilous.
> Under an hell ther is a Cave,
> Which of the Sonne mai noght have,
> So that noman mai knowe ariht
> The point betwen the dai and nyht:
> Ther is no fyr, ther is no sparke,
> Ther is no dore, which mai charke,
> Wherof an yhe scholde unschette,
> So that inward ther is no lette.
> (CA IV. 2989–98)

All is quiet within "Slepes hous."

The cave is surrounded by things "which yifth gret appetit / To slepe": "Popi, which berth the sed of slep," and water, which "Rennende upon the smale stones" (CA IV.3013–14, 3007,3010). There are no trees near "Slepes hous"

> wher on ther myhte crowe or pie
> Alihte, forto clepe or crie.
> (CA IV.3000–03)

Marriage and the Four Wives

It is a delightfully snug and quiet nest for the God of Sleep, whom Iris finds sleeping, of course, on an all black "fethrebed . . . / with many a pilwe of doun" (CA IV.3020–21). Slep assigns Morpheus, "whos nature / Is forto take the figure / Of what persone that him liketh," to go to Alceone in a dream (CA IV.3039–41). That night Morpheus

> Appiereth until Alceone
> In liknesse of hir housebonde
> Al naked ded upon the stronde
> And hou he dreynte in special
> These othre tuo is schewen al.
> (CA IV.3059–62)

Chaucer's Alcione has a similar dream in which her husband appears and speaks with her, saying

> 'And farewel, swete, my worldes blysse!
> I praye God youre sorwe lysse.
> To lytel while oure blysse lasteth!'
> (BD 209–11)

She dies within three days. Gower's Alceone cries when she dreams of Ceix's death:

> Al this sche mette, and sih him dyen:
> Wherof that sche began to crien.
> (CA IV.3064–65)

The dream is too painful to her and she awakens the household with her screams. Her "wommen sterten up" and try to comfort her, but Alceone will take "no confort in hire herte" (CA IV.3077). She fears the worse. In the morning she goes to the seacoast where the body lay in her dream, and sees

> Stark ded, hise armes sprad, sche syh
> Hire lord flietende upon the wawe.
> Wherof hire wittes ben withdrawe,
> And sche, which tok of deth no kepe,
> Anon forth lepte into the depe
> And wolde have cawht him in hire arm.
> (CA IV.3082–87)

Half out of her wits with grief, and unafraid of death, Alceone leaps into the sea. Alceone has not demonstrated any interest or capability in doing anything as forceful and as purposeful as this. For pure love she leaps into the ocean. She is about to catch her beloved in her arms when suddenly the gods intervene:

> . . . for the trowthe of love,
> Which in this worthi ladi stod.
> (CA IV.3090–91)

The gods rescue Alceone from the horror—the "infortune of double harm"—of clasping her dead lord's decomposing body in her arms (CA IV.3088). Alceone "Fro deth to lyve [is] torned," and she and "Hire dreinte lord" are tranformed into "briddes / Swimmende upon the wawe amiddes" (CA IV.3094, 3093, 3095–96).

Alceone's rash response to seeing her husband's body floating on the waves is to leap into the water. More likely than not she cannot swim, and in jumping into the ocean she puts herself at serious risk, but she is not thinking of herself: "sche, which tok of deth no kepe" (CA IV.3085). Neither does she consider that clasping her husband's decomposing body will be an awful and horrid experience. Alceone has lost her reasoning capabilities, yet her actions are not injurious to anyone but herself. This is a woman deeply in love with her husband, and her grief for his death is inconsolable. This action, rash though it is, is the first instance we have of Alceone acting or taking any action in the tale; it is an active, masculine reaction. Alceone never says one word in direct speech, and we do not know her inner thoughts. She is a passive figure throughout the tale except in this scene when Gower shows her leaping into the ocean waves. This is how Alceone speaks; she speaks through her actions, as most of Gower's heroines do—indeed, Gower places more emphasis on the Wives' actions than on their words.[32] In this tale Alceone sheds a feminine text of passivity to embrace a masculine prerogative, and her actions are rewarded.

Truth in love is one of Gower's precepts for married happiness, and in a subtle way, the poet may be suggesting that married lovers who love so selflessly and thoroughly as Alceone and Ceix will receive their reward in kind, as this couple does. The gods watching Alceone reward her for her "trowthe of love" with a chance for the couple to love again. She and her beloved are simultaneously changed into seabirds, and in their new forms they are able to continue to share their bond of truth together. Alceone embraces her husband with her wings and "keste in such a wise, / As sche was whilom wont to do," discovering that she could "do the plesance of a wif, / As sche dede in that other lif" (CA IV.3104–05, 3111–12):

> For thogh sche hadde hir pouer lore,
> Hir will stod as it was tofore,

> And serveth him so as sche mai.
> (CA IV.3113–15)

Alceone is a doting and dutiful wife, even in her new shape as a seabird. This moment demonstrates that the affection Alceone has had for her husband throughout their marriage continues even after their miraculous transformation. It is rare to read of the gods intervening for true love, and Gower's suggestion that as birds the couple can continue to share compassionate love together is unique. Alceone is a "trewe queene" and a paragon among wives (CA IV.3123).

In Ovid Alceone tears at her hair and clothes and leaps into the water, but as she leaps, she becomes cognizant that she is flying over the ocean waves as a seabird. Her husband is transformed by the gods who pity her distress as she tries to kiss his cold lips with the hard bill of her beak. Gower's Alceone is just about to take Ceix in her arms when she sees that he has been transformed into the "liknesse of a bridd swimmende," and when she realizes "sche was of the same sort," her joy is complete (CA IV.3098–99). Unlike Ovid, Gower focuses on the couple's life together as birds; their marital sex life continues and even flourishes:

> many a dowhter and a Sone
> Thei bringen forth of briddes kinde.
> (CA IV.3118–19)

We do not know if the couple had children when they were in their human form, but as seabirds we know their sex life is healthy and prosperous. Alceone is praised for her truth in love and her wifely virtue, and Genius tells Amans that as birds she and Ceix live and love "into this ilke day": the tale has a happily-ever-after quality to it (CA IV.3116).

In the *Confessio*, Gower's married lovers treat each other with compassion and friendship, and they enjoy reciprocal love. In the *Mirour*, Gower echoes the Bible in his admonitions to new wives:

> The husband shall be loyal in governing, and the wife, in her acceptance, shall be modest and gracious, in deed, word, and countenance, without doing anything displeasing to her husband (MO 17689).

Alceone honors her husband, lovingly caring for him as man and as bird, and his love for her is reciprocal. The gods and Gower reward them with a chance to love again, for their love was "honeste" love that set itself in marriage:

> Bot thilke love is wel at ese,
> Which set is upon mariage;
> For that dar schewen the visage

In alle places openly.
(CA IV.1476–79)

Married love in which the partners honor their vows and are comfortable to "schewen" their happiness to the world is the type of love which brings harmony to the lovers and peace to the world at large. This is the type of love Gower advocates for Amans, and for Everyman and Everywoman.

The Tale of Alcestis

Genius recounts the Tale of Alcestis, the "thridde wif" of the Four Wives, within the King, Wine, Woman and Truth tale (CA VIII.2640).[33] Zorobabel, one of the three wisemen in the King, Wine, Woman and Truth tale, tells the Tale of Alcestis to prove that woman's love is second only to truth. The Alcestis story survived in many classical interpretations and medieval commentaries, but it is impossible to know which versions Gower knew.[34] One of the sources for Gower's Tale of Alcestis is probably Boccaccio's *De Genealogia Deorum*;[35] another probable source is the *Ovidius moralizatus*.[36] Alcestis' reputation as a peerless woman was well known; Chaucer praises her and Penelope in a catalog of noble women in the Franklin's Tale (FranT 1442–43), and in Book V of the *Troilus* (TC V.1778), and she presides over the *Legend* as the queen, honored by Eros.[37]

Gower tells the King, Wine, Woman, and Truth tale in the *Mirour* too, but for different purposes. In the *Mirour* the poet seems particularly keen to use the tale to vent his political opinions of the Lancastrian monarchy and the taxing of the clergy for the war with France, but especially towards the controversy surrounding King Edward III and his mistress, Alice Perrers. By the mid-1370s, when Gower wrote the *Mirour*, Perrers' influence over Edward III was notorious.[38] It is generally agreed that Gower is referring to Edward III and the last years of his monarchy in passages from the *Mirour* which rail against a woman controlling a ruler (MO 22801).[39] Writing on the estate of kings in the *Mirour*, Gower focuses on truth, saying that the king—an unnamed ruler—only wants to hear flattery:

> A king should cherish truth and obey it above all things, says Sirach. And yet nowadays we see a king who hates all those who speak the truth; but those who are willing to blandish him become influential. He speaks the truth who says that woman is powerful, and that is visible nowadays. May God save us from these evils, for it is in discord with all laws that a woman should rule in the land and should subject the king to serve her
> (MO 22801).

The *Mirour*'s anti-feminist tone is not found in the *Confessio*, for in the *Confessio* Gower takes a humanistic approach towards women, and he uses the King,

Wine, Woman, and Truth tale and the Tale of Alcestis to illustrate a good woman's love.

It is remarkable that Gower places so much emphasis upon a woman and her love for her husband, but it is in keeping with the poet's proclivity in the *Confessio* to treat women as men's equals; indeed, the Tale of Alcestis "affords a striking example of the sympathetic attitude toward women which pervades the *Confessio* as a whole."[40] Alcestis is an important figure to Gower for she represents fidelity in marriage, and her tale exemplifies the supreme power of woman's love, second only to truth (CA VII.1946). Alcestis' extraordinary gift to her husband marks her as one of the truly exemplary woman, and a Wife beyond reproach. The conjugal tenderness in this tale—and the tale itself—allow Gower to emphasize the importance he places on proper loving, which can lead to a harmony and honest love in marriage.[41] In Chaucer's *Legend*, Alcestis appears as a queen who stands alongside the God of Love, but Chaucer does not tell her tale. The *Legend* had an early reputation as a serious defense of the female sex, but it is now addressed as an ironic poem, and Alcestis is seen as a deeply ambiguous character.[42]

Genius tells Amans that in the "Cronique" there is a story about a ruler named Daires who was honored for his "wisdom and hih prudence" (CA VII.1783–85,1787). Daires sought out wisemen, and he retained three counselors who often gave him counsel in his private chambers (CA VII.1793). He posed a question to his counselors, a puzzle he could not solve himself:

> The kinges question was this;
> Of thinges thre which strengest is,
> The wyn, the womman or the king.
> (CA VII.1811–13)

Arpaghes, Manachaz, and Zorobabel, the three wisemen, each had his own "diverse opinion / Of Argumentz (CA VII.1922–23). Arpaghes argued for the "strengthe of kinges," for a "king hath pouer over man," and because of his "reson" he is the "moste noble creature / Of alle tho that god hath wroght (CA VII.1825,1827–28,1830). Manachaz argued for the power of wine because it can "takth aweie / The reson fro the mannes herte," while Zorobabel stated that "wommen ben the myhtieste" of all (CA VII.1852–53, 1874). He recounts two short tales to prove his point. The first, the tale of the tyrant king Cirus and Apemen, is told in only fifteen lines, yet it illustrates that women can both dominate men and bring out their kinder, gentler natures (CA VII.1884–99). Cirus so loved Apemen that she could "doth with him what evere hir liketh" (CA VII.1895). She clucks the tyrant under the chin, turning him into a meek man,[43] who is firmly in Love's grip, right under Apemen's thumb. Clearly the besotted Cirus has lost control of his ability to reason. The *Confessio* was written thirteen years after Edward III died, but the distaste Gower had for the once-mighty king's foolish actions—or any man's unreasonable behavior—is still apparent in these few lines. However angry Gower may still be with the irresponsible behavior of the deceased Edward, in the *Confessio* he recognizes that women can be accomplished helpmeets to men. A close inspection of the following lines indicates that Apemen was also capable of subduing the tyrant's notorious anger—a very good thing indeed:

> And only with hire goodly lok
> Sche made him debonaire and meke.
> (CA VII.1890–91)

Apemen's influence over King Cirus, then, is both beneficial and detrimental to the state, for a woman and a woman's love can influence a man for better and for worse.

Zorobabel continues his argument in favor of the strength of women by saying that

> A womman is the mannes bote,
> His lif, his deth, his wo, his wel;
> And this thing mai be schewed wel,
> Hou that wommen ben goode and kinde
> For in ensample this I finde.
> (CA VII.1912–16)

This example leads to the story of "good Alcestis" (CA V.1778). The tale of the "goode and kinde" Alcestis is also a short tale, but it supports Zorobabel's argument that a woman's love is stronger than king, wine, or even death. Alcestis' husband Ametus is sick in his bed and everyone waits for him to die (CA VII.1917–18). The distraught Alcestis turns to Minerva, the goddess of intelligence and the feminine arts of spinning and weaving, for help.[44] She does sacrifice to Minerva, hoping that:

> hir lord of his seknesse,
> Wherof he was so wo besein,
> Recovere myhte his hele ayein.
> (CA VII.1925–27)

Alcestis cries and prays until at last Minerva speaks to her.

The goddess tells the supplicant that if she takes Ametus' malady and thus dies, "he scholde live" (CA VII.1931). Alcestis rejoices to hear Minerva's decree, and without hesitation

Marriage and the Four Wives

> So that hir deth and his livinge
> Sche ches with al hire hole entente.
> (CA VII.1934–35)

Alcestis makes her decision to die for her beloved in a heartbeat—there is no hemming or hawing, or wanting to think about this equation overnight. Alcestis knows her mind: she chooses to die for Ametus. Furthermore, Gower stresses Alcestis' strength of purpose with the words "with al hire hole entente" (CA VII.1935). A sliver of a doubt never enters her mind; this Good Wife's self-sacrifice for her beloved is complete. Moments later, she went home to tell her husband the news (CA VII.1936–67):

> In bothe hire Armes and him kiste,
> And spak unto him what hire liste;
> (CA VII.1939–40)

Alcestis makes her decision independently of her husband, she chooses to die so he can be well, she plainly tells him what she thinks, and within a short period of time, she dies, as the accepted plan:

> And therupon withinne a throwe
> This goode wif was overthrowe
> And deide, and he was hool in haste.
> (CA VII.1941–43)

Alcestis does not discuss the plan with anyone; in fact, she makes up her mind quite quickly, in the space of two lines. She does not complain to Minerva, she does not beseech the goddess for another choice. Alcestis prays, seeks help, hears the commandment, and accepts it immediately. There is little dramatic speech but plenty of bold, masculine action in Alcestis' behavior; Alcestis, like Alceone, transgresses her gender and acts purposefully and wholly for her beloved. In most of the sources Hercules rescues Alcestis from hell, but "her demise in the *Confessio* is real and final, a detail which increases the significance and pathos of her sacrifice."[45] In some renditions of the tale the rescue is done at the instigation of her grieving husband; here Ametus is, perhaps, notably silent.

Alcestis' decision to die and the death scene are conveyed in a swift and momentous passage depicting a private and an emotional moment in this couple's marriage. Gower gives us a glimpse of the intimate love the couple shares. The conversation takes place in their bedchamber, and Alcestis holds Ametus in both her arms and talks to him privately—so privately, in fact, that Gower does not tell us what she says (CA VII.1939).[46] In the Marriage Tales Gower depicts several of these private moments and each one is loaded with emotional impact which serves to emphasize the significance and the pathos of the situation—in this case, Alcestis' sacrifice. Gower illustrates these private moments between husband and wife to emphasize the peace a couple can enjoy in a marriage of "honeste" love. By dying for her beloved, Alcestis' full and complete love for Ametus is made manifest; she is the only Wife to commit such a selfless act, and the only heroine in Gower's *Confessio* to perform such a benevolent deed.[47]

It is curious that Gower does not illustrate reciprocal love in this marriage; including Ametus' love for his wife would greatly enhance the story, but he is barely in the tale. We know Alcestis is utterly devoted to Ametus, but his love for her, which we may want to assume is reciprocal, is not illustrated. In Book V of the *Troilus*, Troilus invokes the name and reputation of Alcestis when he angrily tells his sister that her prophecies about Criseyde are wrong, that Criseyde, like Alcestis, is the "kyndest and the beste!" (TC V.1529).[48] Had Gower rescued Alcestis from Hell—at her husband's loving instigation—their marriage would be better illustrated; further, Gower's main point of the tale, that the power of a woman's love is second only to God and God's truth, would have been emphasized. But Gower ends the tale here, and Alcestis remains dead. That she dies so Ametus can live, that her death is a self-sacrifice of the highest kind, makes it all the more surprising that Gower, who continually praises Alcestis, does not rescue her from Hell.

Zorobabel praises women for some of the very same things Gower discredits the sex for in the *Mirour* and in the *Vox*. The wiseman commends women who spur men on to gain fame and honor as knights:

> Thurgh hem [women] men finden out the weie
> To knihthode and to worldes fame;
> Thei make a man to drede schame,
> And honour forto be desired.
> (CA VII.1904–08)

With this passage, Gower's sympathies towards the softer sex are revealed and his unabashed praise of woman's love is heralded. Instead of damning women for their Eve-like tendencies to lead men towards sin, Gower writes that women can "make a man" want to realize his potential and gather "honour" in both knighthood and worldly fame. This is not the same Gowerian voice we hear in the *Vox*, in which Gower writes that a woman's love can sometimes consume a king, resulting in a pitiful state of affairs:

> Now tell me another thing: what honor shall a conqueror have if a women's love can conquer him? (VC 5.1.20)

In the *Confessio* Gower has found a different voice, and he is a champion of love, and woman's love in particular.

Like a skilled Roman orator, Zorobabel states that a reasonable man will "taste" or rely upon his faculty of perception[49] to conclude that

> after the god above
> The trouthe of wommen and the love,
> In whom that alle grace is founde,
> Is myhtiest upon this grounde
> And most behovely manyfold.
> (CA VII.1945-49)

Woman's truth and love, as best exemplified by the wife Alcestis, is second only to God. Alcestis' decision to die for her husband manifests her constancy and devotion to him. There are obvious typological parallels between Alcestis' self-sacrifice and Christ's death, as well as between Alcestis and the Virgin Mary.[50] These parallels heighten Alcestis' standing: seen in this light she is second to the Virgin Mary, who is, of course, subordinate only to God. A more complete display of truth in love is not found in Gower. The wiseman sums up his tale by concluding that

> What strengest is of erthli thinges,
> The wyn, the wommen or the kinges,
> He seith that trouthe above hem alle
> Is myhtiest, hou evere it falle.
> (CA VII.1953-56)

In the Tale of Alcestis, Gower illustrates the strength of truth in a woman's love and her loving actions for her husband. This truth of love "Mai for nothing ben overcome" (CA VII.1958).

The Tale of Lucrece

Gower writes empathetically of the human experience in the *Confessio* and his skill is most visible in the Tale of Lucrece. He accepts Lucrece's virtue without question, praising her throughout the tale for her beauty, wifely chastity, and prudence, while emphasizing her innocence. Lucrece is a woman of action, whether she is sewing clothes for her absent husband, or ensuring her good reputation—and her husband's—at the tale's end through her suicide. Missing from Gower's Lucrece story is the anti-feminist tone found in contemporary renditions of the tale.[51] She is the living embodiment of the high praise Gower reserves for the "praiseworthy women" he singles out in a passage from the *Vox*:

> There was one woman through whom God on high came down, and was made of her flesh. Because of her honor, there are those most praiseworthy women to whom the honor of praise ought deservedly be paid. All good

things come from a good woman, whose chaste love provides love's riches. A good woman is worth more than silver or gold; no fit value can be set upon her. Tongue cannot recite nor pen describe the worth of her whom utter goodness properly distinguishes. Her noble husband dwells revered within his gates and her household contains all that is good. Her servants are fitted out with garments which her hand, busy in its activities, fashions of double strength. No idleness attempts to run through her thoughts; womanly modesty effectively protects them at all times. For her merits, such a good woman should receive everlasting praise which no wicked, gossiping tongue can take away (VC 5.6.295ff).

This praise fits Gower's Lucrece. She is undoubtedly Gower's fullest expression of a "praiseworthy woman" and a good wife. She is full of "womanly modesty," her "utter goodness" is seen in all she does, and, incidentally, she is described in terms which announce her as the most beautiful woman in the *Confessio*. Gower's continual emphasis on "honeste" love is visible in the tender way in which he depicts the married love of Lucrece and Collatin.

Lucrece's story is told by many writers throughout the Middle Ages, including Chaucer who tells her tale in the *Legend*.[52] As usual with the tales in the *Legend* and the *Confessio*, it is difficult to gauge whether Chaucer borrowed from Gower, or Gower from Chaucer, but because some of the details in Gower's rendition of the tale are included in Boccaccio's version, I suspect that Gower may have borrowed from Chaucer, who we know was influenced by Boccaccio. Gower adds several incidental remarks or scenes which are not found in Chaucer, however, and each serves to deepen the pathos in his tale. The source material is from Ovid's *Fasti*, an account of Roman history with the calendar months corresponding to the historical events that occurred from January first through the end of June.[53] Book II, February, recounts King Tarquin's crime and subsequent expulsion from Rome—this is the Rape of Lucrece, a tale Ovid most likely found in an account by his contemporary, the historian Livy. Ovid considerably amplifies Livy's relatively terse account into a dramatic and pathetic tale. Lucrece's tale is treated variously throughout its long history.[54] In the *Roman* Jean's Jealous Husband uses the tale to attack women who are unable to remain faithful wives, unlike Lucrece and Penelope:

> 'But no Lucretia lives in Rome today,
> And no Penelope in all of Greece;
> Indeed, if one should search the entire world,
> He'd hardly find a woman of this kind.'
> (RR 8578–8620)

Livy stresses the public issues in Lucrece's behavior by noting she submitted to the outrage in order to expose the tyrant Tarquin.[55] To Livy, whose concern is history, the self-sacrifice of one woman is well worth the price for Rome; Gower tells the tale for other purposes.

Gower's tale opens during wartime. A siege has been laid around the town of Ardea (CA VII.4762). Arrons, King Tarquin's son, makes a great speech, challenging the other men to a game of boasting: "Who hadde tho the beste wif / Of Rome" (CA VII.4771–72). The men boasted of their wives until a "worthi knyht" named Collatin reminds Arrons, his cousin, that actions speak louder than words (CA VII.4774–75):

> 'It is,' quod he, 'of non emprise
> To speke a word, bot of the dede,
> Therof it is to taken hiede.
> Anon forthi this same tyde
> Lep on thin hors and let ous ryde:
> So mai we knowe bothe tuo
> Unwarli what oure wyves do,
> And that schal be a trewe assay.'
> (CA VII.4778–85)

Without exchanging one word further, Arrons and Collatin leapt on their horses and rode to Rome to spy on their wives (CA VII.4790).[56] Wearing disguises to hide their identities, they ride unrecognized through the Roman streets towards Arrons' palace first (CA VII.4795). They see Arrons' wife

> of glad semblant,
> Al full of merthes and of bordes;
> Bot among alle hire othre wordes
> Sche spak noght of hire housebonde.
> (CA VII.4798–4801)

Arrons' wife is happy and full of mirth, joking with her friends. Gower tells us that she speaks, but she does not speak of her husband. Her concern is wholly for her own enjoyment, and not for her absent husband, away at the siege. Gower follows Ovid here, for in Ovid the men see Arrons' wife and her friends "wearing garlands on their necks, / with drinks set out for staying up late," merriment from which Lucrece refrains (Fasti 739–40).[57] At Collatin's dwelling the men find a completely different scene. Gower illustrates an intimate portrait of a domestic setting from the Middle Ages. Collatin and Arrons see "Lucrece his wif, al environed / With wommen . . . abandoned" to their work (CA VII.4808–11). One of the MED definitions for the word "abandoned" is "to devote (oneself) fully (to religion, to do good)."[58] Lucrece fully devotes all her time to her work. She remains at home, busy supervising her servants in some kind of work, presumably the making of cloth or clothes "for mi housebondes were" (VII.4813). Her first words are for her husband and his safety:

> 'Nou wolde god I hadde him hiere;
> For certes til that I mai hiere
> Som good tidinge of his astat,
> Min herte is evere upon debat.'
> (VII.4817–20)

Lucrece bade the women to hurry, for she wants to send these things to her husband as soon as possible (CA VII.4812). Chaucer's Lucrece is also busy working, and she asks her servants for news of the siege. She too worries about her husband:

> How seyth men of the sege, how shal it be?
> God wolde the walles were falle adoun!
> Myn husbonde is to longe out of this toun,
> For which the drede doth me so to smerte
> That with a swerd it stingeth to myn herte
> Whan I thynke on the sege or on that place.
> (LGW V.1725–30)

Both poets follow Ovid in this passage. In the *Fasti*, Lucrece sits on her couch with "baskets of fluffy wool," and as her "maidservants were spinning their quota," she urges them to work faster (Fasti 741–742). Unlike Arrons' wife, Gower's Lucrece is a portrait of domesticity, keeping herself busy with wifely duties while her husband is away. In the *Mirour* Gower writes:

> a wife should not be idle, but, like the husband, should strive . . . to have a livelihood (MO 17713).

Also,

> . . . the wife should be intent on economy in her house, without wasting or breaking anything (MO 17713ff).

Lucrece well illustrates these precepts from the *Mirour*.

Lucrece misses her husband, and she tells her servants she wishes they were together more than anything else; she speaks the words of a woman in love: "Nou wolde god I hadde him hiere" (CA VII.4817). She is unable to rest or calm her heart until she hears good tidings of her husband. Her concern for Collatin's welfare is apparent. She labors for him, she speaks of him, and news of his safety is "al . . . [her] moste care" (CA VII.4824). Furthermore, this wife knows her husband's character: she fears that when the city walls are attacked, her husband, who is "of such an hardiesse," will "noght himself spare"—that he will, in other words, put his own body in harm's way, thereby sacrificing himself to the wars in order to spare others (CA VII.4821–22).

It is obvious from this description that Lucrece and Collatin share a good relationship. She praises her mate, as he has praised her as one of Rome's best women; theirs is a marriage of reciprocal, "honeste" love. Lucrece is a portrait of a loving wife who misses her beloved husband. She wishes she could turn the city walls into a endless pit and end the siege so that she could see Collatin (CA VII.4827,4829). The differences between Lucrece and Arrons' wife, and their two marriages, are apparent. In the *Mirour* Gower writes that a married woman should honor her husband in her thoughts, actions, and labors, as Lucrece honors Collatin:

> A woman owes honor to her husband, just as a subject to his lord, without despising or abusing him (MO 17605).

It is clear Arrons' wife does not "honor" her husband or miss him, and he easily forgets her as he plans and commits the act of rape.

As Lucrece talks about her beloved husband, tears fall upon "hire whyte cheke" (CA VII.4834–35). She breaks down and she cries woeful tears which "sche ne myhte it stoppe" (CA VII.4835,4831). Collatin, who secretly watches this scene, is deeply moved to hear "The menynge of . . . [his wife's] trewe herte" (CA VII.4838). Overcome with emotion, he steps out from his hiding place and greets her as "mi goode diere" (CA VII.4840). Lucrece, "with goodly chiere ayein / Beclipte him in hire armes smale" (CA VII.4841–42). Immediately, Lucrece's cheeks, "which erst were pale, / To Beaute was restored" (CA VII.4844–45). This is a brief but intimate domestic scene of happiness. Husband and wife, separated by a siege, see each other unexpectedly; Lucrece hugs her husband and is dwarfed by his manly size. Lucrece positively glows as the couple embrace (CA VII.4844–46); Gower does not shy away from illustrating marital affection.[59] Surely Lucrece's happy countenance concurs with the inner love and admiration she has for her husband.[60] Collatin is affected by his wife's emotions, and it is clear that the couple share a deep, reciprocal love. This is one of the fullest expressions of human love that Gower gives us in the *Confessio*, and it is a beautiful scene of marital bliss. The poet's emphasis on "honeste" love is once again illustrated in the tender way in which he draws a married couple, reunited after a period of separation.

Gower's portrait of Lucrece is a rare instance of the poet bowing to a conventional description of feminine beauty: her hair is blonde, she is "so wel adresced," and she speaks pleasantly (CA VII.4881–84). To Arrons, Lucrece is "the beste / And the faireste" woman he has ever seen (CA VII.4872–3). Lucrece's description is the fullest of any of the Four Wives in the *Confessio*, and this merits some attention since Gower usually eliminates physical descriptions of both females and males in his works.[61] Penelope is not described, and neither is Alceone or Alcestis. Gower was certainly steeped in the traditions of the French love lyric, and he knew how to praise feminine beauty, but in the *Confessio*, *Vox*, and *Mirour*, he rarely employs the rhetorical device of description.[62] He seems more interested in what the women do—typically a male prerogative—than how they look, and in their actions, Gower's women are not silent.[63] Gower's women typically transgress their gender and act in non-passive, sometimes aggressive ways, often to aid a husband, like Lucrece and Alcestis do, or, in the case of the Forsaken Women, to strike back at an unfaithful lover. Lucrece's physical description in the *Confessio* is thus a rare illumination. It is as visual as Gower gets: Lucrece is Gower's "most perfect realization of womanliness."[64] Gower has drawn a real woman, a loving wife. Lucrece speaks, but her voice is never described. She is the "faireste" woman Arrons has ever seen; to him, Lucrece embodies the word "wommanhiede" (CA VII.4888). By describing Lucrece in such detail, Gower emphasizes how her beauty affects Arrons, supporting the traditional view that Love enters through the eye. Unfortunately for her, Arrons is struck by Lucrece's beauty with such force that he becomes besotted with passionate desire and evil intent. He becomes a beast and he hunts Lucrece in no uncertain terms. Gower emphasizes her beauty, perhaps, for a specific reason: to show how man can fall into evil if is he unable or unwilling to guard his eye and act reasonably.

Arrons watches Lucrece and Collatin's tender reunion, and its affect upon his inner countenance propels the action in the rest of the tale. Arrons quite suddenly loses "the resoun of hise wittes alle" (CA VII. 4850–51). The culprit is Cupid's fiery dart that hits Arrons and wounds him with the "blinde maladie" of love (CA VII.4852–55). He is overcome with the malady "which no cure of Surgerie / Can helpe" (CA VII.4855–56). Arrons is transformed by Cupid's dart, and from this moment forward he is a man operating without the faculty of reason. Collatin and Arrons return to the siege camp, but Arrons is "so wo besein / With thoghtes whiche upon him runne," that he goes to bed early, not to sleep but to "thenke upon the beste / And the faireste" woman he has ever seen (CA VII.4868–69, 4872–73). Lovesick lovers are often unable to sleep, but few lovesick lovers rape their lady-loves. Thinking of nothing or no one but Lucrece and her beauty, Arrons works himself up to a frenzy. He is consumed with "hire ymage" and carefully goes over every inch of her in his mind:

> Ferst the fetures of hir face,
> In which nature hadde alle grace
> Of wommanly beaute beset,
> So that it myhte noght be bet;
> And hou hir yelwe her was tresced
> And hire atir so wel adresced,

> And hou sche spak, and hou sche wroghte,
> And hou sche wepte, al this he thoghte.
> (CA VII.4877–84)

Lucrece's image is burned into Arrons' mind. Chaucer treats this situation similarly: his Arrons walks about the camp alone, "Th'ymage of hire recordynge alwey newe" (LGW V.1760). Although she is not there "The plesaunce of hire forme was present" and he is overcome by a lustful desire for her, shouting out: "For, maugre hyre, she shal my leman be!" (LGW V.1772). In both renditions, Arrons is determined to take Lucrece by force.

Gower describes Arrons as a "tirannysshe knyht...soupled, bot noght half ariht" (CA VII.4889–90). The MED defines "soupled" as "to become amenable [of the heart], submit,"[65] and it cites the above line from the *Confessio*. Arrons has submitted his heart and reasoning capabilities to Passion. His thoughts are of Lucrece only, and he "non other heide tok," not of his own wife, whom he had claimed was the best wife in Rome, or even of the siege, where his duty lies (CA VII.4891). He is on a path to self-destruction: he has lost his reason and in its place is a passionate, diabolical desire. Like Amans, Arrons burns with lust, a "gret desir, / . . . hotere than the fyr" (CA VI.209–10). In the introduction to chapter four, book five of the *Vox*, Gower describes carnal lust as a power which can "veritably extinguish all chivalrous virtue" in a knight. Furthermore,

> When carnal love holds the mind ensnared, an intelligent man's reason becomes irrational (VC 5.4.230ff).

This is the kind of behavior that Gower abhors, and his lack of tolerance for it surfaces in the manner in which Gower describes the rape. Arrons "degenerates into barbarity and bestiality":[66] Gower first describes him as a "wylde man," then as a "Tigre" stalking his prey, next as a "tirant," and finally, when he is holding Lucrece in his arms, she becomes a lamb and he a wolf: Gower uses an analogy of a "Lomb whanne it is sesed / In wolves mouth" (CA VII. 4905,4959, 4944,4983–84).[67] The poet relies upon similar bestial imagery to describe the ravisher Tereus, in the Tale of Philomela. In the *Mirour*, Gower uses the image of a lion to describe the sin of Rapine:

> By the prophet I find written that as the lion, when it roars, leaps to commit its rapine and immediately kills its prey, so the rapacious man does his business in an even fiercer way. His violence is greater because it is nature that attracts the lion, but the rapacious man acts against reason. The one takes its fill and then withdraws; the other, on the contrary, always keeps his appetite (MO 6841).

Arrons acts without reason as he rides back to Lucrece's house, intent on satiating his appetite with violent rape.

The contrast between the earlier scene of domestic bliss is heightened by the manner in which Arrons arrives at Lucrece's home: he is described as setting a "net / Hire innocence to betrappe" (CA VII.4914–15). Christine de Pisan often complained that women are "traditionally . . . presented as animals to be caught, trapped, and possessed"[68] in medieval literature, a tradition Gower follows here and in his other tales of rape.[69] Notably, however, Gower focuses upon the woman's pain and suffering, empathizing with her predicament, while pointing out the man's unreasonable behavior. Ironically, Lucrece, the Good Wife, welcomes Arrons into her house cheerfully (CA VII.4922,4924). It is only in Gower that Collatin and Arrons are cousins, and this is a noteworthy addition. Lucrece allows her husband's cousin entry to her home, feeds him and gives him a room in which to stay. This hospitality further emphasizes her wifely goodness; she honors her husband well by giving his cousin, who also happens to be the king's son, due reverence. The conversation turns to her husband, and Arrons praises Collatin, hoping to please her.[70] She is the perfect hostess, but her naïve innocence makes her rape all the more horrendous: she welcomes the very man who will defile her. Gower dwells on Lucrece's hospitality, creating both suspense and irony.[71] Arrons keeps up the "frendly speches," abiding his time (CA VII.4943),

> as the Tigre his time awaiteth
> In hope forto cacche his preie.
> (CA VII.4943–44)

Lucrece is unaware of Arrons' violent desire for her; "he hath no word assaied / To speke of love in no degree" (CA VII. 4939–40). Arrons does not profess his love to her, giving her no indication that he is besotted with desire for her. Neither Arrons or Tereus, another rapist in the *Confessio*, vocalize their deep erotic desires to their victims, something which may correlate with Gower's depiction of his ravishers as wild beasts, creatures unable to talk—animals who utterly lack humanity. Overcome with passion, bereft of his reason, Arrons stalks his prey, intent on satiating his ill-placed, passionate lust: he is fully a wild beast.[72]

Alone in his chamber, Arrons has no intention of sleeping. He gets out of his bed and "leide his Ere / To herkne" until he is sure the household has gone to bed (CA VII.4961–62). He creeps down the hall and "the Dore unschette / So prively that non it herde" (CA VII.4968–69). This glimpse of Arrons' cunning is Gower's addition, not seen in either Ovid or Chaucer. Arrons surprises Lucrece in her own bed, grabbing and holding her with both arms while she is still asleep (CA VII.4973). Lucrece is then unable to speak for fear—a very realistic touch which is also found in Ovid. Gower writes:

> thurgh tendresce of wommanhiede
> Hire vois hath lost for pure drede.
> (CA VII.4975–76)

Lucrece is terrified. Arrons threatens her with his sword, saying he will "slen hire and hire folk aboute" if she cries for help (CA VII.4981). He terrifies her and "lich a Lomb . . . sesed / In wolves mouth," she is helplessly mauled by this deranged man (CA VII.4983–84). She swoons from pure terror and "tendresce of wommanhiede," and lies "ded oppressed," in a scene that foreshadows her final death[73] (CA VII.4986, 4975, 4987). Continually Gower emphasizes Lucrece's innocence and Arrons' loss of self-control.

Following Ovid and Boccaccio, Chaucer's Lucrece is threatened that if she calls out for help, Arrons will kill one of her servants and say he surprised them in bed together. In Gower there is no hint of adultery in Arrons' threat (CA VII.4981). Lucrece swoons and Arrons

> tok thanne what him liste,
> And goth his wey.
> (CA VII.4989–90)

Gower and Chaucer both ensure that their heroine is guiltless, and by passing out, in no way can be accused of collusion; in Ovid and Boccaccio she does not swoon. Ovid's Lucrece is described as yielding because she has no other choice; Boccaccio's rendition is similar.

Once his violent passion is spent, Gower's Arrons calls upon his chamberlain to ready his horse, and rides back to his duties at the siege (CA VII.4992). Lucrece waits for him to leave her house, and then gets up and dresses in mourning clothes:

> And up aros long er the day,
> And caste awey hire freissh aray,
> As sche which hath the world forsake,
> And tok upon the clothes blake.
> (CA VII.4999–5002)

Her immediate desire to act is typical of Gowerian heroines.[74] Lucrece buries the events of the immediate past by changing her countenance and her clothes to that of a woman mourning. Then "sche wept" (CA VII.5007). It is an emotionally charged, realistic scene; her suffering is vivid. One can imagine her dressing in a daze, and then letting the tears which filled her heart flow freely.[75]

She lets her once carefully combed hair now "hangende aboute hire Eres" with apparent disregard to her appearance (CA VII.5006). Lucrece summons her husband Collatin and her father, and together they and her cousin Brutus come to her chamber. (CA VII.5016). Gower borrows this detail from Ovid, whose Lucrece also calls her husband and her father to her chamber; Brutus is of the party, but he is not specifically summoned. The three men find the "wofulleste" woman on earth, weeping profusely:

> The wofulleste upon this Molde,
> Which wepte as sche to water scholde.
> (CA VII.5017–19)

Her appearance has drastically changed, indicating the turbulent nature of her inner countenance: she "hirself despised." She kneels at her husband's feet, unable to utter words. He speaks to her in a soft, tender voice, calling her "mi goode swete" (CA VII.5029). Lucrece, however, feels she is unworthy to be thus addressed, believing herself to be "the lest worth of wommen alle" (CA VII.5030–31). This is a rapid fall: from the best of all women to the least in one day! Lucrece tries many times to tell her husband why she is so upset, but each time she attempts to speak, her "tendre schame" does not allow it (CA VII.5042–43). In a marked difference from Gower's rendition, Chaucer's Lucrece summons "hire frendes alle," including her mother, to tell them that she has been raped.[76] (LGW V.1827) She too has a difficult time gathering her wits so she can speak, but Gower has gone to great lengths to depict his Lucrece as a demure, gentle women who is now faced with the very difficult task of telling the men in her life that she has been raped. The poet succeeds in creating a remarkably shy version of the motif frequently used in women's Complaints;[77] she does not raise the hue and cry typically seen in classical literature. Whereas Chaucer's Lucrece wants the world to know of Arrons' crime, Gower's Lucrece speaks only to those dearest to her heart, a realistic detail. Gower continually keeps the focus small to reflect his belief that it is in the microcosm—in an individual man, or in this case an individual marriage—that the world becomes ordered.

It is "noght withoute peine" that Lucrece is finally able to tell of her ravishment. This is another private scene "full of intimate details and speaking gestures."[78] Collatin, in great sorrow, comforts his wife as best he can, in an attempt to restrain her woe (CA VII.5049–50). He and Lucrece's father do not blame Lucrece and they forgive her. Her concern is of the world and what people will say and think of her:

> Nevere afterward the world ne schal
> Reproeven hire.
> (CA VII.5063–64)

Lucrece's words are focused upon her reputation. She now moves quickly and decisively. Under her mantel she had "A naked swerd" which (CA VII.5066–67)

> Betwen hire hondes sodeinly
> Sche tok, and thurgh hire herte it throng.
> (CA VII.5067–68)

Stabbing herself, Lucrece falls to the ground while modestly arranging her mantel around her legs:

> Whan that sche fell, so as sche myhte,
> Hire clothes with hire hand sche rihte
> That noman dounward fro the kne
> Scholde eny thing of hire se:
> Thus lay this wif honestely,
> Althogh she deide wofully.
> (CA VII.5071–76)

Lady to the end, Lucrece covers herself "dounward fro the kne." Both Gower and Chaucer get this detail from Ovid, who illustrates Lucrece's modesty with a simple statement:

> Even then, on the point of death, she made sure her collapse
>   was not unseemly—her last concern as she fell.
> (Fasti 833–34)

It is possible that with this scene both medieval poets are attempting to elevate Lucrece to the status of a saint.[79]

Collatin and Lucrece's father both helplessly watch before swooning—a woman's prerogative—on top of her bleeding body, as they do in Ovid, but not in Chaucer. Brutus pulls the bloody sword out of Lucrece's body and vows to the gods that he will avenge her death. Gower's Lucrece seems to wink or nod at Brutus, approving his pledge:

> And sche tho made a contienance,
> Hire dedlich yhe and ate laste
> In thonkinge as it were up caste,
> And so behield him in the wise,
> Whil sche to loke mai suffise.
> (CA VII.5088–92)

He follows Ovid:

> As she lay, she turned her glazed eyes toward his voice,
> and seemed to shake her head in assent.
> (Fasti 845–46)

Ovid calls Lucrece a woman "with the courage of a man" (Fasti 847). In Chaucer the men do not swoon, and although Brutus vows that "by hir chaste blood . . . / That Tarquyn shulde ybanysshed be," his Lucrece does not stir (LGW V.1862–63). As Arrons represents man without proper rule over himself, Brutus is his opposite, a man who can govern himself with reason, even in the horrid circumstance of witnessing a suicide. A funeral bier is made and Lucrece is carried throughout the town in all three versions.

Gower's Lucrece only tells three people of her rape, and she is barely able to speak for "tendre schame" (CA VII.5052). Gower adds this human aspect to Lucrece's womanly character, thus keeping the rape-telling confined within an intimate, private environment. Rape is a horrendous crime and a difficult topic to discuss, perhaps especially with one's husband and father. It is not a topic Gower's Lucrece wants to announce to the world. Earlier in the tale, Collatin states a precept which Gower honors throughout the *Confessio*, but perhaps most pointedly in this tale: that actions speak louder than words. Instead of ranting and raving to publish her innocence, Lucrece kills herself. To Gower's audience, suicide is a presumptuous and blasphemous act; the Church views it as a sin. In *The City of God* Augustine writes that had Lucrece been innocent, there would have been no need for her to kill herself and thus commit a second sin, murder:

> That highly extolled Lucretia also did away with the innocent, chaste, outraged Lucretia. . . . But perhaps she is not there, because in killing herself it was no innocent which she killed, but one conscious of guilt
> (CG I.19).[80]

Augustine anachronistically uses his Christian law to condemn pre-Christian behavior,[81] but Gower is careful not to condemn his Lucrece. Gower emphasizes that as a pagan, Lucrece plays by different rules: her "excessive fear of . . . shame . . . is part of her Roman heritage," as is suicide, which was viewed as an honorable death.[82] By committing suicide Lucrece takes into her own hands the care for her and her husband's reputation: "the world ne schal / Reproeven hire." Her act of suicide is a very forceful and determined act, and, moreover, it is a masculine action. Lucrece is Gower's most womanly woman—she is the only Wife described, and her tender innocence is emphasized throughout the tale—but in the final scene Lucrece acts with the boldness of a man when she thrusts the hidden knife through her body. Phyllis' tears and Ariadne's hair-pulling are not for her. Difficult as it is to understand Lucrece's desire to kill herself, we can at least recognize and acknowledge the sheer courage and strength of purpose in her decisive action. Lucrece's suicide "serves her quest for vindication as a woman,"[83] and in Gower and Chaucer, she is cleared of all guilt.

Gower's Tale of Lucrece illustrates his "preoccupation with the actions of his characters rather than with their thoughts or conversation."[84] Arrons does not tell Lucrece he loves her, and although we know he is determined to carry out some sort of treachery, we are not privy to how he plans to fulfill the "lustes of his fleissh" (CA VII.4894). His love for Lucrece is "noght resonable," and these words indicate that something evil is afoot. Genius tellingly warns that dishonorable actions ought to be avoided (CA VII. 4895–96). Arrons is operating without reason and without honor, a deadly mix of "melled love and tirannie" (CA VII.4899). He is determined to satisfy his desire upon the unsuspecting Lucrece, an act described as treason, for as a king's son who commands a regiment of knights, it is treasonous for Arrons to attack one of his men's wives (CA VII.4900). In the *Mirour* Gower writes that "great troubles" will befall the rapist, and indeed, as a direct result of his rape, Arrons and his father are banished from Rome, and their monarchy ends. In the *Traitié* X.2 Gower emphasizes this point, indicating that a high sin by a ruler such as Arrons reverberates throughout the land, for the people and for Arrons' lineage (Tr X.2.13–14). The Latin sidenote reiterates this point: Arrons and his father are exiled as are their heirs (Tr X.2.8).

Arrons is guilty of rape and of adultery, too, and as Gower notes in the *Mirour*, three punishments await the man or woman guilty of infidelity: mutilation, defamation, or sudden death (MO 9025). One of the three reasons why a man should take a wife is to prevent him from committing the sins of lechery:

> A man rightly should take a spouse when he cannot otherwise maintain control of his body without committing the offense of lechery (MO 17221).

Also, a man should

> cherish his wife in order to avoid lechery, not in order to commit lechery. For great troubles may befall whoever takes her in wanton desire, and we have many examples of this (MO 17437).

Arrons commits lechery, or more specifically the sin of rapine, by violently attacking Lucrece, another man's wife. As a married man Arrons should have embraced his wife if he was in danger of losing "control of his body." Arrons foolishly disregards his reason, thereby leaving the good and taking the evil. Gower condemns this behavior in the *Mirour*.

> Ah, man, you who give yourself to sin, you act foolishly against your reason when you leave the good and take the evil.... But certainly you are very disloyal and unnatural toward God if you arrange your reason so ill that you lose the spiritual life and also put all the world out of harmony in your temporal life (MO 27169).

Arrons has become evil in his tyrannical behavior and he has put his world "out of harmony" by his violent actions against the innocent Lucrece. Furthermore, he loses his kingdom—the ultimate disharmony for a man born to be king.

Although Chaucer is sensitive to Lucrece's plight, he is as consistently ironic in his portrayal of the Roman Wife as he is with his other Good Women.[85] He continually undermines the goodness of the women in the *Legend* with troublesome phrasing and details which serve to weaken the points he appears to be making.[86] He does this within the first few lines of his Lucrece tale in the *Legend* by referring to Augustine's praise for Lucrece's wifely fidelity, a reference often taken to be ironic,[87] for Augustine damned Lucrece for her suicide, while hinting at her collusion in the rape itself:

> For suppose (a thing which only she herself could know) that, although the young man attacked her violently, she was so enticed by her own desire that she consented to the act and that when she came to punish herself she was so grieved that she thought death the only expiation. Yet not even in this case ought she have killed herself, if she could have offered a profitable penitence to false gods (CG I.19).

Patristic writers like Augustine "dismissed Lucretia straightaway in his *Confessions*,[88] and cast doubts on her virtue which have long shaded her literary reputation: if Lucrece was innocently raped, why did she kill herself? If she is innocent of collusion, she is now most certainly guilty of murder, and he condemns her for that. In his *The City of God*, I.11–18, Augustine focuses on the female Christian martyrs who rely on the omniscience of God to prove their innocence in public.[89] When suicide follows rape, it fastens penalties upon the victim, rather than punishing the rapist. Saint Thomas Aquinas, in his *Summa Theologiæ*, also writes on female Christian martyrs, noting that only those women who are physically violated and die because of their Christian faith are martyrs; Lucrece, a pagan woman, is therefore not a martyr (ST Q.124.4.2). Aquinas writes that it is unclear to the public if a violated woman is innocent, for it is impossible to know if she "suffers this for love of the Christian faith or because she puts little stock in chastity" (ST Q.124.4.2). Aquinas, like Augustine, leaves the door open for conjecture: is the woman guilty of adultery or not? Only God, he posits, who can see into men's—and women's—hearts knows who is guilty and who innocent.

Gower eliminates all references to Augustine, and his presentation of Lucrece is sincere. The *Confessio* contains little or none of the irony found in Chaucer's *Legend*. Gower is not writing a palinode. By exemplum Amans is taught the proper and the improper way to love and thus secure Love for himself; events leading up to Arrons' crime are described most explicitly as reckless comportment, and the rape itself is vilified. Gower places Lucrece in his Company of Lovers at the end of the *Confessio*, and honors her in one of the revered positions among the Four Wives. Perhaps he followed Saint Jerome, whose praise for Lucrece in his *Against Jovinianus* lacks the skepticism of Augustine and Aquinas: "Lucretia . . . who would not survive her violated chastity, but blotted out the stain upon her person with her own blood" (AJ I.46,382).[90] Lucrece follows Dido, Alcestis, and Penelope in Jerome's list of pagan women who "were reluctant to survive the . . . violent death of their husbands . . . and who entertained a marvelous affection for the only husbands they had" (AJ I.46 381–82).[91] Robert Holcot, who held the Dominican chair of theology at Oxford during the fourteenth century, also lists Lucrece along with Penelope and Dido as examples of faithful wives in his commentary on the *Book of Wisdom*.[92] Minnis writes that Holcot retained a "nominalist brand of theology [which] held out the possibility of salvation for those virtuous heathen who had . . . lived by the best law available in their age";[93] perhaps Holcot's beliefs influenced the manner in which Gower treats Lucrece's tale in the *Confessio*.[94]

Lucrece is treated cynically by Jean de Meun in the *Roman*, but this is not surprising since the text as a whole is anti-feminist, it ends in a rape, and no one is punished for the crime. In the *Roman* Ami recounts the Tale of Lucrece and then cynically suggests that good women such as Lucrece and Penelope do not exist anymore (RR 8608–60). Gower's rendering of the Lucrece story, however, lacks this anti-feminist tone and he is both sympathetic to her plight, and empathetic to her suffering. Gower removes the possibility that his heroine betrayed her husband—she passes out—thus maintaining her innocence throughout. Gower and Chaucer are among the few poets who portray Lucrece in this compassionate manner,[95] but the two poets portray her differently. In Gower, Lucrece's innocence is particularly emphasized by her open hospitality to her husband's cousin, a detail not found in Chaucer, and in Gower she wishes to keep knowledge of the rape within the private confines of her home. Rape is common occurrence in the old tales that Chaucer and Gower tell, and in contemporary medieval England as well.[96]

In the fourteenth century rape was considered a crime as well as a sin, and the legal system, in theory, was supposed to protect women from rape. Rape was punishable in the ecclesiastical sphere by excommunication, and in the civil courts of fourteenth century England, punishment included "loss of life and of member."[97] For rape of a virgin, the punishment was blinding and castration.[98] However, there is a large discrepancy between declarations of legal theory and the practice of the legal system, and part of this is due to how the judicial system was developing. The system "came only slowly to rationalize the criminal law and was impotent to handle the criminal cases presented to it. It was particularly so in cases of rape."[99] Patricia Orr, who has studied the court rolls on rape appeals and cases during the years 1194–1222, found that "the court rarely convicted and never severely punished a defendant in case of rape, and most women did not bother to prosecute their case."[100] There are several possible reasons for this, of course, but the most probable one is that a woman accusing a man in a legal system run exclusively by men was at a real disadvantage. If a rape victim hoped to punish her attacker in court, she must prove the crime was committed by finding witnesses to the condition in which she had been left after the attack. This could be a particularly trying experience for a woman, as it continues to be for rape victims today. The rape victim must first seek out trustworthy men and expose her injuries to them; the law made no allowances for feminine modesty, and was similar for men who made an appeal of wounding.[101] But exposing their injuries to men may have been a hardship for women, as Eileen Power has demonstrated in her discussions of women who hesitated to expose their diseased bodies to male medical practitioners.[102] Some women sought to settle the injury out of court, perhaps because "after 1215, those who pursued their cases were more likely than not to lose them."[103] Even if punishment is well deserved, some women sought and received private satisfaction in the form of monetary payments and even marriage; both were of practical use to the victims.[104]

Gower has illustrated Lucrece as a virtuous good wife: her thoughts and labors are all for her absent lord, and her very being blossoms in his presence. She is a woman deeply in love. She is all "wommanhiede," and the "frailty and vulnerability" of her sex is visible within her, but her suicide is a "hard-won triumph of self-assertion."[105] Gower's Lucrece chooses suicide with her eye on public opinion, but her story is a complicated one because, as Schmitz sees it, she is "only allowed to make negative choices."[106] Negative choices are usually what are available to the women in the *Confessio*, most notably to the Forsaken Women, all of whom make unreasonable choices in Love, as I will detail in chapter three. Lucrece's actions, though deplorable to a modern audience, are to be admired for their strength of purpose. Hers was a difficult decision to make, and she chose suicide in order to spare her and her husband's name for future generations. This tragic tale engulfs us emotionally, a tribute to how well Gower recounts a tale with which we are already familiar.[107] Gower recounts a tragic tale of rape, but throughout he emphasizes the love and mutual admiration a husband and a wife can share. In Lucrece we have the perfect portrait of a virtuous wife, the last of Gower's paragons of chastity, the Four Wives. The Tale of Lucrece demonstrates that Gower is quite capable of depicting human emotions, and in this marriage tale we have a glimpse of the sensuality and loving concern Gower invokes when he describes lovers who share the "honeste" marriage bond. Lucrece and her husband honor each other, even while separated by the siege; in death, the pagan Lucrece continues to honor Collatin. In Gower's hands Lucrece and Collatin are one of his fullest and finest examples of a married couple, happily in love.

Conclusion

In the *Mirour* Gower reminds his audience that wives are to obey their husbands graciously, "in deed, word, and countenance, without doing anything displeasing to her husband." The passage continues:

> On the contrary, in order to please him she should suffer and be silent when she sees it is time to do this; and she should speak and take action when she sees it is time to do so, and when she thinks best, without doing anything contrary to the pleasure of her husband. A woman who does this observes marriage (MO 17689).

This edict is something that each of the Four Wives manages to follow completely and well. When Ulysses finally arrives home, Penelope greets him with open arms and is "silent"—not a nag—because she knows "it is the time to be silent." Alcestis, on the other hand, "speaks and takes action" in order to save her beloved's life. She does not question the goddess's decree, she simply bows her head and does as she must in order to save her man. This is self-sacrifice of the most selfless kind. Alceone is very "gracious in deed, word, and countenance" to her husband's wishes. When she sees her husband's body floating on the waves, she "takes action" in a final effort to care for him. Her faithful love is miraculously rewarded and their marriage continues in a new form. Lucrece, the fourth Wife, knows it is best to "take action" in order to keep any blemish from her or her husband's name, and she selflessly commits suicide, according to the Roman laws in which she lives.

Gower depicts several private and emotional moments between husband and wife in the *Confessio*, and each conveys the bond of love and trust that the couple shares. Gower is a poet of private moments. As Bennett asserts,

> most of Gower's protagonists are shown in isolation. As Chaucer is the poet of society, his friend is the poet of solitude—which is why he puts his tales within the frame of private confession.[108]

Lucrece tells her husband she was raped while they are in her chamber, and when Alcestis explains to her husband that her death can cure him, she holds him in "bothe hire Armes" and talks to him privately (CA VI.1939). In the Tale of Philomela, a tale which I do not include in the "marriage group," Gower illustrates a private moment between husband and wife which unfortunately initiates calamitous events. It is while lying beside her husband in bed that Progne with "goodly wordes" tells Tereus her desire to visit Philomela (CA V.557). The fact that the rape destroys their marriage is all the more painful for this glimpse which we have had into their once-happy marriage. Gower often illustrates married couples interacting, and he does so with a realistic touch.[109] Private time is part of the allure and the benefit of having a spouse, and as the poet who advocates marriage, Gower makes sure his audience is aware of the private pleasures matrimony can bring.

The Marriage Tales of the Four Wives demonstrate Gower's belief that "love which is founded on mutuality, on what both Gower and Chaucer call 'common profit,' is the only love which is consistently satisfactory and fruitful."[110] The Wives are chaste women who are faithful to their husbands whom they love. The husbands, although they are not as virtuous as the wives, fully return that love, and their marriages reap the rewards as "satisfactory and fruitful" relationships. Their individual worlds are harmonious, for their love is mutual and reciprocal. In the Latin sidenote to XVIII.1 of the *Traitié* Gower emphasizes the joy man and woman can find in marriage:

> Note here according to the authors that faithful spouses because of the prudent goodness of their own governance keep their wives completely faithful to them. Whence they rejoicing mutually enjoy a happier life in the lord (Tr XVIII.1.1).

Men and women who commit to each other in marriage and who honor and observe the marriage vows are rewarded with a harmonious life for they have reconciled the dueling forces of *kinde* and reason within them by fully embracing the bonds of marriage. In the *Mirour* Gower writes that when men and women enter a marriage, they should "cherish" each other "in friendship" according to the teachings of the Church:

> He who by divine Providence is destined to such a spouse should rejoice greatly in his heart and should treat her with great reverence, without any violence, pride or other wickedness. He should cherish her in friendship as his companion and well-beloved; for they are one body (as the law of Holy Church teaches us), so they should have in unity only one heart without any difference (MO 17509).

Marriage offers man and woman a friendship unsurpassed by any other. In the *Traitié* he writes:

> Then God who made the law [of marriage] made of two persons one flesh. Right is it then that man and woman by this design have all one heart—faithful friend with faithful friend: It is retained in a very beautiful love in accordance with the due law of Holy Church (Tr III.3).

The Marriage Tales of the Four Wives depict men and women matched in conjugal tenderness who do indeed cherish each other and live "without any violence, pride or other wickedness."[111] Gower illustrates those lovers who live with violence and other sins in the love tales of the Forsaken Women, the following chapter. To see these sins embodied, we turn now to the Tale of Deianira, the first of the Forsaken Women.

Chapter Three
The Love Relationships of the Forsaken Women

G OWER TREATS WOMEN IN A KIND LIGHT, EXAMINING THEIR FOIBLES, good and bad, never damning all women for one woman's bad choices. In the *Mirour* he writes:

> ... and if I blame the offenses of bad wives, it is not an accusation or reproach to good ones. Each gets what he deserves (MO 17677).

Gower does not suggest that all women are evil temptresses, and in so doing he contradicts the misogynist writers who feared women and their supposed insatiable natures.[1] Traditionally medieval literature is dominated by misogynous and misogamous discourse, and women such as Medea and Dido are essentially characterized by their sexuality. Marilynn Desmond states that

> the misogynous strain in medieval literature reflects the extent to which the institution of marriage was the building block of secular society, and marriage required the regulation of female sexuality—the explicit purpose of medieval misogyny as well as the standard aim of medieval discourse of chastity.[2]

The *Confessio*, however, completely lacks this misogynous strain, for Gower never suggests that women are evil, or that marriage's purpose is to regulate female sexuality or is something to be avoided. Gower views marriage as a way for both man and woman to control their passionate natures and thus live a life ordered by reason. He is a humane poet who continually urges all mankind to be guided by reason, and throughout the *Confessio* he advises lovers to marry, while stressing that the stability of the community depends upon the mutual accord and fidelity between married couples. In the *Traitié* IV.1. he writes

> When faithfulness acquaints itself with love, then the marriage is good and joyous. (Tr IV.1)

The Marriage Tales of the Four Wives illustrate his message of "honeste" love thoroughly, for not only are their marriages filled with love and accord, their worlds are blessed with harmony. On the other end of the Love spectrum are the five Forsaken Women who march by Amans at the end of the *Confessio*. Deianira, Medea, Dido, Phyllis, and Ariadne are deceived by Love and abandoned by their lovers. The *Traitié* passage above continues:

> But deceivers often make themselves doubtful by false seeming when to the eye [externally] they appear to be lovers. Thus it is like a cord of tows when the thought is at variance with the appearance. (Tr IV.1)

The lovers of the Forsaken Women are faithless and deceitful to a man, yet passion rules supreme in the hearts of the Forsaken Women, and thus their decisions in Love are irresponsible and foolish. Their world is mired in *discordia* and overrun with the Sins of Envy, Sloth, Avarice and with those sins' sinful daughters. In this chapter I will focus on how the irresponsible love choices of the Forsaken Women affect their marriages or love relationships, and their world.

Deianira, Medea, Dido, Phyllis, and Ariadne all believe false and self-serving men's pledges of fidelity and are incredulous when they find themselves abandoned. Truth-in-marriage is an important theme in the *Confessio*, and in the tales of the Forsaken Women truth is often pledged by a dishonest man who speaks well. At the beginning of the Tale of Medea, Genius tells Amans that women are often deceived when they believe men who swear love and undying affection to them (CA V.3236,3238). As Genius says, it is quite common nowadays for an innocent woman to be seduced by a false lover:

> I not hou it schal be ascaped
> With tho wommen whos innocence
> Is nou alday thurgh such credence
> Deceived ofte, as it is seene,
> With men that such untrouthe meene.
> (CA V.3208–12)

The Forsaken Women are all innocents who are gullible enough to believe deceitful men. At the poem's end, Deianira, Medea, Dido, Phyllis, and Ariadne appear in the Company of Lovers who have received bad fortune in love's cause (CA VIII.2548–49). In a vision Amans sees them walk by:

> And overmore
> Of wommen in the same cas,

The Love Relationships of the Forsaken Women 79

> With hem I sih wher Dido was,
> Forsake which was with Enee;
> And Phillis ek I myhte see,
> Whom Demephon deceived hadde;
> And Adriagne hir sorwe ladde,
> For Theseus hir Soster tok
> And hire unkindely forsok.
> I sih ther ek among the press
> Compleignende upon Hercules
> His ferste love Deyanire,
> Which sette him afterward afyre:
> Medea was there ek and pleigneth
> Upon Jason, for that he feigneth,
> Withoute cause and tok a newe;
> Sche seide, 'Fy on alle untrewe!'
> (CA VIII.2550–66)

Medea is the spokesperson for the group, and her "'Fy on alle untrewe!'" is the sum of their cry to Venus. The Forsaken Women mishandle the precepts for a good relationship or marriage because they misunderstand the importance which truth plays in a marriage, and too early pledge their precious selves.

Women who give away their hearts to seafaring strangers do not fare well in Ovid or in Gower. Medea, Dido, Phyllis and Ariadne all fall in love with a stranger from afar; only one, Medea, reaps the benefit of a marriage, a bond cruelly broken by Jason. All the women are deceived, but perhaps they were ready to practice self-deceit: they bestow their love, virginity, complete trust, and, in some cases, their kingdoms, upon men whom they barely know. Deianira and Medea are the two married women in this lot of Forsaken Women, but the marriage vows they pledge in secret do not guarantee them true husbands, and both are deceived. The Forsaken Women place their trust in men they do not know, an action Gower regards as sheer folly, and although the poet is sympathetic to their plights, and he tells the tales from the women's perspectives, he is unwavering in his decision to use their foolish behavior as a lesson for other lovers. Gower often strips away some of the Ovidian details from the tales he tells to reveal the human element, to focus on the woman's emotional response to her predicament. He may be compassionate to women, but he does not alleviate their wrenching heartache. The tales examined in this chapter feature women and men who are ruled by *kinde* and who live in a world mired in *discordia* from which Genius hopes to rescue Amans. In the *Confessio* Gower is a poet of man and of woman, especially the woman in love.

The Tale of Deianira

One of fidelity's opposites is the sin of "Falssemblant," a daughter of the sin of Envy. Falssemblant—"the welle / Out of the which deceipte floweth" (CA II.1880–81)—has grieved many worthy men, and in order to help Amans avoid this sin, Genius tells the Tale of Deianira (CA II.2145). Gower's most likely sources are the ninth letter of the Ovid's *Heroides*, Deianira's letter, and the commentaries on this text, as well the *Metamorphoses*. Chaucer mentions Deianira in the *House of Fame* and he recounts a short version of her story in the Monk's Tale (HF I.402–03; MkT 2119–42). Genius notes that he really does not have to tell an old tale in order to illustrate this sin to Amans, for the trickery and great envy of Falssemblant is visible daily:

> For al dai in experience
> A man mai se thilke evidence
> Of faire wordes whiche he hiereth.
> (CA II.1899–01)

Genius warns Amans that Envy is often difficult to detect:

> For whan his semblant is most clier,
> Thanne is he most derk in his thoght,
> Thogh men him se, thei knowe him noght.
> (CA II.1918–20)

He draws a nice metaphor of the barge which Envy steers downstream, with Falssemblant manning the oars, and untrue Hypocrisy as "his conseil in compaignie" (CA II.1902,1892,1891). This barge flows everywhere but stops nowhere. It remains on the waves, driving great tempests and debates which damage Love and Love's legacy (CA II.1907–09).

The image of Envy fully permeating in the world while destroying Love is cleverly used by Gower. In the tale Hercules and Deianira wander through the wood and come upon a flooded river. While trying to figure out a way to cross the unfamiliar waters without dropping his love, the fair Deianira, into the raging waters, Hercules sees the giant Nessus, who knows how to navigate the river safely (CA II.2159, 2164). Nessus has "gret envie / Which he bar in his herte" towards Hercules (CA II.2173–74). He is jealous of Hercules' might, fame, and perhaps his luck in love. An envious man

> ... wole sette himself behinde
> To hindre with an othre wyht,
> And gladly lese he oghne riht
> To make an other lesen his.
> (CA II.282–85)

The Love Relationships of the Forsaken Women

Nessus is the type of person Gower labels a Talebearer, "a talkative man [who] harms other people like a second plague, and he often strikes as suddenly as a whirlwind" (VC 5.16.880ff). In the *Vox* we are told that the Talebearer's

> tongue loosens marriage bonds, and makes into two what God has declared to be one. Slandered wives shun their husbands, and husbands shun their wives, and they talk incessantly about the evils being done to them (VC 5.16.890ff).

Although Nessus does not slander either Deianira or Hercules, he is envious of their marriage. In the *Mirour* Gower writes that jealousy destroys the jealous man:

> Foolish is the one who thinks of jealousy, for he contends with his own heart so that he himself suffers the worst (MO 17569).

This axiom is true of Nessus and later of Deianira.

While feigning friendship the giant Nessus offers to help the couple: he is "outward profitable / And . . . withinne deceivable," (CA II.2201–02). He carries Deianira across the river while Hercules follows in his footsteps. Once on the other shore, with Hercules still behind him, Nessus (CA II.2225)

> sette his trowthe al out of mynde,
> Who so therof be lief or loth,
> With Deianyre and forth he goth,
> As he that thoghte to dissevere
> The compaignie of hem for evere.
> (CA II.2226–30)

A brief but fast-paced scene follows. As Nessus runs through the forest with Deianira on his shoulders, Hercules shoots a poisoned arrow through Nessus' body (CA II.2234, 2237, 2239). The false giant gets his due and dies for his false-semblance and his envy, but before he dies, he removes his bloodstained shirt and gives it to Deianira:

> And tolde how sche it kepe schal
> Al prively to this entente,
> That if hire lord his herte wente
> To love in eny other place,
> The scherte, he seith, hath such a grace,
> That if sche mai so mochel make
> That he the scherte upon him take,
> He schal alle othre lete in vein

And torne unto hire love ayein.
(CA II.2247–54)

Trusting naively in this false giant's goodwill, Deianira is pleased to have the magic shirt: "Who was tho glad bot Deianyre?" (CA II.2255). By accepting the shirt and agreeing to hide it from Hercules, she assents unaware to Nessus' treachery, and her actions will eventually kill the man she adores:

> The profit that dishonesty acquires is not lasting, and love does not endure as the comrade of envy (VC 5.16.995ff).

Deianira is now as false as Nessus, for dishonesty between husbands and wives causes strife.

False-semblance fills Deianira's heart, and Envy slowly permeates her unsettled mind; the deadly sin takes control of her reasoning capabilities. Genius explains that often

> hertes waxen lasse and lasse
> Of hem that ben to love untrewe.
> (CA II.2260–61)

Gower has set us up to expect something to trigger Deianira's envious mind, and therefore we are not surprised to learn that Hercules sets his heart on a fair maid, Iole (CA II.2262–65). Hercules is "to love untrewe," and disaster is sure to follow (CA II.2261). Hercules and Deianira do not share a truthful relationship—she keeps a secret from her husband—or a tender marriage as do Alcestis and Ametus, where her love is so great that she is willing to die for him, nor is it a balanced marriage: Deianira's heart remains constant, while Hercules' is untrue. In the *Metamorphoses* Deianira is a "violent and jealous wife," but Gower draws his Deianira independently of the Deianiras from the Ovidian myths. He concentrates on the injury done to his Deianira, making it apparent that through no fault of her own, she is forsaken by Hercules, who takes a lover. This is a pattern of falseness that we will see again in the characters of Aeneas, Jason, Demephon and Theseus. In the *Mirour* Gower describes the sin of hypocrisy:

> Hypocrisy the proud looks very heavenly; for by her talk she reproves all evil, but in her malicious heart she is exceedingly worldly and vicious. Hypocrisy is outwardly clothed in saintly habit, just like a lamb full of grace; but in the end, when she strips herself, she looks cruel and full of danger, just like the wolf that kills the lamb (MO 1093).

The Forsaken Women's lovers are false men who practice hypocrisy.

Gower illustrates more of the Hercules-Iole love affair than the marriage of Hercules and Deianira. Iole controls Hercules much like Cirus controls Apemen in the King, Wine, Woman and Truth Tale. Passion rules this pair of lovers so much so that Hercules, the mighty hero, is defeated by Iole and made her fool: she "made Hercules so nyce / Upon hir Love and so assote" that they wear each other's clothes (CA II.2268–69).[3] Cast-off Deianira hears the news that her husband has a new lover, and she knows no other recourse but to use Nessus' love-charm to turn Hercules' love towards her (CA II.2275,2277). With a heavy heart and eyes full of tears, Deianira takes the shirt, described now as an "unhappi scherte," and gives it to Hercules; her tears hint at the future pain the shirt will bring her (CA II.2279–80). He dons the shirt, and immediately his body is set on fire (CA II.2292). Gower names Ovid as his source, who tells how Hercules becomes a wild man who builds his own funeral pyre, leaps upon it, and burns to death (CA II.2297,2295, 2300–01). Hercules' death is inadvertently Deianira's fault—she did not know the poisoned shirt would kill him—but he is to blame for discarding his wife and disregarding their marriage vows. He made a grave error when he abandoned Deianira for Iole, and his punishment is death. Deianira, whose actions kill Hercules, is never explicitly blamed for his death. Genius ends the tale by reminding Amans that all this came from the sin of Falssemblant (CA II.2303).

In Book IV of the *Confessio*, Gower tells another version of the Hercules-Deianira myth, a tale Macaulay labels the Tale of Hercules and Achelous (CA IV.2045–2134). In this brief account, Hercules wins Deianira as his wife in a hand-to-hand battle with the shape-changing Achelous. Gower also summarizes the Tale of Deianira in the *Traitié*. In *Traitié* VII.1–3 he utilizes a refrain: "It is a great peril to break a marriage," and his example is the Hercules-Deianira tale (Tr VII.1.7). He recounts it with few alterations from the version in the *Confessio*.[4] The narrator relates that Hercules is set aflame by a shirt, but there is no mention of who gives it to him (Tr VII.3.17–18).

Curiously in the *Confessio* Gower downplays Deianira and Hercules' marriage so much so that we do not know they are married until the last lines of the tale, when Gower uses the word "wif" in reference to Deianira; he uses it only once (CA II. 2305).[5] The fact that Gower deliberately holds back this information is odd for he freely uses the words "husband" and "wife" throughout the Marriage Tales of the Four Wives, and in the *Traitié*. Indeed, in the *Traitié* VII, he is quite clear, in both the French verse and the Latin sidenotes, that Hercules and Deianira are husband and wife (Tr VII.1.1–7;VII.1.1). Perhaps Gower is loath to sully the words "marriage," "husband," or "wife" by associating them with false Hercules and envious Deianira.[6] In the *Metamorphoses* Deianira is described as Hercules' new bride in the first line of the story, and in the *Heroides*, she refers to herself as "wife." In Ovid Deianira is mostly concerned with the injury to her wifely status, not her husband's infidelity. Deianira's letter to Hercules focuses upon the real possibility that she will lose her valued standing as Hercules' wife; she is loath to give up her share of his glory.[7] Traditionally Hercules enjoyed a hero's status and a reputation as a great lover with "an insatiable sexual appetite";[8] Ovid's Deianira may be accustomed to his dalliances. Not so in Gower. The poet never condones infidelity, although he sometimes ignores it, most notably in the Tale of Penelope. Gower's firm belief that marriage affords man the opportunity to adhere to both the law of *kinde* and reason does not allow room for adulterous behavior.

Gower concentrates on the injury done to his Deianira, making it apparent that Hercules shuns her through no fault of her own; there is no explanation for his fickle and faithless behavior. Passion's power overcomes even Hercules who falls in love with Iole, acquiescing to her every whim. In the *Vox* Gower often subscribes to the prevalent misogynistic thought, writing that the "poison of woman's love takes away common sense," something which is true of Hercules and Iole (VC 5.6.420ff). Iole may control Hercules with her love, but Deianira is the woman who utterly defeats him. Under the influence of powerful Envy and her daughter Falssemblant, Deianira resorts to revenge. Ironically, the mighty Hercules is conquered by his wife, as is Jason. The *Vox* warns:

> When a knight thinks he has vanquished a woman's power, and with tender affection she grants everything he has asked, then he himself is thoroughly defeated, just when he thinks he is thoroughly victorious, and the conquered woman reconquers him (VC 5.5.270ff).

Without his reason to guide him, Hercules is simply a puppet for Iole and a sitting target for his embittered wife. Passion leads everyone in this tale, and no one escapes without great suffering for his or her folly.

In the *Traitié* Hercules' death is the retribution of his misdeed, the adultery which broke his marriage (Tr VII.3.20). In the Latin sidenote, which sums up the verse, we are told that because of his love for Iole, Hercules went utterly mad (Tr VII.1.1).[9] Like lovesickness, madness is an imbalance that causes a man to be ruled by his passions, not his reason.[10] Hercules' adulterous and excessive love for Iole leads to his death, his punishment for breaking his marriage vows to Deianira. This is an instance in which the *Traitié* illuminates a tale in the *Confessio*, a practice Gower does not consistently employ.

It is peculiar that Deianira accepts an enchanted love-charm from Nessus, a stranger who meant her bodily harm, and to keep it a secret from her husband. There are no indications whatsoever that Hercules will be untrue to her; on the contrary, his every concern is shown to be for Deianira in the one scene in which we see the couple together, the river-crossing scene. Deianira's ability to reason is severely damaged by Envy, and the self-destructiveness of this Deadly Sin pervades the tale.[11] These are signs of a troubled marriage; the mutual affection and concern illustrated in the marriages of the Four Wives is not visible here. Deianira's actions indicate mistrust and envy, while Hercules' infidelity destroys their marriage bond.

With this tale Gower further reiterates his belief that truth is the key to peace and loving harmony in a marriage—and thus the world. Trust and "honeste" love are important factors in a marriage, and there is no trust between Deianira and Hercules. Deianira is not loyal to her husband, and she is pulled into Falssemblance's wake until finally she drowns in Envy, bringing Hercules down along with her. Genius says that Deianira is "sori for everemo," but she never finds relief for her anguish (CA II.2307). Gower draws Deianira with great sympathy, and he emphasizes her role as victim, yet he refuses to reward her folly or pacify her heartache; he does not follow Ovid and allow Deianira the chance to seek a pagan solace in suicide. Their marriage is doomed from the start. She mistrusts and he has a wandering heart. The couple is illustrated without any of the mutuality or "honeste" love needed to make a love relationship a lasting one, and their tale ends in death and destruction.

The Tale of Medea

Amans prompts the Tale of Medea from the Confessor when he asks him to express how the "vice of Covoitise / Hath yit Perjurie of his acord" in a love tale from long ago (CA V. 3224–25,3228). Genius agrees to the task, and states that he will also tell

> Hou the wommen deceived are,
> Whan thei so tendre herte bere,
> Of that thei hieren men so swere.
> (CA V.3236–38)

Genius prepares us for another tale of a woman deceived. Gower's Tale of Medea has been called "a most admirable example of sustained narrative, simple and yet effective and poetical, perhaps on the whole Gower's best performance."[12] The tale is well documented, and most scholarship has noted that the poet's unusual depiction of their mutual love serves to enhance the magnitude of Jason's crime of perjury in love.[13] It is quite remarkable what Gower does with his Jason and Medea, for they are portrayed as a couple who are undoubtedly in love. That Gower chooses to depict this particular literary figure as a loving wife in a mutually satisfying marriage is extraordinary, for Medea is known throughout antiquity and into the Middle Ages as an evil witch, a barbarian who dabbled in black magic. Gower's rendition of the Medea tale is notable for its shift towards Medea, his portrayal of her as a selfless woman, and his emphasis upon Jason as a perjurer. Gower eliminates both the Troy story and Jason's prior marriage to Hypsipyle.

Medea is a fascinating figure in literature,[14] and Gower adds a dimension to her which is unique to the *Confessio*. Throughout the tale he stresses Medea's qualities which will endear her to the reader. He transforms her into an unselfish, kind, and confident wife who loves deeply; except for her horrid crime at the end of the tale, she displays all the "good wife" qualities Gower exhorts in the *Mirour* and *Vox*. Gower's Medea is a woman capable of great love. Like Alceone she deeply loves her husband: before and after their marriage, Medea fulfills all Jason's desires (CA V.4189). Gower works to present Medea in a gentle light, and by the poem's end we have taken her side against Jason: if she did not murder her children and Creusa, we would perhaps admire her almost as much as we do Penelope, Lucrece, Alcestis or Alceone. Notwithstanding this black stain upon Medea, Gower presents her as a sympathetic character, in accord with how he treats the other women in this chapter. Medea, like the Four Wives, will do whatever it takes to be a helpmeet to her husband. However, along with Deianira, Dido, Phyllis, and Ariadne, she will be chastised for her aggressive and excessive love, for Gower does not reward any lover, male or female, who does not use his or her reason in matters of the heart. That he does not hold Medea accountable for the murder of her two children, a horrendous crime against Nature and God, is remarkable. Instead, the poet affords her a safe harbor with the goddess Pallas (CA V.4220).

Gower adapted this popular tale from various sources including Benoit de Sainte-Maure's *Roman de Troie*, and Guido delle Colonne's *Historia destructionis Troiae*, and, of course, Ovid.[15] He probably also relied upon the *Ovide moralisé* and the *Ovidius moralizatus* for some elements of the myth,[16] as well as the Ovidian commentaries. Medea is typically dismissed as a barbarian witch, someone whose actions are, in our vernacular, over the top.[17] As a literary character Medea is a dangerous and an educated woman, capable of diabolical deeds, and subsequently she is a model for other women, such as Deianira and Dido.[18] In Guido Medea is a beautiful and well-educated woman who has devoted herself to her studies: she seems unconcerned that she does not have a suitor.

> For the daughter of King Aetes, named Medea, was an extremely beautiful maiden, the only daughter of her father and his sole heir in the kingdom. She, although, had already reached marriageable age and was indeed ripe for marriage, had nevertheless from her childhood given herself up eagerly to the study of the liberal arts, so completely drinking in the Helicon of science with eagerness of heart that no man or woman could be found in those days who was more learned than she (Troy II.175–181).[19]

Gower tells us he borrows from Guido, as does Chaucer: their Medeas are beautiful, wise, and the sole heir of King Aetes (CA V.3245; LGW 1396). Chaucer wrote of Medea in the *Legend*, and she is one of the women whose name is engraved upon the wall in the *House of Fame*. Gower's Medea is a many-sided woman, a truly fascinating study, and he renders her most sympathetically.[20] In Medea Gower has achieved his finest portrait of a powerful woman who loves her husband.

In some versions of the Jason and the Argonauts myths, Medea is a character in the background: Jason wins the Fleece and takes a bride. The Medea myth is unusual in that when the hero is knocked from his pedestal, it is not by a giant, but by his wife. Similarly, Hercules is murdered by his wife. Deianira inadvertently causes Hercules' death, while Medea quite consciously murders Jason's new bride and then wounds her husband by killing their children; the similarities between the flaming shirt Deianira gives to Hercules and the poisoned robe Medea designs for Creusa are apparent.[21] Deianira does not actively seek vengeance against her unfaithful husband, but Medea most assuredly seeks and achieves it; she is the only Forsaken Woman to do so.

We first meet Gower's Medea when her father King Oetes summons her to greet the worthy knight Jason (CA V.3256). Jason is a visitor to their island of Colchis, and he plans to try and win the famous Golden Fleece that resides there (CA V.3265). Gower's simple introduction shows Medea to be the dutiful daughter of a king:

> After Medea gon he bad,
> Which was his dowhter, and sche cam.
> (CA V.3368–69)

Medea is pleasing to Jason, and after she welcomes him to Colchis, she softly takes him by the hand, and leads him to a place where they could converse (CA V.3372–74). She knows who he is for his reputation is well-known:

> in every lond
> Alle othre passede of his hond
> In Armes, so that he the beste
> Was named and the worthieste.
> (CA V.3257–60)

She looks at this fine knight with such intent that his image impresses itself upon her mind. As Russell Peck notes, like so many lovers in the *Confessio*, "Medea fails to guard well her 'yhe.'"[22] Love, of course, enters through the eye, and for Medea Love enters in just one look:

> Forthi sche gan hir yhe impresse
> Upon his face and his stature,
> And thoghte hou nevere creature
> Was so wel farende as was he.
> (CA V.3378–81)

Medea's sudden love is fully returned by Jason. It is a Gowerian invention:

> And Jason riht in such degre
> Ne mihte noght withholde his lok,
> Bot so good hiede on hire he tok,
> That he ne thoghte under the hevene
> Of beaute sawh he nevere hir evene,
> With al that fell to wommanhiede.
> (CA V.3382–87)

Both Jason and Medea fall in love at first sight. Jason has never seen another woman to equal Medea's beauty, and he simply cannot stop looking at her. Gower whets our appetite for a good love tale, for an electricity between the two young people has been sparked. Both characters are drawn fully, and the tale that follows is picturesque and fantastical.

Genius tells Amans that no one knows exactly what the two spoke about, but: "Here hertes bothe of on acord / Ben set to love" (CA V.3389,3390–91). A welcome feast follows and soon after Medea and Jason retire to their rooms. Gower does not elaborate on the feast, showing his independence of the romance conventions which points tellingly towards "his main focus of interest, relationships between human beings."[23] After the festivities are over Genius tells us that Jason cannot sleep—"Al was Medea that he thoghte" (CA V.3403,3407). He is tormented by Love, and tosses back and forth on his bed (CA V.3412). Meanwhile, Medea spends the night thinking "Hou sche that noble worthi kniht / Be eny weie mihte wedde" (CA V.3424–25). Medea is the first woman whom we see contriving a way to marry the knight of her dreams. She does not hesitate to make plans once she has seen the man she wants; indeed, Gower's Medea continually plans to act or is acting upon one of her plans. She spends the night trying to figure out a way that she and Jason will have a moment in which to speak privately, for she is concerned that if she does not tell him how to win the Golden Fleece, he will die in his quest for it, and there will not be any wedding to plan (CA V.3433–36;3630,3429).

The next morning Jason besought her favor, and she listened patiently as this knight wooed her with his good words (CA V.3440–41). Although Medea spent the night scheming, it is Jason who seeks her out. Medea warns him of the dangers of this quest, as her father has already done. Gower allows his heroine to speak several times in this tale, and in her first speech to him, she boldly asks for his covenant of love:

> ... bot as I lieve,
> If thou wolt holde covenant
> To love, of al the remenant
> I schal thi lif and honour save,
> That thou the flees of gold schalt have.
> (CA V.3448–52)

Jason readily agrees: he would be a fool to turn down her offer to help: "Ma dame, I schal treuly fulfille / Youre heste, whil mi lif mai laste'" (CA V.3454–55). He promises to love her in exchange for a guarantee that will ensure his success, his honor, and his life. He prays a long time for her favor, and when she grants it to him, they plan a midnight rendezvous alone in her chamber (CA V.3456,3461).

Chaucer treats this part of story differently, and the effect is that of a business transaction. In Chaucer Medea is undone by the whims of Fortune, which plots her undoing (LGW IV.1609–10). While seated next to Jason at the feast held in his honor, Medea remarks to the knight that unless he seek her help in his quest for the Fleece, he will die. She is quite matter-of-fact about it. She states that she wants to help him and he immediately puts himself at her command. As the Narrator tells us, he is familiar with the art of seduction, "And coude of love al craft and art pleyner / Withoute bok" (LGW IV.1607–08). His reply to her is calculated:

> 'Youre man I am, and lowely yow beseche
> To ben my helpe, withoute more speche;
> But, certes, for my deth shal I nat spare.'
> (LGW IV.1626–28)

Medea foolishly believes he is at her service, and then point by point tells Jason the dangers of his adventure and how to succeed (LGW IV.1629–33). It is then decided that they will wed. Chaucer's Medea gives up the secret too easily. Later that night they seal their bargain with an oath that he

> Ne sholde nevere hire false, nyght ne day,
> To ben hire husbonde whil he lyve may,
> As she that from his deth hym saved here.
> (LGW IV.1640–43)

This marriage vow, especially told as it is by the untrustworthy Chaucerian Narrator, emphasizes that Jason promises to marry Medea because she will save him from certain death. That they are in love is not found in Chaucer's text.

In Guido Medea tells Jason at the banquet that she will save him from certain death if he pledges himself to her counsels. Her terms are quite specific:

> If you will join me to you as your wife, Jason, if you will take me from my father's kingdom, carrying me off to your country, if you will be faithful and do not desert me while I am alive, I shall certainly bring it about and arrange it so that you will eventually fulfill your desire by obtaining the Golden Fleece. . . . For I am the only one among mortals who can. (Troy II.400–406)

Guido undermines Jason's intentions, by describing his response to her as "his perjured oath" (Troy III.111–15). They make plans to consummate their love that night, and in the morning she tells him how to secure the Fleece. In the *Metamorphoses*, just as Medea has convinced herself that "filial affection and modesty" require that she control her untold passion for Jason, he speaks to her, "humbly begging her help, promising to marry her" (Met. VII.94ff). She bursts into tears for she sees her own undoing: "'I see clearly what I am doing: love, not ignorance of the truth, will lead me astray'" (Met. VII.95ff). She then gives into her passions, and trusts the faithless Jason. In the *Heroides* Jason begs Medea for pity and for help, and then, humbling himself before her, he swears he will die "before / one other than you becomes my bride" (Her. VII.116–17). Ovid's Jason calls upon the gods to witness their marriage, and his begging, oaths, and tears convince Medea to tell him the secret of the Golden Fleece. This Jason seems more interested in the Fleece than in the woman, whereas Gower's knight genuinely falls in love with the loveliest woman he has ever seen under heaven (CA V.3385).

Gower's tale is remarkably different from Guido's, Ovid's and Chaucer's texts. That Gower's Jason and Medea love each other is clear: after the first dinner, neither of Gower's lovers can sleep for thoughts of the other; Jason is particularly enamored of Medea (CA V.3403–12). Their midnight rendezvous is one of sensual passion, not a business transaction sealed at a public dinner, as in Chaucer. And instead of having his Medea tell Jason how to win the Fleece at the feast, Gower turns the scene into whispered pillow talk.[24] In Gower Jason speaks confidentially with his friend Hercules, asking him to keep watch so no one knows of the secret meeting with Medea (CA V.3470, 3473). Medea sends a maiden to Jason, who leads him back to her room where

> that he fond redi to bedde
> The faireste and the wisete eke;

> And sche with simple chiere and meke,
> Whan sche him sih, wax al aschamed.
> (CA V.3478–80)

Scholars have pointed out that Gower's Medea sends a maiden to Jason; in Benoit, the go-between is an old woman, with the clear connotation that she is a procurer.[25] In the *Confessio* Medea hugs her maid out of sheer joy when she tells her how Jason was greeted in town after he won the Fleece. It may be a lady-servant relationship, but the maid is a trusted friend. Gower paints the scene in much lovelier tones than Benoit by having Hercules and the maiden work with the lovers: young friends of the young lovers aid them in the love quest.[26] Jason asks his trusted friend Hercules for help, and Medea tells her faithful maid her heart's secrets.

Gower's Medea is an unusually aggressive lover, but she has clear and admirable motives for being so. She has decided she wants to marry this worthy knight, which means she must tell him how to succeed in his quest for the Golden Fleece or he will die in the effort (CA V.3256). But Medea values her knowledge too much to bestow the secret upon him without first exacting a promise of marriage. She brings out a statue of Jupiter[27] as security, and asks Jason to swear a solemn oath of love before she gives him her invaluable help (CA V.3483–85). Her plan seems a very prudent one, and she displays her cunning well. They ask the god to help Jason win the Fleece, and then Jason swears

> That if Medea dede him helpe,
> That he his pourpos myhte winne,
> Thei scholde nevere parte atwinne,
> Bot evere whil him lasteth lif,
> He wolde hire holde for his wif.
> (CA V.3488–92)

Medea exacts a marriage promise from Jason in a very deliberate manner. Every care is taken by Gower to demonstrate that they have pledged love in a serious and solemn manner; their witness, it seems, is a maid who "ded hem bothe full service, / Til that thei were in bedde naked" (CA V. 3496–97).[28]

Jason and Medea's marriage ceremony and the lovemaking that follows is every bit as lovely as the consummation scene in Book III of *Troilus and Criseyde*. Their lovemaking is mutually pleasing, for as Genius says: "Thei hadden bothe what thei wolde" (CA V.3499). Usually Gower uses a phrase such as "Sche granteth him al that he wolde" to indicate sexual relations, but here Gower carefully changes the phrase, implying there is reciprocal delight for both man and woman (CA IV.770). The frank sensuality between this couple resembles what we have seen between Penelope and Ulysses, thus elevating Jason and Medea's love to an honored place in the *Confessio*—and making their fall that much more significant. After the lovemaking, in leisure, Medea tells Jason exactly what he will encounter in his quest step by step. This is a lovely private moment shared by the new lovers: they make love, and then she tells him the secrets needed to defeat the guardians of the Golden Fleece (CA V.3500–01). It is a peaceful and satisfying romantic liaison.

Immediately Medea adapts and acts the role of wife who looks after her husband,[29] but she is far more than an obedient helpmeet, she is a helpmeet with not only the answers but the necessary magic. Medea knows what Jason will encounter in his quest to gain the Fleece, and this is information he is not going to find anywhere else. She tells him when to pray and when to offer sacrifices to the gods. And she provides him with magical charms—a ring to make him invisible, ointment to protect him from the Dragon's fire, among other dangers, some glue for the oxen, and her enchantment. Armed with these amulets Jason is ready for battle. Genius continually reminds the reader of Jason's debt to Medea with lines such as "as he was tawht," and "As Medea him hadde bede" (CA V.3692,3695).[30] Medea has made this feat so easy for him that his glory upon winning the fleece is diminished. Jason wins the prize and receives the praise, never telling anyone he succeeds because of Medea's love, "hir oignement, / Hir Ring and hir enchantement" (CA V.3613–14). She is not a braggart, and never seeks to take credit for Jason's victory, a credit she justly deserves; perhaps she recognizes that in helping Jason she has deceived her father, a moral sin which will catch up with her. From the onset of the tale, she is seen to be a woman who selflessly gives of herself to the man she loves; not once does Jason show his gratitude for her much-needed aid. When Jason returns with the Fleece the townspeople gather about him saying "Ha, wher was evere under the hevene / So noble a knyht as Jason is?" (CA V.3766–67). Ironically, this is the same phrase that Gower's Forsaken Women utter incredulously when they realize that they have been played the fool and their lovers have left them.

The second secret night of romance between Jason and Medea is just as lovely as the first. Once everyone is asleep, Jason walks to her chamber, where a Maid is ready to receive him (CA V.3859,3861,3862). Medea waits for him in bed, and he is all haste to undress (CA V.3866,3867):

> Anon he tok hire in his arm:
> What nede is forto speke of ese?
> Hem list ech other forto plese,
> So that thei hadden joie ynow.
> (CA V.3868–71)

The Love Relationships of the Forsaken Women 93

Gone are Medea's blushes. The couple is very comfortable in bed together, and there is joy in their lovemaking. Afterwards, they plan how Medea will run away with Jason to Greece:

> And tho thei setten whanne and how
> That sche with him awey schal stele.
> (CA V.3872–73)

Medea defies her father, steals his treasure, and foolishly turns her back on her royal heritage (CA V.3897). Gower eliminates the part of the Ovidian myth in the *Heroides* in which she or Jason kill and dismember her brother, throwing his body parts into the sea to slow down the Colchian fleet. In Gower she is her father's only heir and running from her responsibilities as that heir is a serious crime, one from which she is never able to make recompense. By running away, disobedient Medea ends her father's lineage, a sin which further marks her as guilty of passionate folly. The pair are guilty of avarice too, and their greedy actions also contribute to their moral downfall; later, Jason will be charged with avarice in Love. When the morning comes and the lovers are gone, Medea's mother weeps and her father is crazy with rage; he orders his ships to follow the traitors (CA V.3911,3912). He is unsuccessful in regaining his treasure, his Fleece, or his daughter.

Medea's new life has begun: she, Jason, and the Golden Fleece are greeted in Greece by a cheering crowd. They become the parents of two sons:

> Togedre ben these lovers tho,
> Til that thei hadden sones tuo
> Wherof thei weren bothe glade.
> (CA V.3937–39)

Gower draws Jason and Medea's marriage in loving terms—there are two sons, of whom the parents are proud, and there is a doting grandfather (CA V.3940). It is a picture of a happy Greek family, except that the old man is ill and approaches death. Jason gathers up his nerve, "made him bold," and asks his wife to save his aging father (CA V.3946). The sense we as readers get from this line is that Medea has not performed any magic since the couple fled Colchis. Medea, who Genius reminds us is true to Jason, agrees to Jason's request readily (CA V.3950). This is a truly selfless act on her part, but Jason does not repay her in kind for this deed or any deed of love she has performed for him.

What follows is a fantastical scene, rich in descriptive detail and romantic power. Gower borrows it from Ovid's *Metamorphoses*, or perhaps from one of the illustrated romance legends.[31] As Medea stirs the witch's pot, she undergoes fascinating physical changes. Medea, barefoot and with her head uncovered, goes out on a starlit night, when the world is completely still, and calls upon the Goddess Hecate for help (CA V.3958, 3962, 3963, 3981):

> Doun fro the Sky ther cam a char,
> The which Dragouns aboute drowe:
> And tho sche gan hir hed doun bowe,
> And up sche styh.
> (CA V.3988–91)

She drives the chariot to various lands for nine days and nights in search of ingredients for her magical potion so she can grant Aeson his first youth (CA V.4019, 4058). She is now a midnight magician, the sorceress who can restore youth, a woman with awesome powers. Genius describes her as wilder than a wild beast as she runs around lighting altars (CA V.4081, 4080, 4079):

> Aboute hir schuldres hyng hir her,
> As thogh sche were oute of hir mynde
> And torned in an other kynde.
> (CA V.4082–84)

As her cauldron boils, Medea stirs it with a dry branch until the branch is all fresh and green again, an indicator that the potion is ready (CA V.4141, 4143, 4145). Deftly she slices a wound in Aeson's side and the "blod withinne, which was old / And sek and trouble and fieble and cold" drains out (CA V.4157, 4159–60, 4158). The sorceress carefully fills Aeson with her medicinal concoction which includes a horned owl, a 900–year old raven, and a shark (CA V.4131–39). As Aeson drinks some of the concoction, "his youthe ayein he cauhte" (CA V.4166, 4167, 4168). It is essential to note that Medea uses her gift of sorcery for good only: she does not perform any magic which can be considered evil. She uses her magic out of love for Jason twice: she teaches him how to win the Fleece, and she restores his father to youth, at his request. Her magic is an outward sign of her love for Jason.

Genius sums up Medea's acts of kindness as motivated by love for Jason:

> Lo, what mihte eny man devise,
> A womman schewe in eny wise
> Mor hertly love in every stede,
> Than Medea to Jason dede?
> Ferst sche made him the flees to winne,
> And after that fro kiththe and kinne
> With gret tresor with him sche stal,
> And to his fader forth withal
> His Elde hath torned into youthe,

> Which thing non other womman couthe.
> (CA V.4175–84)

As Genius phrases it, no man could invent a woman to love him more than Medea loves Jason, but their relationship has altered considerably: their love is no longer reciprocal, and "Medea [is] most deceived" (CA V.4193). Jason takes and takes from Medea without acknowledging her generosity. In his ingratitude, Jason is very much like Theseus, who readily accepts Ariadne's help in killing the Minotaur and then without hesitation deserts her. The *Mirour* states several rules about the sin of Ingratitude:

> The ingrate who is so against nature is by nature worse than a dog; for a dog, in its fashion, loves and defends its master dead or alive, but an ungrateful man never bears you love or loyalty. For your kiss he bites you in return; do right to him, he will do you wrong; for your honor he dishonors you. He it is who returns evil for good, so that for his very wicked behavior, God hates him, and every creature hates him too (MO 6673).

Medea aids Jason, but he does not bear her "love or loyalty"; he abandons her for Creusa, returning "evil for good, . . . and every creature hates him too." Although Medea's future crimes are unspeakably horrid, Jason is a character who garners hate: he is the original scoundrel, "by nature worse than a dog." Gower's sympathies clearly lie with Medea.

With Medea's help, Jason has all he ever desired: the Fleece, her treasure, two children, a restored father, and now he succeeds to his uncle's throne as king (CA V.4189,4187):

> Bot whanne he scholde of riht fulfille
> The trouthe, which to hire afore
> He hadde in thyle of Colchos swore,
> Tho was Medea most deceived.
> (CA V.4190–93)

Jason should honor Medea, but instead he incredibly marries another woman, Creusa (CA V.4195-96):

> . . . and thus Jason,
> As he that was to love untrewe,
> Medea lefte and tok a newe.
> (CA V.4196–98)

Without a warning, and without a reason, unfaithful Jason abandons Medea. In the *Traitié* Gower writes about adulterers:

> It is a marvel and very much against reason that man should choose his wife of his own choice and then confirm that choice by marriage and then disown his faith when day after day he desires a new love more the best. An honest man does not belie his faith (Tr V.1).

Jason denies his pledges to Medea, an action which is contrary to reason. Furthermore his ingratitude to his wife is outrageous, especially since she has just restored his father to youth.

Medea the sorceress wastes no time in wielding her magic as an evil power for the first time. With her art she made

> ... cloth of gold a mantel riche,
> Which semeth worth a kingesriche,
> And that was unto Creusa sent
> In name of yifte and of present,
> For Sosterhode hem was betuene.
> (CA V.4200–05)

Even though Genius has not told us of Medea's anger, it is inherent in her actions: she sends a gift to Creusa in the name of the "Sosterhode" which they share, presumably for being wives of Jason. As Creusa dons the garment "Anon therof the fyr sprong oute / And brente hir bothe fleissh and bon" (CA V.4208–09). She dies what must be a painful death; no physical remains are left of this young, fresh queen (CA V.4206). Medea next goes to Jason

> With bothe his Sones on hire hond,
> And seide 'O thou of every lond
> The moste untrewe creature,
> Lo, this schal be thi forfeture.'
> With that sche bothe his Sones slouh
> Before his yhe, and he outdrouh
> His swerd and wold have slayn hir tho,
> Bot farewel, sche was ago
> Unto Pallas the Court above.
> (CA V.4211–19)

Gower deliberately employs the word "forfeture" in Medea's curse to connote the legal bond to which Jason and Medea were bound, again underscoring their marriage contract, and Jason's inability to honor it.[32] Their deaths are proof of Jason's forfeiture—he broke the bond and she ensures that nothing is left from it nor from his lineage.

The murders are sudden and the horror of it catches us off guard. Medea enacts her revenge upon her once-trusted husband by cruelly killing their children in front of him. Within seconds his sword is drawn, but Medea vanishes.

She escapes death, but not her heartache: in Pallas' "Court above, / . . . sche pleigneth upon love (CA V.4219–4220). While she complains of Love to the goddess, Jason is left in great distress, horrified at the sight of his slain children (CA V.4221, 4222). Jason has lost his new wife, his children, and Medea, the woman from whom he once could not withhold his gaze (CA V.3383). Genius concludes the tale by warning Amans:

> Thus miht thou se what sorwe it doth
> To swere an oth which is noght soth,
> In loves cause namely.
> (CA V.4233–34)

Jason is censored for his perjury, but not one word is said against or about Medea's loathsome, murderous actions; this is quite notable. Gower never denies her criminality, but he does not elaborate on it. He merely presents it in all its horror as part of the exemplum to Amans.

Jason is guilty of bearing false witness against Medea, against Love, and against the god Jupiter. He is also guilty of selfish greed, one of the daughters of the Deadly Sin of Avarice upon which Book V focuses. He lusted after the Fleece and Medea, and then he yearned for a new love. In the *Heroides* Jason deserts Medea for Creusa's wealth and power,[33] but in Gower, Jason has inherited his uncle's throne, and presumably he has all the power and wealth he needs. Thus he marries Creusa even though Medea has given him everything. This tale is particularly unsettling because Gower has taken pains to illustrate the mutual love of one accord between Jason and Medea. They had a peaceful existence, with precious moments of lovemaking, and children as proof of their love. Nonetheless, through Jason's perjury, they lose it all. This is a Gowerian invention; in Guido the Jason-Medea tale ends when the couple arrive in Greece.[34] In the *Heroides* Ovid writes that Medea, who has been cruelly banished from their home by Jason, does not believe that he is remarrying until one of their children sees his father at the head of the marriage procession and tells his mother; it is a particularly heartbreaking moment for Medea (Her. 188–210).

In the Medea myth Medea's revenge is rarely legitimized, yet men avenge and are praised for it in heroic tales. If this tale were gender reversed, and it was Jason doing the avenging, striking out at Medea's new husband, he would receive vindication.[35] But it is a woman who avenges, killing Jason's new wife and her own children, and Medea is damned for it in centuries of literature — but not by Gower. Her murderous actions go beyond the "normal" revenges even of men; Ruth Morse argues that Medea has "usurped a male prerogative: her usurpation is a multiple offense" and it is difficult to "overemphasize just how unusual this is."[36] Yet Gower allows Medea to seek revenge and to usurp Jason's throne; and like a male avenger she acts—and acts swiftly. Murdering their children ensures that they, a traitor's children, cannot grow up to inherit their father's kingdom nor to repeat their father's crimes.

Guido and other misogynist writers do not trust women who wield this kind of power. Although Guido has described Medea's scientific knowledge and "art of magic" in detail, thus illustrating her intelligence and skill—"no man or woman in those days could be found who was more learned than she"—he reminds his audience that she is a woman, and women are cunning, never contented, and always scheming (Troy II.180ff). He laments that on the evening that Medea and Jason meet, her father orders her to sit next to the hero.

> Is it wise to trust to feminine constancy or the female sex, which has never been able, through all the ages, to remain constant? (Troy II.244ff).

Ironically, it is Jason who cannot remain constant. Guido goes on to remind his readers of women's voracious sexual appetites and how they use their cunning to entrap men, thus undermining Medea's powers.[37] Gower, however, studiously avoids the anti-feminist rhetoric Guido favors. Although Medea is undoubtedly a powerful witch, she resorts to using her magic for vile revenge only when she realizes that Jason has deceived her. She murders her children by hand, not magic, but she calls upon her magic to escape from Jason's dangerous wrath.

In Gower's tale Jason is truly the villain and Medea is a lifesaving and lifegiving woman and sorceress who aids Jason in his hours of need. Gower illustrates Medea's side of the story, and he gives the good with the bad. He presents Medea's two murders and does not try to hide them, but his sorceress is scooped up by the gods and rescued before Jason can run his drawn sword through her. While most of the other Forsaken Women are not allowed the satisfaction of revenge, Medea, like Deianira, retaliates against her husband. Medea and Deianira are married women, and their husbands, Jason and Hercules, break the marriage bonds which Gower believes are sacred. Gower takes the women's side, and allows these two abandoned wives an opportunity to strike back at their cheating spouses. The outcome, however, is not productive for anyone involved—destruction and death follow close upon revenge in both Gower and Ovid.

In the *Traitié* VIII.1–3, Gower also recounts the Tale of Medea. Medea is given full credit for aiding Jason in his quest for the Golden Fleece (Tr VIII.1.1–3). After bearing him two sons, Jason changes the purpose of his original bond and utterly rejects her, and marries Creusa (Tr VIII2.8–13). Then Medea

> whose heart is enclosed with sorrow, in her anger, as a madwoman (and this was a great pity), killed her young sons before the eyes of Jason. God will avenge a broken marriage. (Tr VIII.3.15–21)

The narrator has pity for the murders Medea commits in a fit of madness; nothing else is said of this pair of unhappy lovers. The refrain, "God will avenge a broken marriage," echoes the one in the Hercules-Deianira verses, "It is a great danger [peril] to break a marriage" (Tr VIII.1.7; VII.1–3). The Latin sidenote sums up the tale, noting that Jason abandons Medea and copulates with Creusa, whence he and his sons tragically died (Tr VIII.3.1.1). Medea's crimes of infanticide are arguably the worst crimes in all the *Confessio*, yet Gower does not damn her for murder, here or in the *Confessio*. Genius, in fact, does not even comment upon it.

When Medea walks by Amans at the end of the *Confessio*, she cries out "'Fy on alle untrewe!'" (CA VIII.2566). She is the only one of the Forsaken Women and the Four Wives to speak as she walks by Amans; her heartache lingers. Medea's sudden vengeance for Jason is indicative of her sudden love for him. Her aggressive pursuit of Jason, seen in Ovid, Guido, and Chaucer, is unique among the women in this chapter and those in chapter two; it perhaps contributes to her downfall. Her error is compounded by the fact that she chose to disregard her responsibilities to her father and her future kingdom, a disobedience stressed by Guido, too. Enchanted by Jason, Medea loses her ability to reason: she is seduced by his beauty and his reputation. In Book I Genius tells Amans that when Man is blinded by Love, he will not recognize Reason:

> Yit myhte nevere man beholde
> Reson, wher love was withholde.
> (CA VIII.2197–98)

Reason and Love are not governed by the same master, a precept which is especially clear in Medea's actions, as well as the other tales examined in this chapter (CA VIII.2199).

Throughout her literary history Medea is a powerful and threatening woman, and the historical accounts often silence her, making her a fearsome creature, or a part of different tale altogether.[38] The story of Medea is one of rewriting, and that story has its origins in classical antiquity and in other styles of historical representation: medieval romance, historical texts, and in stories which draw and draw upon ideas and perceptions about women.[39] Medea informs the characterization of women: she is a princess, an heiress, a disobedient daughter, a knowledgeable sorceress, a lover, a queen, a mother, a healer, a murderer, and a woman who receives shelter from the gods. She is all things which embody the word "woman," and for some writers, and readers, she represents something to be feared. This "multiplication of 'Medeas,'" as Morse puts it, "influenced depictions of "Woman" which went well beyond genre categories to create an essentialist definition by which women were judged."[40] Gower's Tale of Medea certainly informs the tales of the Forsaken Women as a whole. Morse points out the similarities with the Dido tale, and I note that Deianira is a woman born from Medea, too.

Gower has drawn Medea as a complicated character. She is the fairest maiden Jason has ever seen, and a wise and confident woman who provides him with precise and precious information enabling him to win the Fleece. Although Medea masterminds their entire love affair, Gower is careful to illustrate Jason's reciprocal love: the tender moments the couple share in bed are among the most memorable in the *Confessio*. Yet for all her cunning Medea is unable to restrain the passions of her tender heart, and in the end, this fault destroys her world (CA V.3237). In her selflessness, Gower's Medea resembles Alcestis, a woman who traditionally garners great praise as an exemplary wife. Alcestis and Medea both save their husbands' lives; for their efforts one woman dies and the other is forsaken. Medea disregards her duty as heir and her responsibilities to her kingdom; her behavior is irresponsible, and Gower cannot abide it. In the end she suffers greatly for the mismanagement of her heart, a failure which echoes throughout her world, and in centuries of literature.

The Tale of Dido

Virgil places Dido in the Aeneas myth, but before Virgil there was no connection between the two figures.[41] Originally Dido was an exemplary wife, who remained chaste and shunned suitors after her husband Sychaeus died; when Iarbus tried to marry her, she killed herself for love of her husband. The Church Fathers were "staunch champions" of the chaste Dido story, and some who favored this version of the tale considered Virgil "a blasphemer of her character."[42] Saint Jerome praises Dido along with Lucrece, Alcestis and Penelope in *Against Jovinianus* as previously noted.[43] Among the Ricardian poets Dido's love story is a favorite, but according to Gotz Schmitz, the medieval audience was more familiar with Ovid's version of the tale in the *Heroides* than with Virgil's.[44] Ovid probably relied heavily upon the *Aeneas* for his tale of Dido,[45] but Gower makes no reference to Virgil, and it is doubtful that he knew him.[46]

Gower's sources are the *Heroides* and the medieval commentaries on it. Ovid's letters are written from a heroine's point of view, and from Dido's vantage point Aeneas looks more like a faithless lover than a hero: this is the view which dominates the Dido myth in the Middle Ages. It was strengthened by Dares Phrygius' and Dictys Cretensis' eyewitness reports of the fall of Troy and its aftermath, which branded Aeneas as a traitor to his town.[47] Chaucer tells Dido's tale in the *Legend*, and in the *House of Fame*, and the Narrator says he follows the *Aeneid* (HF I.240–381).[48] Chaucer takes Dido's side in both versions. Ovid mentions Dido along with other ladies in the *Ars* who die for what he terms "Erotic ineptitude, lack of technique," and he briefly mentions her suicide in the *Metamorphoses* (AA 31–49,42).[49] In the *Roman* La Vieille evokes the Dido story to demonstrate the dangers that await the woman who places all her hope in one man.[50] However La Vieille is not to be trusted, and she regards Dido as a fool, rather than one of love's victims.[51] She ridicules women such as Dido for their gullibility: "God love me, he is but a fool / Who would believe a lover on his oath" (RR 13147–48).

In Gower's hands Dido is another woman abandoned by her lover, and Aeneas is a knight in the same mold as the *Confessio's* Jason and Demophon, "anti-heroes" whose chivalry is questionable.[52] In telling her tale in the *Confessio* Gower focuses on the ill-treatment Dido receives from her guest Aeneas, while ever-mindful of her own culpability in the love affair. Gower's lovers are imperfect: she loves to excess and he is faithless. The Forsaken Women are abandoned by men who lie and disregard their bonds of honor, but Gower implies throughout that women must govern themselves more wisely in affairs of the heart too. The Forsaken Women are victims of unscrupulous men, but they ignore reason and embrace their passions, and in Gower's lexicon of love they are culpable for their own errors. Blaming others for one's mistakes has no place in Gower.

In Book Four of the *Confessio*, Genius focuses on the sin of Sloth. The Confessor asks Amans if he is guilty of lachesce, or procrastination, and he freely admits it. He tells Genius that when it is time to pursue his lady, he finds himself tarrying, debating whether it might be better to visit her or to send a letter; thus he procrastinates (CA IV. 35, 38, 41–42). Genius promises to teach the Lover how to avoid sloth by telling him the Tale of Dido (CA IV.68). Aeneas and his great navy arrive at the city of Carthage, whose queen is Dido. Genius never recounts how she came to be queen, nor does he describe her feminine allure. The first thing he tells Amans is that she

> . . . loveth Eneas so hote
> Upon the wordes whiche he seide,
> That al hire herte on him sche leide
> And dede al holi what he wolde.
> (CA IV.88–91)

We do not know what Aeneas says to Dido, but his words must have dripped with sweetness and love for she immediately gives him her heart. Dido is another woman who relinquishes her heart, that priceless commodity, to a man she barely knows. Gower's brief tale moves at a quick pace. Immediately after they make love, Genius says that Aeneas leaves for Italy, never to return (CA IV.92,93,95). Despite the intimacy they shared, Aeneas leaves Dido without so much as an *adieu* scene at the docks. His leave-taking is a reported "as it be scholde," with no explanations (CA IV.92). From our perspective we know Genius is referring to Aeneas' imperial destiny, but since Genius does not relate that part of the myth, Dido is not aware of her lover's call to duty. All she knows is that he is gone, and she, who believed what he said, has been left behind. Since Gower does not use the words "husband" or "wife" in the tale, we may assume the couple is not married.

In Chaucer's *Legend*, Dido and Aeneas' affair begins in friendship. Aeneas is an honored guest in Dido's court, and Chaucer describes their time together with sumptuous scenes from fourteenth-century medieval romances—there is music and revelry, feasting, merry-making, and hart-hunting. Richly embroidered tapestries hang in Dido's chambers, they dine on spice cakes and drink wine, the horses they ride are swift, and the saddles they sit upon are embroidered with gold (LGW III.1099–1110). Chaucer's Dido is too magnanimous with Aeneas, much like Medea, who is too trusting and too generous to her father's guest Jason. In the *House of Fame*, the Narrator tellingly warns that Dido "loved al to sone a gest" (HF I.288). Dido lavishes Aeneas with gifts, which Chaucer lists—from horses to jewels to falcons to gold goblets—and he gives her treasures in return. Soon she suffers from lovesickness: she is tormented by dreams and cannot sleep.[53]

Gower greatly shortens the tale as he found it in the *Heroides*, and he is not influenced by Chaucer's much longer and fuller version. Chaucer seems to follow Virgil—in the *Legend* he includes the cave scene and narrates the couple's love pledges (LGW III.1225–39; Aen.IV.91–132). In the *House of Fame*, Dido's long and loud laments as Aeneas prepares to leave Carthage are augmented by the Narrator's warnings for women to beware of men who "shewen outward the fayreste, / Tyl he have caught that what him leste" (HF I.281–82). This description of men in general and Aeneas in particular is the very essence of Hypocrisy as Gower defines it in the *Mirour*. Hypocrisy is

> ... outwardly clothed in saintly habit, ... but in the end, when she strips herself, she looks cruel and full of danger, just like the wolf that kills the lamb (MO 1093).

In Gower Aeneas matter-of-factly sets sail as if he were leaving on a crusade; he does not run from Dido, he simply leaves. Gower was either unfamiliar with Chaucer's work or consciously chose not to incorporate it; the latter is more feasible. The love affair Gower draws is decidedly one-sided: his Aeneas never promises Dido anything, but nonetheless she gave him all that he wanted.

Abandoned, Gower's Dido suffers from the hot pangs of Cupid's fiery darts (CA IV.97,96). She writes Aeneas a letter, begging him to return to her without delay, threatening that she will kill herself "'for thi sake,' / ... 'wel I wot,'" if he tarries too long (CA IV.99; 114–15). This is one of only two times we hear Dido's voice directly; several lines later, she complains of his sloth (CA IV.128–31). Aeneas receives Dido's letter, but he ignores it:

> Bot he, which hadde hise thoghtes feinte
> Towardes love and full of Slowthe,
> His time lette, and that was rowthe.
> (CA IV.118–20)

Aeneas' response, or rather his lack of one, stings even after reading the passage several times. In the *Mirour*, Gower writes about Slackness, the third daughter of the Deadly Sin of Sloth:

> Of the cases Slackness has in hand, she says, "Tomorrow, tomorrow," and lets the present day pass. When seated beside her neighbor, she gives many vain excuses . . . ; and thus she slowly puts off everything, both the divine and the secular (MO 5605).

Aeneas is rendered guilty of this sin in the secular sphere of love.

While Aeneas can barely remember the passions he shared with Dido, she still burns with love (CA IV.122). Her desire feeds on itself, and she is overrun with wantonness,[54] another sin from which Gower warns lovers in the *Mirour*:

> . . . for in . . . her heart she recites her wanton thoughts, and she excites her body so that it desires more than nature. Her appetite increases in the flame that spares no one (MO 9193).

Dido's passion for Aeneas burns bright, but he has forgotten about her and about their love. Her heart is "so full of wo," and she complains, in her own voice:

> 'Ha, who fond evere such a lak
> Of Slowthe in eny worthi kniht?
> Now wot I wel my deth is diht
> Thurgh him which scholde have be mi lif.'
> (CA IV.128–31)

Like Ariadne, Dido is incredulous that such a worthy knight as Aeneas could have such a fault of sloth in him. He should be true to his knightly status, if nothing else, and embody the virtues of prowess and steadfastness, both of which are necessary on the battlefield and are commonly known to battle the sin of sloth. Aeneas is a lazy lover—like Ulysses. Ulysses, however, shares a bond of reciprocal love with his wife, while Aeneas entertains mere faint thoughts of Dido's love.

Realizing that Aeneas is not going to return, Dido believes she has no other recourse but to kill herself. She prepares for her death, although she had once hoped that Aeneas would be her life:

> Riht evene unto hire herte rote
> A naked swerd anon sche threste,
> And thus sche gat hireselve reste
> In remembrance of alle slowe.
> (CA IV. 134–37)

Without Aeneus by her side, Dido believes her life is over; killing herself affirms it. It is interesting to note that Dido, Deianira, and Medea do not display excessive emotion in their distress: there is no pulling of hair or river of tears in their tales. Gower's Dido does not blame anyone but Aeneas for her heartache.[55] Although Gower depicts Dido as a victim of Aeneas' slothful and faithless behavior in Love, he does not spare her from her heartache or death. She is responsible for her actions, as are all of Gower's Forsaken Women.

Gower's Dido seeks peace from her heartache in death. Suicide is not a solace Genius recommends, but he does not damn her for it.[56] We expect to hear Gower as a Christian echo Chaucer and condemn this suicide, but there is only silence.[57] Dido is unable to withstand the pangs of unrequited love. She resorts to drastic measures to find peace; she kills herself thinking it is her only recourse. Had she considered her situation with this stranger more carefully, she might not have been in this dire predicament. As Chaucer writes in the *House of Fame*, "Loo, how a woman doth amys / To love hym that unknowen ys!" (HF I.269–70).

Dido and Aeneas are not married, and no pledges of love are exchanged. In the *Legend* Dido begs Aeneas to marry her before he leaves so she can "deyen as youre wif"; their love pledges do not constitute a marriage (LGW III.1322). Aeneas, now described as a traitor, ignores her pitiful cries and cowardly steals away at night (LGW III.1328). Green asserts that Chaucer's willingness to call the *Legend's* "betrayers 'traitors,' a heavily loaded term in the feudal vocabulary," is indicative of "the underlying seriousness" with which he treats the heroines.[58] In Gower Dido's folly is clear throughout the tale, and he will not forgive her for her actions, neither for succumbing to her burning desires, nor for committing suicide.

Although this tale is told from Dido's perspective, her words are only heard twice; she is another one of Gower's silent women who is described through her actions, not her words. Dido's passion for Aeneas is excessive: her heart belongs to him, then she suffers from lovesickness, her desire continually increasing. There is a vast difference between how Genius describes Dido and how he draws Aeneas. Aeneas never says he loves Dido, he never pledges his truth to her, he does not burn with hot desire for her, and he never promises to return. He says something to her that successfully seduces her, and sexually speaking, he receives everything that he wants from her, but no promises of love are ever made. Once in Italy he has faint memories of love, but the contrast between the lovers' degree of loving is striking. There is no reciprocity in this love affair, and without mutual accord there will never be a good relationship, let alone an ideal marriage. Dido places all her heart on a man who does not return her love, and that turns out to be the sum of her error. She has succumbed to her passions and not governed her body or ruled her mind with her reason. Dido's misplaced passion for Aeneas parallels Amans' lovesickness for his lady-love, and both Dido and Amans suffer unrequited love. As he does in so many other of tales in the *Confessio*, Gower chooses to focus on the human element, one woman's and one man's moral responsibilities. Genius uses the tale to warn Amans from sloth in love, but the underlying premise is the same as it is always is in the *Confessio*— that the Love one seeks must be a balanced and "honeste" love. Faithless Aeneas has no intention of remaining with or returning to Dido, and therefore he may be deemed culpable for her suicide. But Dido disregards her royal responsibilities, and in acting unreasonably in matters of the heart she is thus held accountable for her mistakes in love, and certainly for her suicide.

The Tale of Phyllis

The Tale of Phyllis is another tale which Genius uses to cure Amans of his Sloth in Love (CA IV.711). The Deadly Sin of Sloth has five daughters, and each one affects faithless lovers in her own way. "Foryetelnesse" is the daughter vice which effectively eliminates reason from a man's heart, a sin which thrives in both Amans and Demephon (CA IV.541,542–45). A forgetful man has no memory of either his words or his actions, and to reiterate his point, Genius says that if a forgetful man hears a tale he will not be able to remember it for he cannot hold the memory of anything, from what is in his wallet to what is in his heart (CA IV.547). In matters of love, a forgetful man's words are the ruin of many lovers; he rarely means what he says:

> And skarsly if he seith the thridde
> To love of that he hadde ment:
> Thus many a lovere hath be schent.
> (CA IV.552–54)

Demephon is a man who matches Genius' description of a forgetful lover entirely; he speaks well of love, but he does not speak from his heart (CA IV.762). Amans admits that he is intimidated in his lady's presence and is therefore forgetful (CA IV.572). Overcome with fear, and he stands in front of her like a deaf and dumb man, unable to say what he had planned:

> Al is foryete for the while,
> A tunge I have and wordes none.
> (CA IV.690–91)

When he tries to find the nerve to look at her, he is a "couard herte of love unlerned" (CA IV.609,611). In contrast Demephon is no coward, and his skills as a lover are sharpened, perhaps from years of practice. Poor Amans' heart is so "Al out of reule" that when he sees his lady he thinks he is in paradise, and is so ravished by the mere sight of her that he is unable to speak (CA IV.682–83; 694–97). Demephon is not afflicted by forgetfulness in the same manner as Amans. He is not a sputtering lover who attempts to speak words of love but ends up standing amazed and dumbfounded; he is skilled in what the Gawain poet calls "luf-talkyng."[59] He has no difficulty speaking words of love to Phyllis, although not one word that he speaks is true. He is false from the beginning of the tale and Phyllis is utterly deceived.

The Confessor hears Amans confess to his forgetfulness and pusillanimous behavior in love, and he tells the penitent that he must speak up for himself (CA IV.706,707,710):

> For love his grace wol noght sende
> To that man which dar axe non.
> (CA IV.712–13)

To remind him to allow nothing to keep him from the business of Love, Genius tells Amans the Tale of Phyllis, which is a pitiful story of a forgetful lover (CA IV.725,729). Gower's drew upon Ovid's *Heriodes*, the *Remedia Amoris*, and on later medieval commentaries for the Phyllis Tale.[60] Chaucer recounts her tale in both the *Legend* and the *House of Fame*, but as always between Gower and Chaucer, it is difficult to determine who borrowed from whom. King Demephon sails from Troy and by happenstance ends up at Rhodes, where he moors his ships (CA IV.733,734, 739). Phyllis is the queen of Rhodes, a woman Genius describes in a few brief lines. She is

> of yonge age
> And of stature and of visage
> Sche hadde al that hire best besemeth.
> (CA IV. 743–45)

This is the only picture Gower draws of his Phyllis, except during the suicide scene, where we learn she has a white neck, a symbol of feminine beauty in medieval literature.[61] Phyllis shines among women, and as an added bonus to her beauty, she bears the scepter, which makes her both a target for wooing and a good choice as a marriage partner. Demephon recognizes her value as a female commodity and he acts upon it.

Although the Tale of Phyllis is a "recurrent variation . . . of the romantic seafaring stranger with a girl in every port,"[62] their subsequent love affair—while similar to the tales of the Forsaken Women examined in this chapter—is unique in that Demephon schemes to steal Phyllis' heart. Like the other Forsaken Women, Phyllis is betrayed by her man, but "in medieval exegesis of *Heroides II* she was regarded as having been culpably foolish to have fallen in love with a seafarer (in moralistic medieval criticism, the nice girls do *not* love a sailor)."[63] Minnis' succinct parenthetical statement applies to Gower's Phyllis as well as his Medea, Dido and Ariadne, none of whom manage to avoid sailors. Demephon, however, seems particularly a scoundrel for he executes his seduction in a calculated manner which the other men do not display. In the *Legend* Chaucer emphasizes his crafty and untrustworthy character by making a point of telling the reader that his father is a scoundrel too. Following Ovid, Chaucer emphasizes that Demephon is Theseus' son,[64] and has inherited his father's faithlessness (LGW VIII.2459–64).[65] Gower does not make this familial link.

Gower's Phyllis is quite pleased with what she sees: "Of Demephon riht wel hire qwemeth" (CA IV.745). She seems to be impressed with this knight's physique, much like Criseyde is taken aback by her first glimpse of Troilus, whom she sees riding by her window, prompting the exclamation: "Who yaf me drynk?" (TC II.651). In the *Legend* Chaucer emphasizes that Theseus' reputation precedes him and everyone in Rhodes gives him due honor. Chaucer's Phyllis welcomes him to her court, and Demephon swears he will wed her almost immediately. In the *Confessio* Demephon moves quickly too. He realizes he cannot avoid falling in love with the beautiful and powerful queen: "ne myhte asterte / That he ne sette on hire his herte" (CA IV.749–50). He contrives to speak words of love to Phyllis:

> So that withinne a day or tuo
> He thoghte, how evere that it go,
> He wolde assaie the fortune,
> And gan his herte to commune
> With goodly wordes in hire Ere.
> (CA IV.751–55)

Demephon is a crafty fellow. To him, love is "bot a game," a phrase Amans uses at the end of the poem, and Phyllis' heart is something with which Demephon will gamble (CA VIII.2152). He plans to tempt Fortune and whisper sweet nothings into Phyllis' ear, and whatever the outcome is is fine with him. A skilled con-artist who plays the role of a lover well, Demephon is false from the beginning, a trait we have not seen before in Gower's lovers.

Demephon is a confident, nay, brazen man: who is he to whisper into the ear of the Queen of Rhodes? But that is what he does, and Phyllis allows it. He begins by telling her to rest easy:

> And forto put hire out of fere,
> He swor and hath his trowthe pliht
> To be for evere hire oghne knyht.
> (CA IV.756–58)

He swears to be her "oghne knyht," a promise of fidelity that Phyllis accepts, and with his ships safely anchored in her harbor, he has ample "time and space / To speke of love and seche grace" (CA IV.759,760–63). With crafty tongue, bold Demephon seeks Phyllis' grace, and as she eagerly listens to his word of love, she gives him her heart (CA IV.763):

> And hou he swor and hou he preide,
> Which was as an enchantement
> To hire, that was innocent.
> (CA IV.764–66)

Gower uses the word "enchantement," a word he uses rarely in the *Confessio*.[66] To be enchanted is to be under a spell, and it often carries a sinister connotation. Phyllis is an innocent woman, and Demephon becomes the enchanter.[67] She believes Demephon's words to her

> As thogh it were trowthe and feith,
> Sche lieveth al that evere he seith,
> And as hire infortune scholde,
> Sche granteth him al that he wolde.
> (CA IV.767–70)

Demephon is a very smooth seducer, and Phyllis is under his considerable power. She is mesmerized by his pledges of love, although he never promises to be her husband, only her own knight.

Demephon gains access to Phyllis' heart and to her body, and is thus described as being full of joy; his plan proves to be a success (CA IV.771). Despite Phyllis' sorrowful protestations, Demephon prepares for a journey. He pledges that he will return to her within a month, and "forth he wente / To Troie, as was his ferste entente" (CA IV.776,779–80). Gower reminds us that Demephon's first intention is to travel to Troy, and Phyllis, it is implied, is merely a stop along the travel route. Just as he does with Aeneas' imperial destiny, Gower does not elaborate on Demephon's original intentions. Gower, following Ovid, is not interested in telling the heroic adventures of men like Demephon and Aeneas. Gower writes from a woman's perspective, as Ovid does in the *Heroides*, and from this vantage point the men who desert these women are scoundrels and dishonest lovers, not heroes. In the *Heroides* and in the *Confessio*, Phyllis and Dido do not care if their lovers have destinies to fulfill; their only concern is that they have been tricked and unceremoniously abandoned. Gower draws the men in all their ignominy, as he emphasizes their irresponsible behavior: Demephon and Aeneas are guilty of Sloth and perjury, and neither attribute is heroic.

In the *House of Fame* Chaucer describes Demephon as a man who swore "ful falsly, / And traysed Phillis wikkidly," and he blames him for her death (HF I.389–90). In the *Legend* Demephon is more diabolical and false than he is in Gower; he even dares to speak of their impending wedding. Once he has slept with Phyllis, he says he must return home:

> For there he wolde hire weddynge aparayle,
> As fel to hire honour and his also.
> (LGW VIII.2473–74)

Phyllis utterly believes him. Chaucer writes that as Demephon prepares for his journey, he gives commands to repair his shipwrecked boats as if he were already the lord of her country (LGW VIII.2479). He sets sail, and, as in Gower, he never returns. In the *Heroides* Ovid draws a lover's leave-taking that neither Gower nor Chaucer chooses to use. It appears to be a tender farewell between a lover and his beloved, but Demephon, we know, beguiles Phyllis. The scene is permanently set in Phyllis' mind:

> I cannot lose sight of the day you sailed off.
>   Your ships were waiting on the waters
> of my harbor, ready to leave, and you closed
>   your arms around me putting your lips
> on mine mingling tears and lingering kisses;
>   a whispered pledge of undying love,
> you cursed the breeze that played into your sails. Your last
>   words were even shouted in the wind:
> 'Phyllis, do not forget that I will return.'
> (Her.II.26–33)

Ovid underscores Demephon's treachery.

Gower writes that a month passes and Phyllis has not heard from her lover, yet she falls deeper and deeper under the spell of the false Demephon (CA IV.718):

> Hire love encresceth and his lasseth,
> For him sche lefte slep and mete
> And he his time hath al foryete.
> (CA IV.782–84)

She stops eating and drinking, one of the classic responses to those afflicted with lovesickness. While she pines for him, he has completely forgotten all about her. Phyllis writes a letter, telling him how she is overcome (CA IV.788):

> With strengthe of love in such a wise,
> That sche noght longe mai suffise
> To liven out of his presence.
> (CA IV.789-91)

She begs him to remember the promises he made to her, and in her letter she writes that she fears she may die if he does not return to her as promised (CA IV.793,794,797). Chaucer's Phyllis also writes Demephon a letter, blaming herself for being too generous with her body:

> 'But I wot why ye come nat,' quod she,
> 'For I was of my love to yow to fre.'
> (LGW VIII.2520-21)

Phyllis is abandoned and angry: she prays that the gods will avenge her, and that Demephon will "be nat suffisaunt to bere the peyne" (LGW VIII.2524).

Gower's Phyllis still seems to believe Demephon will return. His lovesick heroine takes some comfort in her letter, hoping against hope that he will return to her, but Genius comments that it is a pity to write what happened next: "he foryat / His time eftsone and oversat" (CA IV.800,805-06). Gower describes Phyllis' misery and pitiful way she scans the horizon, looking for his ships' sails.[68] Sometimes she thinks she sees a ship, and her hopes rise as she imagines it carrying him or his letter. Her misery and demented mental state are apparent (CA IV.811). Phyllis is obsessed: she stares at the seacoast "al the longe day / . . . into the derke nyht" (CA IV.814-15). Deluded in his love, Phyllis lights a

> lanterne on hih alofte
> Upon a Tour, wher sche goth ofte,
> In hope that in his cominge
> He scholde se the liht brenninge.
> (CA IV.817-20)

This pathetic scene is original in Gower; her gullibility is fully exposed. It is pitiful how subservient this queen has become.

Deceived by Demephon and ignored by Venus, the queen of Rhodes finally gives in to her despair. She runs from the tower to her private garden, moaning woeful moans (CA IV.832,833,844,845). Swooning, and with tears streaming down her face, she accuses Demephon of his sins in the first dramatic narrative we have in this tale[69] (CA IV.838-40):

> 'Helas, thou slowe wiht,
> Wher was ther evere such a knyht,
> That so thurgh his ungentilesce
> Of Slowthe and of foryetelnesse
> Ayein his trowthe brak his stevene?'
> (CA IV.843–47)

Phyllis' despairing cry of disbelief is strikingly similar to Dido's lament. Phyllis hangs on to the thread of hope as she readies herself for suicide, still talking to an absent Demephon, who she thinks may return to find her:

> If that thee list to come and se,
> A ladi ded for love of thee.
> (CA IV.851–52)

Tying a green silk scarf around her white neck, she hangs herself and thus dies for a false lover (CA IV.857,859). It is her first bold move, but it comes too late. Genius says that the gods were moved by the pitiful sight of Phyllis hanging from a tree, and they transformed her into a nut tree (CA IV.857,859,861,867). This metamorphosis is unique to Gower. Word of her death reaches Demephon, who too late curses his sloth (CA IV.877,878). Why he experiences this fleeting moment of regret is unexplained.

Phyllis is the only one of the Forsaken Women whom Gower allows a metamorphosis to rescue her, as it were.[70] Gower uses the nut tree transformation to emphasize that while Demephon's actions are contrary and *unkinde*, Phyllis' love and steadfastness are in harmony with Nature and God. That she was completely duped is beyond her control—the word "enchantment" allows this difference —and he grants her this metamorphosis for her innocence. Her excessive love, however, is misguided, and her behavior in Love is foolhardy. Phyllis does not conduct herself reasonably in this love affair, and her error is compounded because she is the queen. Gower's pity for this woman is carefully marked throughout the text, and although she behaves foolishly, we are continually reminded that she is innocent and Demephon is guilty of forgetfulness and perjury. Amans is warned from this sin which wounds many lovers:

> For noman mai the harmes gesse,
> That fallen thurgh foryetelnesse,
> (CA IV.881–82)

Forgetfulness in love is an unpardonable sin in Venus' eyes, and Genius wants to ensure that Amans is not guilty as is Demephon. Demephon's calculated cruelty is unlike any we have seen in the *Confessio*. His intentions towards Phyllis are never honorable, and his carefully planned seduction successfully attains his desires. Phyllis' misfortune is that she believes whatever this smooth-talker says. She is a gullible woman, and although we may pity her, her actions announce that she has willingly traded her self-control for a passionate love affair.

Phyllis is infatuated with Demephon and her actions correspond appropriately: she is operating without her reason, and is governed by her passions.[71] She has succumbed to her emotions and taken

> ... delight in Wantonness as long as she can, without limit, without rule, without moderation (MO 9445).

In an earlier passage on wantonness in the *Mirour*, Gower notes that when the object of one's passion leaves, a lovesick lover such as Phyllis will languish:

> But when the follower of Wantonness cannot have his desire of the one his heart is set upon, he languishes in foolish love; he cannot eat, he cannot sleep, his laughter all changes to tears, as if he has been robbed of everything (MO 9421).

Phyllis, like the lovesick Troilus, suffers greatly, and despairs.[72] Phyllis has lost all her joy, and Demephon has indeed "robbed [her] of everything." In the *Mirour* Gower writes about Magnanimity, a daughter of the virtue Prowess, which fights against Idle Despair and Sloth:

> The heart of Magnanimity is like a square die: no matter on what side it falls, it always stands up. Likewise, Magnanimity, however adverse or kindly Fortune the fickle may be to her, is always equally stable in herself; so that neither adversity nor changeable prosperity can make her out of harmony with anything that is her duty (MO 14305).

Phyllis is unable to manage her heart, and therefore she neglects "her duty" as Queen of Rhodes; had she some store of magnanimity, she might have withstood Demephon's utter treachery.

Phyllis is seduced in a very calculated way by a man who enchants her. We have not met a seducer like Demephon before. He is false from the word go, and he is a confident and self-centered lover. Gower makes it abundantly clear that Demephon has planned the whole seduction. Whereas Aeneas, another slothful lover, is lazy in love matters, Demephon is calculating, ungrateful, and forgetful. The parallels between the Tale of Dido and the Tale of Phyllis are ringing familiar: a seafaring man arrives on the coast, he seduces the local queen, and with promises to return, he leaves. Time passes, and she slowly comes to the realization that he will never return. In Gower's hands Demephon is another selfish and ungrateful lover, another man who counterfeits emotions of true love, and leaves his lady. As queen it is Phyllis' ultimate decision as to who can anchor in her harbor; like Dido, she graciously allows a stranger to moor. Phyllis treats Demephon, a stranger to her lands of Rhodes, very kindly, as does Dido, and as we will see, Ariadne, too, yet none of these women receive reciprocal treatment. Minnis' comments on Medea, Dido, Phyllis and Ariadne in Chaucer's *Legend* apply to the *Confessio* as well; he states that "we are dealing with a legendary of good *gentle*women, whose behavior lives up to their privileged birth and breeding."[73] The importance of giving hospitality to strangers is stressed in classical literature as well as in the Old English tales such as *Beowulf*. Gower's Medea, Dido, Phyllis, and Ariadne all welcome these handsome strangers to their lands with great hospitality, but unfortunately the men do not honor them in return.[74] The women compound their foolish judgment by trusting the men with their most precious gifts, themselves, and each woman suffers the consequences. Dido and Phyllis both commit suicide, while Ariadne is left stranded on a remote island; all are victims of faithless men.

The Tale of Ariadne

The last of the Forsaken Women Tales in the *Confessio* is the Tale of Ariadne in Book V, the Book of Avarice. Ariadne walks in the Company of Lovers with those who were hurt in Love's cause (CA VIII.2549). She has been wounded by "unkindeschipe," a form of ingratitude:

> And Adriagne hir sorwe ladde,
> For Theseus hir Soster tok
> And hire unkindely forsok.
> (CA VIII.2556–58)

Genius tells Amans the Tale of Ariadne to warn him against the sin of Ingratitude, a daughter of the sin of Avarice. The Confessor says

> For ther mai be no such grevance
> To love, as is unkindeschipe.
> (CA V.5224–25)

"Unkindeschipe" is "Of covine and of felaschipe / With Avarice he is withholde" (CA V.4888–89). An unkinde man will take what any man will give him, but will begrudge anyone else help or thanks (CA V.4903). To illustrate his point, Genius tells the Tale of Ariadne (CA V.5226).

Gower once again borrowed from Ovid. He would have found details for the myth in the *Metamorphoses* and in the *Heroides*, but some particulars are from the *Ovide moralisé*, *Ovidius moralizatus*, and the glosses.[75] Chaucer told the tale in the *Legend*, and he summarizes it in the *House of Fame*.[76] Genius begins his tale by telling Amans of the bizarre peace treaty struck between King Mynos of Crete, Ariadne's father, and King Egeus of Athens: each year nine Athenian men are sent to Crete to meet their deaths in a cruel sacrifice. The men are forced into the maze-like house of the monster Minotaur and eaten alive. One year King Egeus' son Theseus is among the nine men who must travel to Crete and meet his fate (CA V.5315). Cruel Mynos sends one man to be devoured by the Minotaur each day, "Bot Theseus was so favoured, / That he was kept til ate laste" (CA V.5327–29). Ariadne hears about Theseus' fame and with one glance at him she falls in love (CA V.5334–36):

> Hire hole herte on him sche leide,
> And he also of love hir preide,
> So ferforth that thei were al on.
> (CA V.5337–39)

The phrase "thei were al on" frequently indicates that a couple is sexually intimate, but not in this particular context; several lines later it is explicitly stated that they slept together (CA V.5382). Ariadne takes a risk in befriending this knight; indeed, in giving him her whole heart she makes a senseless mistake. She is foolish to consort with a prisoner, and her behavior is especially unseemly as the king's daughter; she is clearly mislead by her passions. Without any prompting from Theseus, Ariadne tells him "what manere he scholde him save" from Minotaur's clutches (CA V.5341). She knows how to get out of the labyrinth, and she readily offers him this secret. Handing him a ball of thread, she tells Theseus to tie it to the door he enters through, and then follow it back out (CA V. 5343). She also gives him some pitch to throw into the Minotaur's throat (CA V.5349–50). These are clever tricks, and they work. Theseus does as this maiden has taught him and slays the monster (CA V.5359–61). He returns from the prison-like house a victor, thus ending the war between Athens and Crete (CA V.5366–67). This is cause for public celebration, but Genius announces he will now focus upon the sweet Ariadne (CA V.5368).

The "faire Maiden Adriane" has a beauty that is "withoute wane," a very pretty line which Gower does not use to describe anyone else in the *Confessio* (CA V.5370, 5369). Ariadne is thrilled to see Theseus alive. Mynos invites the knight to stay at the palace as a guest for several days, and he and Ariadne become sexually intimate (CA V.5373–74). They whisper together and Ariadne fully "abandouned" herself to Theseus,

> In al that evere that sche couthe,
> So that of thilke lusty youthe
> Al prively betwen hem tweie
> The ferste flour he tok aweie.
> For he so faire tho behihte
> That evere, whil he live mihte,

> He scholde hire take for his wif,
> And as his oghne hertes lif.
> (CA V.5379–86)

Ariadne loses her virginity to Theseus, and he promises to marry her. It is unclear whether he promises to marry her before or after they make love, but either way she has given herself to a man she barely knows.[77] Genius tells Amans of Theseus pledges:

> He scholde hire love and trouthe bere;
> And sche, which mihte noght forbere,
> So sore loveth him ayein,
> That what as evere he wolde sein
> With al hire herte sche believeth.
> (CA V.5387–91)

Ariadne so intensely loves Theseus that she is unable to do anything but fully believe whatever he says (CA V.5388). Ariadne gives herself up to her passions; she is completely seduced by Theseus and his reputation. Like the other Forsaken Women, Ariadne finds herself in the irrational position of secretly pledging oaths of love with a man. There are no witnesses to the vows she and Theseus exchange, and therefore no obligation for Theseus to honor what he so ardently pledges to Ariadne.[78] The ceremony is illicit and takes place without King Minos' knowledge or permission. The love the couple shares in this brief moment quickly unravels.

Ariadne is so "assured of his trouthe" that she leaves Crete with Theseus, and that, says Genius, is "routhe" (CA V.5393–94). An editorial comment such as this is very rare in Gower. Chaucer's Narrator frequently interjects his opinion,[79] but Gower's Genius does not. In the *Heroides* Ariadne runs away with her lover, against the wishes of her parents, and Gower seems to follow this source with the simple statement "Hire fader lefte" (CA V.5401). Ariadne runs away; she has knowingly and willingly betrayed her father. She strips herself of her royal legacy and, with a lover by her side, willingly deserts her homeland; her actions parallel Medea's. Ariadne's disobedient and aggressive behavior contributes to her downfall. In the *Legend* Chaucer emphasizes Theseus' sorry predicament in prison as he waits to be thrown into the Minotaur's house. Chaucer's Ariadne and her sister Phaedra appear together in his version of the tale, and together they help him escape from the Minotaur's labyrinth. It is Ariadne who suggests marriage in Chaucer's version of the tale; indeed, she barters quite aggressively (LGW VI.2078–2102). When the conniving Theseus mentions that he has been in love with Ariadne for "This sevene yer," the deal is struck (LGW VI.2114–20). Chaucer's Ariadne seems like an astute businesswoman, but she is seduced by flattery, and things do not go according to her plans.

In the *Confessio* Theseus forgets his promises to marry Ariadne as soon as their journey begins (CA V.5403). Seasick from the excursion, Ariadne begs to rest, presumably on land, thus providing Theseus with an opportunity to rid himself of her. Theseus is now described as a "beste unkinde" who "no trouthe kepte" (CA V.5424–25). As Ariadne sleeps, Theseus sets sail:

> Whil that this yonge ladi slepte,
> Fulfild of his unkindeschipe
> Hath al foryete the goodschipe
> Which Adriane him hadde do.
> (CA V.5426–29)

Theseus has quickly forgotten the generosity of Ariadne's two gifts to him: his life and her heart. In the *Mirour* Gower writes of the sin of Ingratitude:

> Never rely upon an ungrateful man. For even if he had pledged you his faith and sworn by God and all the saints that he would never fail you but would unfailingly love you in sickness and in health, you will never be sure of him (MO 6649).

Gower also writes about the virtue of Generosity, which contends against the sin of Avarice and Ingratitude, and guarantees that one good deed deserves another:

> With regard to human creatures, the civil law of ancient Scripture summarizes in a few words all that law that touches reason and moderation, namely, 'Do to another as you wish him to do to you'
> (MO 15217).

Ariadne does not get her due reward. Theseus forgets the kind deeds which she has done for him, and he is without remorse. Heartlessly, Theseus

> ... bad unto the Schipmen tho
> Hale up the seil and noght abyde,
> And forth he goth the same tyde
> Toward Athene, and hire alonde
> He lefte.
> (CA V.5430–34)

Theseus' order to set sail and thus abandon her on the island is an extraordinarily barbarous act, and it is a wonder that his shipmen obey him. The fact that

Gower uses the phrase "and noght abyde" may indicate that some of the sailors, at least, were concerned about leaving the young woman behind on the island.

Ariadne awakens from her nap to find herself alone on the island: "Hire herte was so sore aflyht / That sche ne wiste what to thinke" (CA V.5438–39). Theseus' cruelty has stunned Ariadne. She runs to the edge of the water, but the ship has already vanished from the horizon. Genius tells us what she says in her own words, the first dramatic speech in the tale:

> 'Ha lord,' sche seide, 'which a Senne,
> As al the world schal after hiere,
> Upon this woful womman hiere
> This worthi kniht hath don and wroght!
> I wende I hadde his love boght,
> And so deserved ate nede,
> Whan that he stod upon his drede
> And ek the love he me behihte.'
> (CA V.5444–51)

Ariadne cries, "Hire faire tresces sche todrouh," and she swoons "betwen the deth and lif" (CA V.5464, 5466). Although the circumstances differ, Ariadne's emotional state contrasts sharply with someone like Penelope, who maintains her calm and poised demeanor throughout her years of waiting for the slothful Ulysses to return. Ariadne is incredulous that Theseus has forgotten his promises to her:

> 'It is gret wonder hou he mihte
> Towardes me nou ben unkinde,
> And so to lete out of his mynde
> Thing which he seide his oghne mouth.'
> (CA V.5452–55)

But Theseus forsakes Ariadne, and takes her sister Phaedra, who had come along on the journey, in place of her (CA V.5482).[80] Genius tells Amans that Theseus, once a "noble kniht," has "the lawe of loves riht / Forfeted hath in alle weie" by abandoning one sister and embracing another (CA V.5475, 5476–77). In the *Traitié* Gower writes that marriage is a matter of faith which cannot be destroyed:

> The sacrament of holy church brings this blessing to marriage. It is a bond, without dissolution, which man must guard. For whoever would read the past he would have reason to say, for fear of vengeance and harm. An honest man does not belie his faith (Tr 5.3).

Theseus has repudiated his pledges to Ariadne. His bond of honor is worthless, but Gower never tells us if Theseus meets death for his misdeeds.

At the tale's end Genius reminds Amans that "Unkindeschipe" weakens the truth in a man's heart:

> Unkindeschipe, where it falleth,
> The trouthe of mannes herte it palleth,
> That he no good dede aquite.
> (CA V.5486–88)

Truth in love is a necessary component in the marriages of happy lovers, as seen in the marriages of the Four Wives. Without truth, man's heart becomes feeble; Theseus' untrue heart must be very weak indeed[81] (CA V.5487). Theseus is "unkinde" and no better than the "fend," for the Devil, like Theseus, seeks to satisfy himself only: "Bot al toward himself al one" (CA V.5491,5493). Theseus is first described as a worthy knight, then he becomes a beast, and finally, a fiend. He is a self-centered man whose "Unkindeschipe" towards the too-generous Ariadne costs her her life.

Like the other women in this chapter, Ariadne gives up everything she has—her virginity, her heart, her homeland, her inheritance—for a wayfaring man she barely knows. Not surprisingly, Theseus leaves her with empty promises and no wedding ceremony. Sadly, Gower's Ariadne is the agent of her own destruction in more than one way: she too willingly helps a stranger, too quickly gives him her heart, and foolishly "With al hire herte sche believeth" his promises; she even inadvertently provides him with a woman who will supplant her in his heart, her sister. Unlike the virtuous Alceone who receives a reward for her well-placed loving, Ariadne gives up her virginity and her father's kingdom for an unscrupulous knight, and subsequently finds herself utterly alone on a barren isle in the Aegean.

Ariadne's letter in the *Heroides* conveys a sense of inevitable doom: Ariadne knows she is going to die and in her misery she complains not of Theseus' infidelity but of her loneliness in death. The hopelessness in Ovid which defines the poem is apparent in Gower too. Gower presents his heroine in a bleak landscape, uselessly searching the horizon for Theseus' ship (CA V.5442). She is alone on the island, and as she stands on the shoreline scanning the ocean the pathos of her situation is realistically conveyed. Her grief and the despair in her cries for help emphasize Gower's ability to tell a story skillfully despite little adornment. In Ovid's *Metamorphoses* the god Dionysus takes pity on Ariadne and transforms her into a constellation; Chaucer relates that her crown only becomes a constellation. In some traditions of the story, Dionysus rescues and marries Ariadne, but Gower does not employ a rescue or a metamorphosis.[82]

Ariadne's over-hasty actions indicate her readiness to love and her willingness to trust the word of a stranger. She falls in love with Theseus on his reputation alone in what seems to be an instant. Theseus does not ardently woo Ariadne, but she gives away her whole heart, a very valuable commodity especially in a king's daughter, before he even so much as begs for her love. She bestows valuable gifts without exacting a promise from her lover and, to compound her errors, she does this twice: first with the elusive secret of how to exit Minotaur's house, and secondly with her valuable heart. She is a very eager young woman, and this type of aggressive love behavior has no place in Gower; furthermore, it is to her detriment. She is far too generous, and she is unkindly repaid for her magnanimity. The parallels between this tale and the Tale of Medea are obvious but should be stated. Theseus, like Jason, has a woman to thank for both his victory and his life. Again, like Jason, Theseus promises to marry that woman, and although Jason does marry Medea, he does not keep his marriage vow, and so neither man honors their promise. Theseus journeys home a victor—and perhaps to a victor's return—but he is unable to honor the woman who guaranteed his very success.

Theseus is an ungrateful man brimming with avarice.[83] Gower illuminates the sin of Ingratitude in the *Mirour*:

> Ingratitude is one who always associates with Covetousness. She is the one who in the evening forgets the good things of the day and gathers together everything for herself, considering nothing to be common property. She is the one who has a heart without love, for she renders neither thanks nor gratitude to her Creator, who gave her all her sense and vigor. She is the one who, if you had given her every honor, would not in the end give back to you a prune (MO 6637).

The Latin headnote to Book V of the *Confessio* epitomizes the ingrate Demephon's dishonorable behavior:

> All that's made, and God who made it all,
> Together damn an ingrate's words and deeds.
> Grief's not far off when he a mistress takes,
> And finally she ceases to be his.[84]

Gower lets Ariadne languish on the island with no Dionysus to rescue her, for her quickness to satisfy her own passion and her inability to wait for a proper marriage ceremony deserve punishment, not rescue. Moral control in matters of love is a serious matter to Gower, and Ariadne had no control over her budding sexuality. In any love affair reason is needed to keep passion from turning the relationship into a tragedy. Ariadne's excessive love and her aggressive behavior are volatile components unchecked by her reason. Her passion boiled too quickly and it overflowed into Theseus' greedy hands, and her naiveté and her willingness to be seduced contribute to her undoing. Theseus is to blame for his dishonest heart and his avaricious desires, but he is not blameworthy for heating up Ariadne's passions. She did that herself. Ariadne meant well, but her behavior is unreasonably excessive, and that is something Gower abhors and will not reward.

Conclusion

Gower continually reminds his readers that the harmony of the world is tenuously held in balance. When man acts unreasonably and embraces passion over reason, disharmony and havoc rule. Genius tells Amans the love tales of Dido, Phyllis, and Ariadne, the three unmarried women in this chapter, to remind the Lover that man must uphold the law of reason, and anyone who satisfies his or her sexual desires without the sanctity of marriage will fail in the affairs of Love. The difference between these three women and a woman such as Alcestis, and it is a significant difference in Gower, is that Alcestis is a wife, while the unmarried women engage in secret sexual relations with men who give them only promises, and empty ones at that. Medea, Dido, Phyllis, and Ariadne each commit the same mistake, that of giving in to their desires and giving what Gower calls their "all" to a seafaring stranger. Each of these women is ready for love and willing to believe any and all of the lies her seductive sailor speaks, and each suffers cruelly for her imprudent love decisions. The Forsaken Women are not rewarded by Venus, and except for the brief moment when they feel the warm rays of love emanating from the fickle goddess, they suffer deeply for their foolish love choices.

In the *Confessio* Gower doles out punishment to those whose sins of excessive passion and foolish behavior are beyond the realms of reasonable behavior. As he writes in the *Mirour*, "each gets what he deserves" (MO 17677). Ariadne suffers utter solitude and lives on a deserted island, and Phyllis is transformed into a Nut-tree after she commits suicide; she is the only Forsaken Women to be granted a metamorphosis. Dido also commits suicide, but neither she or Phyllis is damned for that sin against Nature and God. The tales of Deianira and Medea, the two married women in this chapter, illustrate how jealousy and rage can destroy reciprocal love, especially if love is shadowed by hypocrisy. The contrast between these two marriages and the four marriages examined in chapter two are significant. Medea gives of herself and her art to Jason, and in return he gives her falseness. In the Tale of Medea, the destruction of their love is especially disheartening for we have seen evidence of a mutual love and affection. In the Tale of Deianira the heroine is overcome by Envy and seduced by "Falssemblant." While her husband Hercules is guilty of both deception and adultery, Deianira's passionate and malicious response to his infidelities result in his and Iole's deaths. Gower does not grant her immunity for her murderous sins, rather she must pay the price for her misdeeds by living out the rest of her days in anguish. Deianira and Medea are both guilty of cruel murder, but most curiously for a Christian poet, Gower does not condemn them for this grievous sin against Nature, Love and God.

Gower barely hints that the men in these tales, Hercules, Jason, Aeneas, Demephon, and Theseus, either have a call to a higher cause, or are part of a larger myth. Each man has a reason for deserting his lady-love in the heroic renditions of these tales, and the women are not deserted so much as merely a part of the background landscape which nurtures the heroes. This is not so in the *Confessio*. In the *Confessio* and in the *Traitié* Gower follows Ovid's stance in the *Heroides*, and sides with the women, seeing only that the men have deserted women to whom they promised love and truth, chastising them for their infidelities and false oaths.[85] Although Gower censures the men, he does not commend the women because their imprudent actions are excessively passionate. To love well one must seek and maintain the balance that the Marriages of the Four Wives exhibit, but Gower's Forsaken Women's passions know no bounds, and the poet disdains unreasonable behavior in men and women alike.

Linda Barney Burke correctly points out that the *Confessio* "is imbued with a tone of mellowness, sensitivity, and compassion for the limitations of human nature. What has not been so apparent is that an important reason for this benign atmosphere is the almost total absence of negative female stereotypes and antifeminist propaganda in the *Confessio*."[86] Gower works to present his creations as full and complete women. The poet is sympathetic to the foolish and forsaken women in this chapter because he is a poet who understands the human condition, yet he is fair to men and women alike, most notably in the *Confessio*. Anyone, male or female, who loses his reason is susceptible to censure by Gower. Unmarried and married foolish women, however sympathetically they are treated, are not rewarded with a peaceful existence, and not given a chance to try again. In Gower lost reputations and loneliness are the rewards for foolhardy and hasty decisions in Love. He has no tolerance for unreasonable behavior in mankind, for he believes it is every man and every woman's duty to control his passions and live properly in God's eyes.

In the *Confessio* the women are often the focal point of the tale. This is unusual, and furthers the point that Gower is a poet of humanity. He holds men and women equally accountable for their actions, and in the *Confessio* his concern is the proper management of one's passions. A Dido or an Ariadne is secondary to an Aeneas or a Theseus in the larger and more complete myths to which they belong, but Gower's illustrations of women are drawn with sympathy and humanity. Dido is an example of a woman who has misplaced her love and lost sight of her moral duty to love properly as well as her regal duty to marry before engaging in intimate relations, especially with a stranger. We are familiar with Dido and the other Forsaken Women because they are famous for their love entanglements with men who are mythic heroes, but now in Gower's hands, through Ovid, we learn how they are jilted and understand that they have had a role in their own downfall. Yes, their lovers are slothful or unfaithful, but their choices in men are made without any consideration to their moral responsibilities; in short, they are ruled by passion, not reason. Throughout the tales of the Forsaken Women Gower focuses on the woman's or the man's personal responsibility to do the right thing, as it were. One's moral conduct is indicative of the peace found in the world at large, and Gower takes this responsibility, which includes the responsibility to love properly, very seriously.

Chapter Four
Lovesickness in the *Confessio Amantis*

Throughout his poetry it is evident that Gower believes man's duty and responsibility to God lies within his ability to govern himself in a reasonable fashion at all times; in the *Confessio* he is especially concerned with how man conducts himself in matters of the heart. Gower's penitent is afflicted with the disease of Love known as *amor hereos* or lovesickness, an aspect of love which fells many lovers in medieval literature. Medieval medical practitioners treated lovesickness as a disease which left uncured could degenerate into the more severe mania or melancholy, and practitioners and poets alike treated the disease quite seriously. The frame of the poem, Amans' confession to Genius, affords a good example of Lovesickness in a Middle English poem. Sick with love-longing for a lady who is "further fro my love / Than Erthe is fro the hevene above," a timid Amans begs for mercy from Venus and her angry son Cupid (CA I.105–6). Cupid pierces Amans' heart with a fiery arrow and then flees, but Venus sends her priest Genius to hear Amans' complaints about his "thilke unsely jolif wo" from which he suffers (CA I.88). Peering closely at Amans, Venus' priest remarks that Amans looks ill, and declares that he is suffering from the malady of Lovedrunkenness:

> And as me semeth be that art,
> Thou scholdest be Phisonomie
> Be schapen to that maladie
> Of lovedrunke, and that is routhe.
> (CA VI.108–111)

Amans immediately confesses that he suffers for love's sake—"Holi fader, al is trouthe" (CA VI.112). As Genius absolves Amans of his love sins, we learn the intimate details of Amans' love life as well as the temperament of his mind. Amans' behavior results from his inability to behave rationally in the face of

Love, a human failing considered sinful by Venus' priest.¹ His confession is a thorough and complete one, and serves as a frame for the poem, a poetical device Gower readily found in the *Roman*. Amans lovesickness has poisoned his very soul, and he needs to be cured, something that becomes manifest during Genius' careful scrutiny. Amans' illness is clearly defined at the onset of Book I, and as the poem progresses his suffering and symptoms are fully defined and developed. By the end of the poem the confession, with some help from Venus, has provided Amans with the self-knowledge he needs in order to grasp Genius' lessons and accept the goddess' decree.

Amans has set his heart upon a woman who barely favors him with a kind look, and he suffers endlessly for her sake. His love is selfish and unbalanced, distinctly dissimilar to the reciprocal love Gower recommends throughout the *Confessio*. In his confession Amans complains that his devoted service to the Goddess of Love affords him only misery. His body is racked with hot chills and cold fevers, he cannot sleep, he has no appetite, he experiences mood swings, and most grievously from Gower's point of view, he has lost control of his senses. Any physician of Gower's London would recognize Amans' illness and declare it to be lovesickness. His symptoms are the classic examples of lovesickness found in Ovid's *Ars* and the *Remedia*, works Gower knew, but Amans' symptoms are also found in medical manuscripts and commentaries. *Amor hereos* is first mentioned by Constantine, a ninth century North African monk, whom Chaucer refers to as "the cursed monk" in the Merchant's Tale (MerT 1810). Constantine wrote Latin translations of Arabic, Greek and Hebrew medical books, and he may be the writer responsible for bringing the medical tradition of lovesickness into European culture.² The *Viaticum*, a popular handbook for travelers who lack access to medical care, included a chapter on lovesickness, revealing that in Islamic culture lovesickness was believed to be a serious disease requiring treatment.³ In Mary F. Wack's translation of the *Viaticum* and its commentaries, she argues that these texts "attest that lovesickness was as 'real' for medieval physicians as melancholy, headache, baldness, and scalp lice—as real as the other diseases of the head among which *amor hereos* was classified."⁴

The three most authoritative texts on lovesickness in the medical curricula across Europe were the *Viaticum*, a gloss on the *Viaticum* by Gerardus Bituricensis (Gerard of Berry's *Glosses*), and Avicenna's *Canon medicinae*.⁵ These texts and their commentaries shaped subsequent medical discussions on the subject and agree that the causes of lovesickness are both psychic and somatic. Wack summarizes:

> The sight of a beautiful form may cause the soul to go mad with desire, as Constantinus says. In Gerard of Berry's formulation, the mind 'overestimates' the value of the perceived object and hence desires it excessively. This overestimation, however, can only take place if the material composition of

the brain is corrupt, that is, the imagination must be excessively cold and dry so that the overestimated image adheres abnormally and excites the concupiscible power. An excess of black bile or another humor (some later treatises list semen in this category) may also cause the disease. The etiology is thus both psychic and somatic, but the material composition of the body, particularly of the brain, is crucial in the development of the illness. No ethical valuation is attached to the causal mechanisms in any of the texts—the patient is not held 'guilty' or 'responsible' for his illness.[6]

In the *Confessio*, as well as Chaucer's *Book of the Duchess*, the Knight's Tale, and *Troilus and Criseyde*, afflicted lovers show the physical and psychological signs of love distress, both pale faces and senseless behavior. It appears that Gower, like Chaucer, was aware of the medical thinking and practices of his day, but there is no way of knowing how much the poets knew of the medical texts firsthand.[7] In the prologue to *The Canterbury Tales*, Chaucer lists medical writers with whose work the Physician was familiar, but familiarity with names is not evidence that Chaucer himself actually read the works himself.[8] The pain and suffering which Amans' experiences is analogous to the suffering described in the medieval medical treatises; physicians and poets, then, share a mutual language, the language of human nature.[9]

Gower begins Book I with a Latin headstone which defines Love using the conventional contraries:

> Sick health, vexed rest is love, a warlike peace,
> A wound most sweet, fair ill, a pious fault.
> (CA I.i.7–8)[10]

In the *De Planctu*, Alan describes love as "peace joined to hatred, loyalty to treachery, hope to fear and madness blended with reason" (DP 149). Jean uses similar contraries in the *Roman*: "troubled peace," "amorous war," "treasonous loyalty, disloyal faith," contraries he probably found in Alan (RR 4271–72). In book five, chapter two of the *Vox* Gower develops the inconstancies of love into over thirty lines, beginning with ones that echo the above passage.[11] He continues this discussion of love in the next chapter where he describes how erotic love or lust drives rational judgment from a knight's mind. He writes of women's beauty which can enslave a man and leave him destitute of rational judgment:

> When a man sees her womanly beauty—so sweet, elegant and fine, but more like an angels—he thinks her a goddess, and puts his fate of life and death in her hands. . . . Outwardly, he does not show what the sight of her means to him; inwardly, the sting of love pierces his heart. . . . His mind's eye grows dull, blind from the darkness of lust, and he sinks down to his own destruction. . . . So he goes blindly mad because of his blind love.
> (VC 5.3.130–140ff)

It is conventional, of course, that Love enters through the eyes.

It is not just medieval poets, however, who warn lovers to guard their eyes from Cupid's arrows. Medieval medical practitioners also agree that the sight of a beautiful woman could trigger erotic impulses within the body and cause one to be afflicted with lovesickness. The practitioners recorded that a number of causes must converge at the same time for lovesickness to take hold, but in effect, the medical community and the poets agree upon an important point: Love enters through the eye, is fed by the imagination, and soon dominates the lover's soul. Peter of Spain, a commentator on the *Viaticum* and an expert on both medicine and philosophy, describes eyes as man's "windows to the soul" which allow the woman's image to enter man's imagination.[12] The eyes suffer in love because "the greater connection any member has with the brain, the more it suffers in the brain's illnesses, [and] . . . the eyes are of this sort."[13] Peter writes:

> Love enters through the senses to the interior faculty, namely to the fantasy, and from the fantasy [it progresses] to the estimative faculty, whose function is to recognize friendship and enmity, as Avicenna says, and beyond that in all things. (Peter Viaticum B 233)

In the *Liber de heros morbo*, another translation of the *Viaticum*, Johannes, a student of Constantine's, states something similar:

> Sometimes the cause of this disease heros is the delight of the rational soul in a beautiful object. For if it contemplates beauty in a form similar to itself, a rage to unite with it is kindled. Since therefore grave psychological symptoms accompany this serious disease, that is, the kindling of incessant thoughts.[14] (Johannes *Liber* 328)

The medical practitioners believed that intense contemplation of one's beloved kindles the disease, which is what happens to Gower's Jason and Medea.

When Medea first sees Jason she instantly falls in love with his beautiful form (CA V.3378-81). His image lodges in her imagination where it grows, feeding her erotic desire until she is obsessed with him. Likewise Jason cannot stop starring at Medea; he falls in love at first sight too (CA V.3382-87). Phyllis is also afflicted with love through her first look at Demephon (CA IV.745). In the *Confessio* Genius first questions the penitent Amans about the state of his five senses:

> For tho be proprely the gates,
> Thurgh whiche as to the herte algates
> Comth alle thing unto the feire,
> Which may the mannes Soule empeire.
> (CA I.299-302)

Genius says that sight is "the moste principal of alle / Thurgh whom that peril mai befalle" (CA I.306–07), for Cupid sends a "firy Dart / Of love" into his victim's eyes (CA I.319–24). These examples illustrate how medicine and literature offer similar descriptions of passionate love in the later Middle Ages.[15]

In the *Roman* the God of Love shoots an arrow at the lover's "very heart, though entering by . . . the eye" (RR 1690). In Chaucer's Knight's Tale, when Palamon first sees Emily he cries out as if in pain. He explains to the concerned Arcite that he "was hurt right now thurghout myn ye / Into myn herte" (KnT 1096–97). Moments later Arcite sees Emily's beautiful form, and he, too, is wounded (KnT 1115). During the eleventh and twelfth centuries, when the school of medicine flourished in Salerno, medical practitioners were concerned with defining pleasure and locating the seat of desire.[16] The eyes, the heart, the brain, or the liver were among the organs associated with pleasure, but the subject of where desire began was never resolved for the "scholastic authors did not attempt to resolve or harmonize" the lack of agreement about the geography of pleasure.[17] Eyes, however, were given prominence, a medical theory which is certainly borne out in medieval literature. It was thought that a beautiful sight was imprinted in the memory which in imagining or remembering it stirred up one's passions.[18] Upon seeing his beloved a man's liver becomes warm and sends blood through his body, awakening his sexual desire. Thus the three elements thought "necessary for the performance of the sexual act, heat, moistness and spirit," are present.[19]

Gower states that Book I of the *Confessio* will be about love, a marked transition from the Prologue, in which he endeavors to provide wisdom to England by writing of the vices and virtues and the proper rule of the three estates.[20] Love is common to every man:

> Which every kinde hath upon honde,
> And wherupon the world mot stonde,
> And hath don sithen it began,
> And schal whil ther is any man;
> And that is love, of which I mene
> To trete, as after schal be sene.
> (CA I.11–16)

Immediately the poet notes that "loves lawe is out of reule"—some men get too much and others too little—but nonetheless there is a common denominator: no man, no matter how wise he may be, can restrain love or control its arbitrary willfulness, for Love is "above alle othre strong" (CA I.18;VI.101).[21] Gower describes Love as an incurable sickness:

> For yet was nevere such covine,
> That couthe ordeine a medicine
> To thing which god in lawe of kinde
> Hath set, for ther may noman finde
> The rihte salve of such a Sor.
> (CA I.29–33)

In the *Vox* Gower writes:

> Alas, that love is not curable by any herbs! Neither brawn nor brain can escape its burden. No one can avoid this innate disease, unless it be that divine grace alone watch over him. O how grievous is the nature of man! Driven to his own destruction by it, it forces him to love. (VC 5.3.190ff)

Furthermore, Love has been and will always be his own master:

> It hath and schal ben everemor
> That love is maister wher he wile.
> (CA I.34–35)

Gower relies upon the proverbial "For love is blind and may noght se," reminding his audience that one cannot ever be certain of Love, for "He yifth his graces undeserved" (CA I.47,51). Giving oneself to Love is like rolling the dice, and often man would avoid love if he knew what Love would do to him (CA I.58–60).

Gower begins the Lover's confession by promising to tell the reader of his "wofull care, / Mi wofull day, my wofull chance" in Venus' court, Gower states he "Woll wryte and schewe al openly / How love and I togedre mette" (CA I.83–89) It is May, traditionally a month of mating and love, but instead of rejoicing and enjoying the songs of the birds which are busy choosing their mates, the weary Lover lies down on a "swote grene pleine" (CA I.111). In a melancholy voice he calls to Venus and Cupid in heaven:

> 'Wher is pite? wher is meknesse?
> Now doth me pleinly live or dye,
> For certes such a maladie
> As I now have and longe have hadd,
> It myhte make a wisman madd,
> If that is scholde longe endure.'
> (CA I.126–31)

Amans prays for some of Venus' grace, and suddenly the goddess and god of Love appear before him. Cupid glares angrily at Amans before shooting an arrow into him and departing. Venus stays behind and she asks him what kind of man he is; he replies "'A Caitif,'" a response which is indicative of the way he feels (CA I.161). Amans is held captive to his lady's charms, and calls himself a wretch.[22] His infatuation has filled him with woe and inner turmoil, and he is unable to recognize himself. He tells Venus that he believes he deserves "'Som wele after my longe wo'" (CA I.171). Venus wants to be sure that Amans is not one of the many "Faitours" who claim to be in her retinue but are feigning service, and she asks him to prove his allegiance to her (CA I.174–76). With a spark of wit, Amans says he will, "Be so my lif therto wol laste" (CA I.187). Hearing this statement, Venus decides to send her Confessor Genius to Amans to shrive him of his sins "'In aunter if thou live'" (CA I.189).

Gower did not have to reach very far back to find the character of Genius. In the *Roman* Genius is the priest of Nature; in the *Confessio*, he is the priest of Venus, Goddess of Love. Genius also appears in Alan's *De Planctu*, as Nature's priest; her "other self" and "alter ego" (DP 206–07). As Venus' priest we expect Genius to expound sexual love, but the tales Gower's Genius tells advance married love, and advocate that lovers who make a solemn vow of marriage to one another live a peaceful and mutually beneficent life. Genius' dual nature, which has a marked similarity to man's, was viewed by early critics as "a principal manifestation of Gower's failures to reconcile his subject with his moral framework," but Genius is now regarded as "an effective spokesman for the multifacetedness of Gower's perspective on human love." [23] Genius often expounds a knowledge that would seem more fitting for a Christian priest than one who serves Venus,[24] for he never advocates amorous abandonment in the *Confessio*. He is a character worth a fuller study than I can provide here.[25] J. A. W. Bennett succinctly writes that Genius

> obliquely reflects the struggle between passion and reason, measure and excess, private interest and public weal, that takes place in all lovers and in all men, . . . [while] . . . his humor bespeaks a shrewd and experienced confessor.[26]

Gower's Genius leads Amans through a thorough confession, intent on teaching him the proper way to love, by reigning in his *kinde* and reconciling himself with temperate reason.

Genius employs a confession following the Christian formula. He meticulously tests and teaches Amans, as thoroughly as "a priest of the Fourth Lateran Council . . . could have wished."[27] The Confessor says as Venus' priest he will speak primarily of love, but he will also touch on other subjects; he is "a sort of universal priest."[28] Genius hopes to persuade Amans to speak about his love experiences and adopt the moral norms the priest expounds.[29] As a confessor Genius claims it behooves him to inform Amans how the vices apply to Love so he will understand and hopefully avoid them (CA I.276–80). He may be the priest of Venus, but he is also the voice of rational judgments, advocating the use of reason as man's best defense against foolish love errors, and recommending married love over amorous pursuits without a marriage license. Gower's Genius is a character in whom pagan, Christian, and Gowerian philosophies meet, yet he is not a reliable authority figure.[30]

Genius greets the penitent:

> Benedicite,
> Mi Sone, of the felicite
> Of love and ek of all the wo
> Thou schalt thee schrive of bothe tuo.
> (CA I.205–08)

Amans readily agrees to this confession, saying

> ... 'for I am destourbed
> In al myn herte, and so contourbed,
> That I ne may my wittes gete,
> So schal I moche thing foryete ...
> ...
> Bot now my wittes ben so blinde,
> That I ne can miselven teche.'
> (CA I.221–29)

Earlier Amans complained of his woe, but here he admits to suffering from utter confusion, a loss of wits. The fact that Amans recognizes his illness is a first step towards his cure, as it always is for anyone who seeks help. Genius is not a medical practitioner, but as he shrives Amans of his sins, he helps to ease Amans' pains by unconsciously employing one of the recommended medical remedies—that of a confessional conversation. Ultimately it is Venus who shocks Amans into reality by handing him a mirror and applying a salve which release him from his folly and cures him of lovesickness.

Lovesick lovers exhibit some basic symptoms: they are pale, their eyes sunken, they seek solitary places such as woods and gardens so they can be alone with thoughts of their beloved, they experience hot fevers and cold chills, they have no appetite, and cannot sleep. Gerard of Berry scrutinizes the lover's malady, referring to it as "an incessant preoccupation of the brain with the beloved thing, and the damage is transferred from the brain to all the parts of the body."[31] Amans is incessantly preoccupied with thoughts of his lady, and these continual thoughts keep him awake at night; sleeplessness is one of the most common symptoms of lovesickness. Amans' mind races with fantasies of his lady, and he confesses that he is unable to sleep:

> I mai noght slepe, thogh I wolde;
> For love is evere faste byme,
> Which takth no hiede of due time.
> For whanne I schal myn yhen close,
> Anon min herte he wole oppose.
> (CA IV.3368-72)

At night, Amans

> sighe and grone
> And wisshen al the longe nyht
> Til that I se the daies lyht.
> (CA IV.3170-72)

Amans' soft moans indicate the pain in his heart. Gower's Phyllis is another sleepless lover, who "lefte slep and mete," when Demephon fails to return (CA IV.782-84). The inability to sleep is a serious symptom of lovesickness, and the early medical treatises stated that inducing sleep, naturally enough, is curative.[32] Caelius Aurelianus, a fifth century African, who writes about sleeplessness in a section on mania, notes that "continual sleeplessness" is one of the "observable causes" of mania.[33] Among the cures for sleeplessness that Aurelianus cites are passive exercise, and "the rapid dripping of water . . . for under the influence of its sound patients often fall asleep."[34] The sound of "dripping water appears within the context of sleep both in the *Book of the Duchess* and the Ceyx and Alcyone myth of Ovid's *Metamorphoses*."[35] Gower also retains the dripping water which "Rennende upon the smale stones," as well as a delightful description of the Cave of Sleep, the God of Sleep's house in his Tale of Alceone (CA IV.3010).[36]

A pale and wan lover, lying in bed moaning and sighing, unable to sleep, is a conventional description of a lovesick lover, and a familiar figure to Chaucerians. Arcite, in the Knight's Tale, cannot sleep for love, and he lies awake "waillynge al the nyght, makynge his mone" (KnT 1366). Chaucer's Troilus cannot sleep either (TC I.484-87). Eventually sleeplessness and lack of nourishment takes its toll on Arcite and Troilus both, transfiguring them into pale and thin men. When the newly freed Arcite sees his reflection in a mirror, he realizes his changed looks are to his advantage and will enable him to move about the court of Athens undetected by his enemies as he watches over Emily (KnT 1399-1407). Troilus' illness shows "in his hewe both eve and morwe" (TC I.487). He tries desperately to hide his changed looks for he once scorned lovers, going so far as blasphemously calling Cupid "'Seynt Idiot, lord of thise foles alle'" (TC I.910).[37] Troilus decides his best recourse is to pretend he has another ailment—he "seyd he hadde a fevere and ferde amys" (TC 1.488-491)—but it is too late for Troilus: Love has physically transformed the stalwart knight into a common lover. In the *Roman* the God of Love explains that true love will ravage the Lover, leaving "neither flesh nor blood" (RR 2553). Later, when Criseyde has left for the Greek camp, Troilus becomes so weak and disfigured that he cannot walk without a crutch (TC V.1221–22). The mighty Trojan warrior's wasting body is proof of the serious damage which can befall lovesick lovers.

Genius probes deeper into Amans' psyche and questions the lover of his familiarity with Somnolence, the lazy Chamberlain of Sloth. Amans defiantly states that he is not guilty of this sin (CA IV.2770). Amans spurns Somnolence, telling Genius that if he

> mihte come and duelle
> In place ther my ladi were,
> I was noght slow ne slepi there.
> (CA IV.2774–6)

When near his lady, Amans is "redi to consente" to any of her wishes, and he gives Genius several examples to prove that he is not sleeping or slothful, when Love comes calling (CA IV.2797). Amans says that he could endure without sleep if it meant he would not have to leave her side:

> With al myn herte I curse and banne
> That evere slep was mad for yhe;
> For, as me thenkth, I mihte dryhe
> Withoute slep to waken evere,
> So that I scholde noght dissevere
> Fro hire, in whom is al my liht.
> (CA IV.2834–39)

Amans curses Sleep which puts him "Out of mi ladi compaignie" each night (CA IV.2847). When he does finally fall asleep, and he admits that he dreams dreams "drecched to the fulle / Of love" (CA IV.2896–99). He dreams that his lady's guardian, Danger,[38] has left her, allowing him easy access to her charms, but when he awakens, "al is torned into sorwe" (CA IV.2908). The Lover in the *Roman* is warned that when he finally falls asleep, he will dream of his lady lying naked by his side and be in great joy (RR 2428–33). Like Amans, when he awakens he will suffer deep despair; he will live between bliss and utter dejection (RR 2437–46). Amans is tortured by the hours of darkness, for whether he is unable to sleep or he dreams, he is haunted by love, and in this he is a typical lovesick lover.

Genius notes that "love and Slep acorden noght," and indeed, they are conventional enemies, as Genius' tale of Cephalus and Aurora illustrates (CA IV.3186). Unlike Amans, who is kept awake by the fevers of his lovesickness,

Cephalus stays awake to enjoy being in his lady's "armes all the longe nyht" (CA IV.3192). Cephalus wants a few more hours of darkness in which to enjoy lovemaking with his lady, and when the first light of day is seen, Cephalus "unto the Sonne he preide / For lust of love" (CA IV.3195–96). In the *Amores*, Ovid chastises the Dawn for arriving so soon:

> What's the hurry, Aurora? Take it easy, let Memnon's spirit
> Enjoy the yearly sacrifice by his birds!
> Now, if ever, I love to lie in my mistress's tender
> Embrace, feel her close by my side,
> At this cool hour of deep sleep, with liquid bird-song
> Tremulous in the air.
> What's the hurry? All lovers, men and girls, resent your coming:
> Exert those rosy fingers, rein in awhile!
> . . .
>   Why hurry, spoilsport?
> (Amores, I.13.1–10,31)[39]

On the night of the consummation of their love, Troilus and Criseyde wish for a longer night too. When the sunlight beams into their room, Troilus curses Titan, the sun god and Dawn's lover, for causing lovers everywhere distress:

> 'O fool, wel may men the dispise,
> That hast the dawyng al nyght by thi syde,
> And suffrest hire so soone up fro the rise
> For to disese loveris in this wyse.'
> (TC III.1465–68)

Centuries later, the narrator of John Donne's "The Sunne Rising" also curses the morning sunrise and wishes for a longer night so he and his lady may prolong their lovemaking.[40] Amans, however, curses the night not the morning sun, for he is alone at night, unlike Cephalus, Ovid, Troilus, and Donne's Narrator. Most lovers pray for the cover of darkness, but Amans wants a shorter night. He is turned inside out and upside down by lovesickness, and therefore he craves the opposite of what lovers who are in mutually satisfying relationships want. Gower repeatedly re-enforces the notion that Amans is not in a healthy, balanced relationship. Amans curses the night and the darkness it brings, an inverted situation which points to his inability to rule his passions.

Medieval lovesickness and modern depression share the same symptoms: insomnia, appetite loss, mood swings.[41] Chaucer highlights the inner turmoil of a lover in the throes of lovesickness in both the Knight's Tale and in *Troilus*. Arcite's spirits are so feeble and low that the Narrator guesses that he does not only suffer from "the loveris maladye / Of Hereos," but also from mania, an offshoot of the disease:

> And chaunged so, that no man koude knowe
> His speche nor his voys, though men it herde.
> And in his geere for al the world he ferde
> Nat oonly lik the loveris maladye
> Of Hereos, but rather lyk manye,
> Engendred of humour malencolik
> Biforen, in is celle fantasik.
> (KnT 1370–76)

Excessive love for Emily has driven Arcite crazy. Troilus suffers from erotic desire to the detriment of his health too. He is "wel neigh wood," worrying that Criseyde has a lover, a thought that makes "his herte blede" (TC I.542–43;498–504). Troilus' emotions are ravaged by Love and he wishes for death, believing death to be a better option than languishing as he does now (TC I.526–29). Wishing for death, of course, is a common desire among lovesick lovers: Dido and Phyllis both kill themselves to end their love suffering. Amans thinks of death as a release from the pain which he fears he cannot endure much longer (CA I.126–31).

Obsessed lovers know no moderation. Arcite, Troilus, and Amans all suffer from the same symptoms: they cannot sleep or eat, they are witless, and they pray for death; furthermore, each lover has made his lady his world, a dangerous fixation. It is conventional to suggest moderation to lovers, as Ovid does in the *Ars Amatoria*:

> Moderation's best, as so often: don't play the country bumpkin,
> But equally, don't lay your affectations on
> Too thick.
> (AA 3.304ff)

Clearly neither Arcite, Troilus, or Amans have followed Ovid's advice. One of the treatises on the *Viaticum*, written by a Montpellier master,[42] notes that the disease originates in the brain, and defines it as

> an excitation of the thoughts about an individual or singular form and figure of human likeness, very similar to melancholic worry, aided by unfulfilled desire and concupiscence.[43]

Constantine defines "eros" as "disease touching the brain":[44]

> For it is a great longing with intense sexual desire and affliction of the thoughts. Whence certain philosophers says: Eros is a word signifying the

greatest pleasure. For just as loyalty is the ultimate form of affection, so also eros is a certain extreme form of pleasure (*Viaticum* 187).

Constantine's Latin translation of the popular Arabic medical handbook gave western physicians a term for passionate love. Wack argues that it was Constantine who translated "*Ishk*" to mean excessive love or lovesickness. John Livingston Lowes credits Constantine with the earliest use of the word "*hereos*."[45] In his seminal article of 1914, Lowes defines Chaucer's phrase, "loveris maladye / Of Hereos," from the Knight's Tale, as "the lover's malady of eros" (KnT1373–4). Until Lowes' article was published, Chaucerians translated the word "Hereos" to mean heroes, knights and heroic men, instead of "eros," which connected the phrase broadly to Love. Lowes studied the etymology of *heroes* and proved that Chaucer borrowed descriptions of lovesickness he must have found in medieval medical treatises to describe Arcite's physical and mental condition in the Knight's Tale.[46]

The misinterpretation of Chaucer's line in the Knight's Tale strengthened the link between lovesickness and the upper class, adding credence to the writings of Gerard of Berry, who stressed that lovesickness only afflicted "noble men who, on account of riches and the softness of their lives, are more likely to suffer this disease" (Gerard *Glosses* 203). A man of the noble class has more time for leisure which translates into time to become obsessed with thoughts of his beloved, a "principal feature of the disease."[47] Those in the wealthier classes could also afford to summon a physician, who would pronounce the patient lovesick, and prescribe the proper antidotes. Constantine the African's *De coitu* indicates "a leisured heart . . . and daily joy increase libido."[48] Following this argument, Troilus is a prince, and has the means and the leisure to fall in love.[49] In the *Remedia*, Ovid writes that leisure is the first thing a lover should avoid if he hopes to cure himself of his infatuation:

> No leisure—that's rule
> Number one. Leisure stimulates love, leisure watches the lovelorn,
> Leisure's the cause and sustenance of this sweet
> Evil. Eliminate leisure, and Cupid's bow is broken
> His torches lie lightless, scorned.
> . . .
>   so Venus loves
> Leisure: if you want an end to your loving, keep busy—
> Love gives way to business—and you'll be safe.
> (RA 136–144)

Amans is of the leisure class yet he is a busy lover, ready to satisfy his lady's every whim, although she repeatedly rejects him (CA IV.1746–50).

According to Ovid, Amans makes the mistake of seeking a quiet sanctuary in the woods where he can be alone with his thoughts (CA VI.133–34). Lovesick lovers often wish to be alone, but in the *Remedia*, Ovid writes that lovers who wish to cure themselves should not wander off alone, as Amans does:

> Lonely places, you lovers, are dangerous: shun lonely places,
> Don't opt out—you'll be safer in a crowd!
> You've no need for secrecy (secrecy fosters passions):
> From now on company's what you need.
> If you're solitary you'll be sad, your forsaken mistress
> Always there in your mind's eye,
> A too-vivid presence.
> (RA 256–62)

A solitary lover like Amans becomes listless and melancholy when his lady is not around. He confesses he cannot muster up enough energy to dance:

> I mai noght wel heve up mi fot
> If that sche be noght in the weie;
> For thanne is al mi merthe aweie.
> (CA VI.146–48)

Amans also suffers from an "inly cold" and a "hote chele," the fever of Love (CA VI. 246–47). In the *Vox* Gower also describes this fever, which drives the lover blindly mad:

> Colder than ice and hotter than burning fire, he both freezes with fire and burns with cold. Just as a bird envelopes itself with birdlime by rolling it in, so does he grow the more ardent with love while defending himself against it. (VC 5.3.140ff)

Amans suffers from the "blanche fievere"—"In cold I brenne and frese in hete"—the same feverish sickness from which Troilus suffers: "For hote of cold, for cold of hote, I dye" (CA VI. 249; TC I.420). The MED defines "blanche fievere" as "a stage of lovesickness analogous to chills,"[50] and the term was often used to describe a lover who suffers from unrequited love.

Amans suffers from unrequited love. He beseeches his lady with one thousand words, but she rejects his overtures (CA VIII.2048). The lady rejects him so often that Amans lives "adrad / For sorwe" that she will say "nay" to him again (CA I.2748–49). Nonetheless, he is undeterred. Amans' lady remains uninterested in his overtures, barely tolerating his presence (CA IV.2792–97). Although Gower rarely describes his characters, the lack of information we have about Amans' lady seems especially mystifying and makes the love affair rather suspect.

Lovesickness in the Confessio Amantis

At the day's end, when Amans must take leave of his lady, he puts on an elaborate show, feigning that he has forgotten something so he can steal another kiss; his plan seldom works (CA IV.2826–32). The comical scene is made more ridiculous as it becomes apparent that Amans, like the Lover in Ovid's *Amores*, is humiliated by love—neither of their ladies return their earnest sentiments—yet they continue to love anew, as if unable to stop loving.[51] In both the *Confessio* and in the *Amores* the Lover is thoroughly alone.[52] Amans' love affair is not balanced, and using the Marriage Tales of the Four Wives as a touchstone, we can safely assume that something is seriously amiss. Amans is ruled by Passion and his actions are therefore indicative of an irrational, lovesick man.

In Book VI of the *Confessio*, Genius tells Amans about the "grete Senne original" which "is cleped Gule" (CA VI.10). The first branch of Gluttony is "Dronkeschipe," a vice which can

> make of a wisman nyce,
> And of a fool, that him schal seme
> That he can al the lawe deme.
> (CA VI.18–20)

Genius is concerned with a particular form of drunkenness, something he calls "the jolif wo," a drunkenness so strong that man "knowe noght / What reson is, or more or less" (CA VI.84, 86–87). This strain of sickness is impossible to withstand:

> Such is the kinde of that sieknesse,
> And that is noght for lacke of brain,
> Bot love is of so gret a main,
> That where he takth an herte on honde,
> Ther mai nothing his miht withstonde.
> (CA VI.88–92)

Losing his wits is Amans' biggest complaint against the "jolif wo," which serves to underscore the importance Gower places upon man's ability to reason. He confesses that he cannot tell fact from fiction:

> For so thurgh drunke I am of love,
> That al that mi sotye demeth
> Is soth, as thanne it to me semeth.
> (CA VI.222–224)

Amans is besotted with love, and bereft of wit:

>   al mi wit is herteles,
>   And al myn herte, ther it sit,
>   Is, as who seith, withoute wit.
>   (CA VI.254–56)

Lovesickness and drunkenness are similar: both rob a man of his reason, and both a lovesick lover and a drunken man crave what they mistakenly believe will quench their desire.

Gower returns to his theme of reason over *kinde* repeatedly as he reminds the reader that Amans, and the Forsaken Women too, must regain control of their wits and leave foolish love behind in order to love and live properly. Lovers drunk with love and men besotted with wine have relinquished control of right reason, that faculty which separates man from the lower orders. Both lovers and drunks display the same symptoms: "they lose their bodily strength, their senses, their ability to determine right from wrong; they enter a kind of illusory realm of their own devising."[53] Amans is unable to tell fact from fiction: he lives in another world, one in which he lady grants him favors and Danger is nowhere to be found. Even though Amans' lady is disdainful to him, he continues to crave

>   a newe thorst,
>   The which me grieveth altherworst,
>   For thanne comth the blanche fievere.
>   (CA VI.237–39)

This "gret desir, / The which is hotere than the fyr" fills the Lover as wine fills the drunk, and Amans' thirst for love will not be quenched (CA VI.209–10). Amans says he has taken a draught from the "welle / In which mi deth is and mi lif," and he sees no cure or release from this particular hell (CA VI.276–77). He drinks from his lady's graces, she who has the power to give him life or death.[54] His thirst for Love increases as he drinks more, but his thirst is unquenchable.

Medieval poets often describe love and lovesickness as an unquenchable thirst for the lady. Amans believes just a taste of his lady's love will satisfy his craving, but the more his heart desires the more his "thurst schal nevere ben aqueint," for the god Jupiter, with his two tuns of love-drink, is behind this irresistible thirst (CA VI.265), an idea Gower probably found in the *Roman*:

>   As Homer tells the story, Jupiter
>   Before the threshold of the mansion placed
>   Two tuns, filled full throughout the livelong year;
>   From one of these two tuns each person drinks
>   Who lives on earth—father or bachelor,
>   Maiden or mother, young, old, foul, or fair.

> Fortune is hostess of the well-stocked inn,
> ...
> To some the more, to some the less she grants.
> ...
> Serving each well or ill as suits her mood.
> (RR 6761–75)

Gower changes the situation slightly, and applies it to the subject of love:

> For Jupiter aboven alle,
> Which is of goddes soverein,
> Hath in his celier, as men sein,
> Tuo tonnes fulle of love drinke,
> That maken many an herte sinke
> And many an herte also to flete,
> Or of the soure or of the swete.
> That on is full of such piment,
> Which passeth all entendement
> Of mannes witt, if he it taste,
> And makth a jolif herte in haste:
> That other biter as the galle,
> Which makth a mannes herte palle,
> Whos drunkeschipe is a sieknesse
> Thurgh fielinge of the biternesse.
> (CA VI.330–44)

Blind Cupid[55] arbitrarily passes out the brew as reward or punishment, "without lawe of governance" (CA VI.349–53;364). Perhaps man is not to blame for his inability to withstand love since it is capriciously doled out by a blind man with a nasty streak. Drunk on Jupiter's bitter drink, Amans confesses that he is "torned from miself so clene, / That ofte I wot noght what I mene" (CA VI.119–120). His thoughts are "drunke" and

> mi wit faileth
> And al mi brain is overtorned,
> And mi manere so mistorned,
> That I foryete al that I can,
> And stonde lich a mased man.
> (CA VI.128–132)

Amans stands "lich a mased man"; similarly Troilus is described as "wel neigh wood" (TC I.499). Amans and Troilus suffer from the pains of love described in the *Roman*, in which the God of Love instructs the Lover that there will come a time when he will

> half forget yourself, bemused,
> And long time stand like a graven image mute
> Which never budges, stirs, or even moves.
> (RR 2281–83)

Both Amans and Troilus are stunned by Love. They have succumbed to lovesickness, and recline with the full weight of the disease upon them. A cure is needed before they sink into despair.

In his medical work Avicenna writes that the first step for treating lovesickness is for the physician to learn the name of the patient's beloved. This could take coaxing, something Pandarus does fairly well in the *Troilus* (TC I.596–875). Troilus' body shakes with feverish chills "As though men sholde han led hym into helle" until he finally tells Pandarus that the object of his fondest desires is Criseyde (TC I.872). Avicenna recommends taking the patient's pulse:

> while naming names and repeating them over and over. Whenever there is a great variation in the pulse rate on account of this recital of names, and the patient acts as if he has been slain by the mention of one of the names, then test that name by saying it repeatedly, and it will become evident whether or not it is the name of the one he loves.... Furthermore, when no cure is found except joining the two together with the blessing of church and civil law, then let that be done.[56]

Now knowing the name of Troilus' beloved, Pandarus works to cure his friend of his affliction.

Cures for lovesickness fall into two categories: psychological and physical. Medical practitioners sought to cure the patient foremost with physical treatments that would eliminate or decrease the amount of fluids within him. Many of the authors of the medical treatises on lovesickness highly recommend sexual intercourse as a cure: Avicenna considers therapeutic intercourse as the best cure for lovesickness, "though it must be exercised according to 'law and faith,' a proviso not in the *Viaticum*," while Gerard of Berry claims that lovesickness cannot be completely cured without intercourse.[57] Coitus was thought to expel "superfluous humors, but in addition, according to the widely-quoted Rufus of Ephesus, it also chases out fixed ideas, which is particularly valuable for the melancholic."[58] Constantine also recommends intercourse:

> Sometimes the cause of this love is an intense natural need to expel a great excess of humors. Whence Rufus says: 'Intercourse is seen to benefit those in whom black bile and frenzy reign. Feeling is returned to him and the burden of eros is removed, even if he has intercourse with those he does not love.' (*Viaticum* 189)

If the desired woman is not available, Gerard of Berry recommends "consorting with and embracing girls, sleeping with them repeatedly, and switching various ones" as a useful means to cure the disease (Gerard *Glosses* 203). The medical tradition is sorely at odds with the Church in recommending this cure so persistently, revealing that "medical sexual ethics, at least concerning lovesickness, were less constrained than those of conservative moral theology."[59] Medical discourse found itself facing a host of contradictions, and it tread a dangerous path "between religious repression and the most unbridled freedom of lifestyle."[60] While the medical treatises stated that abstinence could pose health problems for certain types of people, and generally speaking considered abstinence harmful for both males and females,[61] the Church promoted sexual restraint, even among married couples.[62]

A passage from Constantine the African's *De coitu* flatly states that intercourse is healthy, for it "is truly useful and promotes health."[63] In the Middle Ages the principal of moderation "condemns not only overdoing it but also underdoing and thus forms the basis for a medical disapprobation of sexual abstinence."[64] Preaching abstinence in marriage was problematic, and the social case against it supported by the philosophical and medical doctrine.[65] Sexual intercourse as a cure for lovesickness was therefore viewed separately from its moral implications, even though the West's acceptance of Islamic medicine was occurring at a time when the Church "was attempting with some success to regulate sexuality outside marriage and to enforce clerical celibacy."[66] Avicenna, Gerard of Berry and the other commentators who prescribed intercourse as a cure for their patients retired morality into the background, for curing their lovesick patients was their objective.[67] The commentators thus paved the way for a medical discourse free from theological repression.[68] The authority of the medical profession depended upon its ability to prescribe cures regardless of what the Christian Church believed, and "if medicine was to have any practical effect," texts such as the *Liber de heros morbo* and the *Viaticum* had to be "viewed as empirical descriptions of reality, that is, of human beings in health, disease, and states in between."[69]

In an expressive article on lovesickness in *Troilus*, Wack examines how Pandarus prescribes therapeutic intercourse to Troilus. Both Pandarus, as the physician, and Troilus, as the patient, accept that sleeping with Criseyde will cure him of his lovesickness.[70] Instead of being cured after he sleeps with her, however, Troilus loves her even more intensely. We may reject the notion that Criseyde is merely Troilus' cure, and the romantic love in this tender scene is saved from a medical treatise reading. Wack's article on Troilus' lovesickness is illuminating in that it focuses upon how the medical community's oft prescribed cure for lovesickness, intercourse, was accepted as just that—a medical cure, removed from moral ethics. That the medical community is at blatant odds with the Church is not deemed a problem by the *Viaticum*'s commentators. Although "Constantine and his commentators never address the topic explicitly, it seems clear that 'honest' women were excluded from the enjoyment of this therapeutic practice."[71]

The medical texts suggest that once the desire is fulfilled, *amor hereos* would be relieved. While in bed with Criseyde, Troilus realizes the horrible pains he had experienced are replaced with a joy he has never known:

> The blody teris from his herte melte,
> As he that nevere yet swich hevynesse
> Assayed hadde, out of so gret gladnesse,
> Gan therwithal Criseyde, his lady deere,
> In armes streyne.
> (TC III.1445–49)

Sexual intercourse gives Troilus temporary joy, but it does not last: when Criseyde leaves Troy, Troilus visibly suffers anew. Pandarus again tries to prescribe sex therapy, but Troilus spurns taking a new lover. Taking and delighting in new lovers is a lovesickness remedy Ovid also recommends:

> So take a hint from Agamemnon's example,
> Acquire new flames, let your love be split two ways
> Where two roads meet.
> (RA 485–87)

Unlike Troilus, Amans has no hope of receiving sexual favors from his lady, for she barely lets him touch her hand (IV.2783), and he has no Pandarus to procure another lady for him to love in her stead.

After sex therapy, wine-drinking garners the highest praise as a cure by the *Viaticum*. The *Viaticum* commentators wrote that drinking wine counteracts depression by changing the patient's mood and brings him into contact with people, thus ending his solitary condition. In his text, Constantine quotes Rufus:

> 'Wine,' Rufus says, 'is a strong medication for the sad, the timid, and erotic lovers.' (Viaticum 191)

Johannes lists wine-drinking among his cures:

> Drinking wine that is temperate in quantity and quality is one of the better ways of removing the thoughts of patients of heros, as is chatting with intimate friends, listening to sweet songs, and looking at pleasant gardens and meadows, delightfully flowing water, and the beautiful faces of women. (Johannes *Liber* 328)

While Johannes recommends moderation, Ovid bluntly writes that:

> Wine promotes sex—unless you take a skinful
> And drown your wits in drink.
> . . .
> Either keep off drink, or else hit the bottle
> Till you're riding high: nothing between will serve.
> (RA 805–810)

In his *Gloss on the Viaticum* Giles recommends wine-drinking as a cure for lovesickness: "wine truly carries away bad thoughts, for it cheers up the soul, and because of this it is beneficial for sufferers of *heros*."[72] Peter of Spain also ponders whether drunkenness is useful in curing lovesickness. He writes that since drunkenness causes oblivion it is beneficial to the lover for it helps him forget his beloved, but, on the other hand, it does not aid the estimative faculty to return to "rightly ordered love" (Peter *Viaticum B* 249). He defers to Ovid's authority, and notes that in the *Remedia* Ovid recommends thorough drunkenness or no wine at all (Peter *Viaticum B* 249). If Genius were to prescribe cures, he would probably not prescribe wine-drinking because too much wine contributes to memory loss as well as the inability to reason.

Other recommended cures for lovesickness were psychological: travel, walks in a beautiful garden, pleasant conversation with a friend, reading poetry, and listening to soothing music. These popular cures were thought to both soothe the agitated body and to calm the lover's over-active imagination. Peter of Spain writes that travel "causes one to see beautiful things and pleasant places, upon which the patient fixes his thought . . . and consequently he withdraws his imagination from his beloved."[73] Ovid lists travel as a cure for lovesickness, acknowledging that it might not be easy for the lover to tear himself away from his beloved's haunts:

> Though the chains that hold you are strong, you just need to
>   make a lengthy
> Journey, go far away: you'll weep, your mind
> Will dwell on the name of your deserted mistress,
>   Your foot often hesitate midway
> Through your travels. The less you're anxious to go,
>   the more you
>   Should make sure of going, persist,
> Force yourself to hurry regardless.
> (RA 213–219)

Amans does not have any interest in traveling. His obsessive desire is to hover about his lady each day. He refuses to fight the infidels, fearing not his life, but losing his lady to another suitor if he were away (CA IV.1662–65).

Pandarus recommends travel as a cure for the lovesick Troilus. Pandarus suggests they visit a neighboring king:

> And thus thow shalt the tyme wel bygile,
> And dryve it forth unto that blisful morwe
> That thow hire se, that cause is of thi sorwe.
> (TC V.404–06)

Traveling does not cure Troilus, however, even though King Sarpedoun has provided his guests with a social whirlwind of feasts, music, and fair ladies for dancing partners. Troilus cannot enjoy himself, and selfishly thinks no one else should enjoy himself either, for "she that of his herte berth the keye / Was absent" (TC V.460–61). He refuses to enjoy pleasures at Sarpedoun's home because he is fixated upon Criseyde. Troilus makes the mistake of re-reading Criseyde's letters, which re-open his love-wounds (TC V.470–75). Ovid sternly admonishes lovers to burn all love letters in order to bury old and unrequited love:

> Beware
> Of re-reading those treasured letters from your seductive
> Ex-mistress: such letters, re-read,
> Break down the firmest resolve. Grit your teeth and burn the packet,
> Whispering, 'May this prove the pyre of my love!'
> (RR 716–720)

After re-reading her letters, Troilus wants to cut the visit short, and return home (TC V.470–83).

Like Troilus, Amans is obsessively fixated upon his lady, and in Amans' case, the fixation does not vanish until Venus hands him a mirror at the poem's end, and he is able to recognize himself as an old man.[74] Lovesickness has warped Amans' ability to think clearly, one of the dangers of the disease according to the medical treatises, "for the violent appetite and the hope and care associated with it can result in a fury or madness."[75] Peter of Spain defines *hereos* or lovesickness as a disease of the imaginative faculty, the cogitative faculty, the estimable faculty, and of the fantasy. He writes:

> ... there is, in lovesickness, a failure of judgment about non-sensed forms or things, such as friendship and enmity and similarly other things.... in lovesickness, the estimative faculty judges some woman or some other things to be better or more beautiful than all the rest, even though it might

> not be so, and then it orders the cogitative faculty to plunge itself in the form of that thing. And thus in lovesickness there is depressed thought. . . . Moreover, all the emotions of the soul are a suffering of the heart, since all the emotions of the soul follow the heart. . . . therefore [lovesickness] is a suffering of the heart. (Peter *Viaticum A* 217)

Amans admits that he cannot think clearly, and he complains of being "destourbed / In al myn herte (CA I.221–22). The *Vox* acknowledges that

> A knight does not rightly have to fear a bodily wound, since he should receive the world's praises for it. But he should fear the wounds of the spirit, which blind, incurable lust inflicts with fiery darts. Bodily wounds are to be healed, but not even Galen will make a man well who is sick with love. (VC 5.4.225ff)

So strong is love that even brave knights fear it.

The one cure that Genius provides to Amans, and it is perhaps an unintentional outcome of the confession, is that of good conversation. The medical texts recommend pleasant conversation between the lover and a friend, although a beautiful woman is the preferred listening companion. Constantine recommends "conversing with dearest friends" as a cure, and Johannes elaborates on his teacher's advice (*Viaticum* 191). Following the cures of wine drinking and listening to music, Johannes prescribes

> the beautiful and tender faces of friends. Thus some have said that it is cheering to drink wine and to listen to the conversation of friends. Galen said: Talking with intimates removes a burden from the shoulders. If all these things—namely, drinking wine, music, and talking with friends—take place in gardens or meadows with flowing water, everything is altogether more delightful. (Johannes *Liber* 328)

Inadvertently, Genius helps to cure Amans' sick heart by talking the penitent through a long confession, thus lifting his burden and replacing it with a full absolution of peace. Their pleasant conversation takes place in the woods in a "swote grene pleine," the sanctioned location for an intimate talk (CA I.111). The medical texts recommend a "masterful listener" [76] be available to the lover, and this is the role Genius plays so well. Genius hears Amans' confession, listening to "Bothe all . . . [his] thoght and al . . . [his] werk" (CA I.196). Genius gets Amans talking about his lady, much in the same way the Narrator in *The Book of the Duchess* gets the Black Knight talking about Fair White.[77] Amans bares his soul's secrets to Genius—as he should in a confession of love. His questions and Genius' answers and Genius' storytelling—their conversation as a whole—is what helps Amans return to right reason. In the *Troilus* Troilus has a good friend in Pandarus, who actively seeks to cure Troilus of his lovesickness. Ovid says that friends are needed when the lover suffers from Love's malady, noting that Phyllis had no one near her at the time of her distress:

> Don't avoid conversation, don't shut the door on callers,
>   Don't hide yourself away and cry in the dark.
> Always have some Pylades there to back up Orestes:
>   Of friendship's various benefits, this
> Is by no means the slightest. What was it destroyed poor Phyllis
>   But the secret forest? The cause of her death is clear:
> *Being alone.*
> (RA 586–92)

Genius keeps Amans thinking and talking about his lady-love, and he takes Amans through the stages of his lovesickness as he shrives him of his sins. Genius leads Amans in good conversation, allowing him to speak of his lady, thus serving him well. To completely cure Amans of his ailment, however, divine intervention and forced self-introspection are also needed.

A lovesick lover like Amans needs to be educated and brought back to his senses by using his reason. He is so far removed from the center of his soul, however, that he does not even know he is operating without reason. By confessing his sins to Venus' priest, Amans is able to share his burden of unrequited passion with someone. The confession should also serve as a personal educational experience for Amans, but whether or not he is able to apply any knowledge from the tales Genius tells to his own life is questionable.[78] The knowledge that Genius tries to convey to Amans is self-knowledge, that of righting the soul with reason.[79] Peck writes that it should be understood that

> Amans's confession to Genius . . . [is] a reappreciation of Nature. As such it involves a twofold process, both a turning outside himself to discover objectively man's use and misuse of his creative energies throughout history and a turning within himself to rediscover his own neglected creative ability. . . . [Furthermore], as Boethius and Augustine so clearly emphasize, confession is remembering. Memory provides the key to Aman's restoration. It is his means of reclaiming his forgotten, natural self in order that he may be released from its fantastic substitute.[80]

Amans, who has called himself a "caitlif," cannot remember who he is, and until he is able to do so, he will not be restored to right reason (CA I.161).

At the end of the Tale of Apollonius, Genius stresses that a lover must love in "such a weie / As love and reson wolde acorde," and Amans begins to recognize that what the priest says about love has merit. (CA VIII.2022–3). For the first time, Amans asks him directly for help, but Genius' counsel is broad: "Take love where it mai noght faile," "Love is blind," and be "governed / . . . not of will" but by reason (CA VIII.2086, 2105, 2136–7). Amans has reached his limit with Genius' proverbial statements on love, and he accuses him of playing with his emotions, of not taking his painful malady seriously. He attacks Genius, yelling

> Mi wo to you is bot a game,
> That fielen noght of that I fiele.
> (CA VIII.2152–53)

It is a very human accusation: "you just don't understand." Amans is angry with his confessor, and this is a good emotion for him, for by focusing on Genius rather than his lady, he is suddenly able to see himself in a different light. To signal this notable change, Gower shifts the narrative perspective "from that of a dramatic dialogue to that of an onlooking narrator, [which serves to anticipate] . . . the Lover's new perspective which will enable him to disengage himself from his venial infatuation."[81] A cure for Amans seems imminent.

Introspection is a first step towards any inner healing. Amans begins to recognize the value of Genius' lessons and how they may apply to him, yet he cannot let go of his futile desire for his lady:

> Mi resoun understod him wel,
> And knew it was soth everydel
> That he hath seid.
> . . .
> Yit myhte nevere man beholde
> Reson, wher love was withholde.
> (CA VIII.2191–98)

It is a fight between his Reason and his Will, and Reason begins to win when Amans takes action: he writes to Venus, begging for help. When Venus appears, she taunts the penitent, saying the answer to why he receives no pleasures in love lies

> in thi persone;
> For loves lust and lockes hore
> In chambre acorden neveremore.
> (CA VIII.2402–04)

There is a debate among scholars as to whether Amans' age comes as a complete surprise to the reader or it has been hinted at throughout the poem;[82] I interpret this line as the first acknowledgement that the Lover is old.

Amans' love is characterized as degrading, and so it is: he has thoroughly played the senseless fool. Love has ravaged this Lover and removed his wits so thoroughly that he needs to be shocked into remembering his true self and age in order to heal.[83] Amans' type of love, marked by foolish and selfish behavior, is not sanctioned by Gower for a man or a woman of any age. Amans is unfit to love because his desire is excessive, misplaced and misguided, and his advanced years make him that much more unsuitable to serve in Venus' court. Although Amans feigns a "yong corage" (CA VIII.2405), gray hair and lovesick behavior render him unfit for love; he is impotent. Venus tells him that many lovers feign a youthful presence, yet cannot stand up to the trials and tribulations of Love; furthermore, impotency "was an impediment to matrimony in canon law."[84] Therefore the goddess tells Amans he is not "sufficant / To holde" Love's covenant (CA VIII.2410–20):

> Forthi tak hom thin herte ayein,
> That thou travaile noght in vein
> (CA VIII.2421–22)

She cuts Amans to the core with this announcement: he feels a blast of cold, and swoons to the ground.

In this unconscious state, Amans has a vision which Macaulay refers to as the Companies of Lovers.[85] Amans sees Cupid and Youthe leading a jolly parade of young lovers who wear garlands and the newest Bohemian fashions, a reference to Richard II's princess Anne. The lovers sing songs of love and the music is so loud "as al the hevene cride / In such acord" (CA VIII.2480–81). Amans hears them talk

> al of knyhthod and of Armes,
> And what it is to ligge in armes
> With love, whanne it is achieved.
> (CA VIII.2497–99)

The group includes lovers whose tales appear in the *Confessio*, and a few whose tales of love are treated in the *Traitié*: Tristram and Isolde, Lancelot and Guinevere, Jason and Creusa, Hercules and Iole, Theseus and Phaedra, Paris and Helen, Troilus and Criseyde and Diomedes and "a thousand mo than I can sein" (CA VIII.2500–39;2537). Interestingly, Gower includes Jason and Theseus among this happy and youthful Company of Lovers, even though Theseus is described as a faithless man, a lover

> thogh he were untrewe
> To love, as alle women knewe,
> Yit was he there natheles

With Phedra, whom to love he ches.
(CA VIII.2511–14)

The lovers Jason, Hercules, and Theseus are "impenitent in their former faithlessness, while Medea, Deianira and Ariadne are left to complain by themselves."[86] Following them is a group of lovers who complain of Love: Narcissus, Pyramus, "Achilles, which for love deide," Agamemnon, Menelaus and many more (CA VIII.2545). The Forsaken Women, "wommen in the sam cas" as the men who precede them, are next, and Gower gives them each a short biography of how they loved and lost, using words such as forsaken, deceived, "unkindely forsok," complaining, and "feigneth" (CA VIII.2551–65). Medea sums up their collective feelings by uttering "'Fy on alle untrewe!'" as she passes by (CA VIII.2566). Deidamia is next, along with Cleopatra, Thisbe, who also speaks, bewailing of Pyramus' sloth: "Wo worthe alle slowe!'" (CA VIII.2582).[87] Progne and Philomela follow, Canace is next, and even Circes and Calypso, the sorceresses, march by. Although not all of these lovers, men and women, have been lucky enough to have their love relationships endure the test of time, they each have loved and been loved. Unlike Amans, they know "the olde daunce," to borrow a phrase from Chaucer (GP 476).

The Four Wives are the last of this group of successful lovers to walk by Amans. Gower introduces them and immediately elevates their status above the others, "Bot above alle that ther were," and they are recognized by the Company of Lovers who gives them due reverence (CA VIII.2605):

Whos name I herde most comended:
Be hem the Court stod al amended;
For wher thei comen in presence,
Men deden hem the reverence,
As thogh they hadden be goddesses,
Of al this world or Emperesses.
(CA VIII.2607–12)

The "foure wyves" are described in glowing terms as women "Whos feith was proeved in her lyves," and whose good marriages afford them great fame (CA VIII.2615–16). Amans notes that Youthe was too busy to pay him any attention as he lay there on the ground, strengthening the perception that young people are the ones who are fit to endure love's trials (CA VIII.2661–65). Following the Wives is Elde, who "cam a softe pas / Toward Venus," bringing with him a smaller Company of Lovers than Youthe led (CA VIII.2667–68). Most of these lovers "were of gret Age, / And that was sene in the visage" (CA VIII.2671–72). This group is not accompanied by loud music, although the sounds of the harp and lute are heard. They walk softly and display a sober cheer, smiling but not laughing as the young lovers do. Amans sees king David with Bathsheba, Solomon with at least one hundred wives and concubines, Delilah and Sampson, Aristotle, Virgil, Socrates, Plato, and Ovid (CA VIII.2682–2719). The Lover is moved with the knowledge that love is sweet to everyone, and having seen the poets and older company he feels "the lasse aschamed" for his loving, and he dares to hope for grace (CA VIII.2720–25). Even as Amans lies on the ground in this semi-conscious state, after a confession in which his love habits have been thoroughly scrutinized, he still has room to hope that Venus will grant him love.[88] Amans' belief in grace from Venus, even at this point in the poem, illustrates how thoroughly he is afflicted with lovesickness, for he is unable to recognize that his love does not accord with reason.

The old lovers gather around Amans as he lies on the ground, and together "These olde men with o vois alle / To Venus preiden for my sake" (CA VIII.2727–28). The goddess cannot refuse so many requests, and from such a company. Pity "come[s] into hire Ere," and she tells Cupid to send Amans some comfort (CA VIII.2732). The group again prays for Amans, and this time "some of the yonge route" pray too (CA VIII.2740). Cupid, who "may hurte and hele / In loves cause," approaches Amans and the crowd presses in

> To se what ende schal betyde
> Upon the cure of my sotie.
> (CA VIII.2758–59)

Everyone in the company begins speaking and offering opinions; some say that an old man should not behave as Amans has, for he has made a fool of himself by not acting reasonably. Others disagree, pointing out that the "wylde loves rage / In mannes lif forberth non Age"; further, when "the lampe is lyhtly set afyre, / And is fulhard er it be queynt" (CA VIII.2773–76). Thus there are diverse opinions as to whether or not Amans deserves grace until Blind Cupid settles the argument by pulling the arrow out of Amans' heart (CA VIII.2800). Everyone vanishes but Venus and Genius who remain with the penitent (CA VIII.2800–03).

Amans awakens to find Venus anointing his heart, his temples, and his kidneys with a cold salve which seems to calm his spirit (CA VIII.2817–19). The goddess hands him a "wonder mirour," and reflected in it, Amans sees his sorrowful face ravaged by Time—dim eyes, thin cheeks, and gray hair. He does not like what he sees, and states "Mi will was tho to se nomore / Outwith, for ther was no plesance" (CA VIII.2821, 2832–33). Looking into Venus' mirror has shocked Amans into recognizing that he is, indeed, a wrinkled old man.[89] While gazing at his reflection, Amans recalls days past, and reflects upon the passing of time until he shakes himself out of his swoon.[90] Leaving his lovesick heart behind, recognizing his true self, and moving forward into reality is a healing process for Amans; he is cured of his lovesickness. Acknowledging both his age and Nature's ability to heal, he "gan to clepe . . . [his wits] hom ayein" (CA VIII.2861). Once

> Resoun it herde sein
> That loves rage was aweie,
> He cam to me the rihte weie,
> And hath remued the sotie.
> . . .
> I was mad sobre and hol ynowh.
> (CA VIII.2862–9)

Love's rage—the fever, the chills, the loss of wits, the aches and pains—dissipates, and Reason is called home to its proper place. Venus asks the Lover to define Love, but a cured Amans says he "knew him noght" and begs to be excused from her court (CA VIII.2875).[91] Venus puts black rosary beads engraved with the words "*Por reposer*" around the Lover's neck, and calls him by name—"John Gower"—telling him to seek "nomore of love" (CA VIII.2908,2911). She banishes him from her court—"tarie thou mi Court nomore"—and advises him to "let reson be . . . [his] guide" in all things (CA VIII.2924, 2919). Cured of his lovesickness, Amans turns "Homward," thinking upon the "bedis blak" and smiling quietly to himself (CA VIII.2904, 2959).

Amans vows to spend his days writing and praying, "with al myn hol entente" (CA VIII.2967–9). This is a fitting recovery for Gower's lover, for Gower is a poet overtly concerned with how man should properly live his life, and the rule of reason is his conception of the world. Amans' unbalanced love bereft him of his reason, and the lovesick behavior which ensued runs directly counter to the poet's desire is to see man ruled by reason, restraining his passion in a lawful marriage of mutual love. Gower sets forth his belief in "honeste" love in the *Confessio*:

> Bot thilke love is wel at ese,
> Which set is upon mariage;
> For that dar schewen the visage
> In alle places openly.
> (CA IV.1476–9)

Amans' one-sided love affair is not "wel at ese," and his impotency renders him unfit for marriage; therefore his love suit, which can be characterized as unhealthy as well as unreasonable, is not successful. With Genius' help and Venus' intervention, Amans is thus able to call his reason home, and he is granted a life of quiet, scholarly repose. It is not the reward the lover sought from

Venus and Cupid, but as Venus reminds him, he asked for council, and she gave it: "Remembre wel hou thou are old" (CA VIII.2440).

Conclusion

It is in exploring the Aspects of Love that Gower strengthens his firm belief that in order for man and woman to live in peace and harmony an "honeste" love must be sought and nurtured if mankind is to live and love properly and responsibly. Gower is resolute that each man or woman is responsible for his or her behavior. He follows convention and "consistently suggests that love is an irresistible force"[1] in the *Confessio*, yet he nonetheless makes clear that each individual is held accountable for his love decisions. That he maintains this perspective throughout the *Confessio* for woman as well as man is notable and admirable, especially since he employs anti-feminist rhetoric in the *Mirour* and *Vox*, yet refrains from it in the *Confessio*. Gower's poetry often defies the feminist theory which places woman as victim and man as perpetrator. In the *Confessio* he is neither partial to man nor woman, and although it appears his sympathies lie with women, it is rather that he views woman as man's equal; if he is responsible for his love actions, then so is she. Gower's unique insistence upon equality in the *Confessio* proves this point: man cannot blame woman, and woman cannot blame man. In Gower there are no excuses for unrestrained and foolish behavior, although he recognizes that it is often difficult to restrain passion.

This particular aspect—the struggle between *kinde* and reason—is subtly illustrated in the character of Genius. Gower's Genius is the voice of Everyman, for he is torn between his loyalty to Venus, his ecclesiastical training, and his desire to adhere to God's laws. Genius finds himself struggling with the notion of advocating sexual passion unrestrained, something which as Venus' priest he should advance. That he does not, and that he subtly promotes marriage instead, indicates Gower's mastery of his art: the two dueling voices are combined into a priest who advocates passion within a marriage of reciprocal love. He is Gower's master creation, a character who resembles man and woman struggling with the aspects of love. The Confessor is a perfect Gowerian storyteller for in his moral tales lies the predicament facing all men—whether to follow *kinde*, his passionate nature, or his reasoning capabilities, the wise voice within him. Man is capable of choosing right reason,[2] and that is Gower's hope for mankind. Amans chooses reason too, but his lovesickness—not a trivial disease in the Middle Ages—encumbers his ability to make the proper decision until Venus intervenes.

Negligence of one's duties is always a sin in Gower's eyes, for he believes that discordia or concordia in the world at large results from each man's personal behavior. This is a concurrent theme in the *Confessio*, the *Mirour*, and the *Vox*: each man's decisions affect the macrocosm. In his three major works Gower strives to teach man the behavior proper to his station—for peasants, for the clergy, for knights, for ministers of law, and for kings, and in the *Confessio*, for lovers, men and women. In the *Mirour*, the *Vox*, and in Book VII of the *Confessio*, Genius discusses the duties of a king, noting that when a ruler neglects his responsibilities, the structure of society is threatened. This is evident in the Tales of the Forsaken Women. Two of the women, Dido and Phyllis, are queens—Medea is the sole heir to the throne, and Ariadne has no brothers—yet they squander their regal status and neglect their royal duties, and for their transgressions, they suffer. In these tales the man is guilty of faithless behavior to the woman, and she is guilty of a lack of discretion. None of the Forsaken Women receive lasting harmony in their lives or love relationships: two of them commit suicide, two languish, bereft of lover, friends and family, and one escapes to the gods. The Forsaken Women do not realize the importance "trouthe" plays in a love relationship.

In the Marriage Tales of the Four Wives Gower is careful to use the words "husband" and "wife," but in the Forsaken Women's tales those words are rarely used. Perhaps this is Gower's way of indicating that the Forsaken Women are involved in illicit sexual affairs of which he does not approve. The authoritative voice of St. Augustine, who valued marriage for its avoidance of unmarried sex, was enormously influential in the Middle Ages.[3] In a sermon on "Matrimonial Agreements," Augustine recognizes that couples will have marital intercourse for reasons other than begetting children; when this occurs, he reminds his followers to "do it in their own bed and no other," calling it a sin, "but a venial one."[4] In *Sermo LI* for Advent, Augustine stresses that it is not the "exchange of chastities that makes both a husband and a wife; it's the exchange of charities between the two." The "exchange of charities" is a phrase which conjures up reciprocity of compassion and kindness, something which Gower's Four Wives—and Medea—share with their husbands.

It was not until the thirteenth century that marriage and the marriage ceremony itself became recognized as an important sacrament.[5] There are two types of recognized legal marriages in the Middle Ages, one defined by the publication of banns and a public ceremony conducted by a priest, and clandestine marriages, private contracts made in a public or private space with witnesses.[6] To make a marriage absolutely licit, a priest should consecrate the ceremony.[7] Gower's Ovidian heroines are pagans, of course, and therefore they adhere to a different set of rules. He honors the marriage bonds of the Four Wives, and Deianira's and Medea's marriages only; Deianira's because he tells us she is married, and Medea's, for the words exchanged by the lovers in front of a witness. The other marriages are neither church nor clandestine marriages; they are sexual relationships only, of which Gower, and the Church, disproves.[8]

The differences between the language and manner in which Gower treats the Four Wives and the Forsaken Women corroborates his insistence on legal marriages which "dar schewen the visage / In alle places openly" (CA IV.1478–79). He urges his readers to embrace "honeste" love in a marriage of one accord, for not only do solid relationships honorably serve God's purpose, but in a marriage of mutual love a man and a woman will find unending joy in the pleasures of the flesh. No where in the *Confessio* does Gower imply that sexual passion is something which man must avoid; rather he believes that passions can be indulged as long as man heeds the voice of reason, and in Gower this can be achieved in lawful marriage of reciprocal love. The private glimpses of the tender moments shared by married lovers such as Ceix and Alceone and Jason and Medea strengthen his position that in marriage intimate sexual relations may be fully enjoyed. Gower's position in the *Confessio* that married couples can take pleasure in sexual love—for enjoyment and for generation—stands alone from the Church's precept that sex is for procreation only.[9] But in a Latin headnote to *Traitié* IV Gower echoes Augustinian thought:

> ... an honorable marriage takes its origin not from lust or avarice but only to honor god by generation lawfully. (Tr IV.1)

In the *Mirour* he further reiterates Augustine's message about marriage:

> Whoever wishes to cherish Matrimony cannot be wanting in honor; for a pure loyal marriage permits us to do the natural act (which is otherwise a mortal sin), without injuring ourselves according to nature and at our pleasure. And furthermore, it particularly causes us to earn merit if we loyally keep the estate of matrimony according to the law. (MO 17185)

In the *Vox* and the *Mirour* Gower affirms the Church's position on generation, but in the *Confessio* he never denies sexual passion between married lovers.

The lack of anti-feminism in the *Confessio* is evident in several instances. Notably there are no sexually insatiable females in the *Confessio*, yet this is the most persistent charge made against women in literature of the Middle Ages.[10] Rather, Gower illustrates reciprocal sensual passion, most notably in the Tales of Penelope and Medea. Traditionally, husbands, no matter how young, are unable to satisfy their wives' voracious sexual appetites; cuckoldry is the inevitable consequence[11] in many of the texts from which Gower drew. Jean de la Meun reiterates this view of women in the *Roman* through the mouth of La Vieille. Misogynistic expression in various medieval texts is prevalent: women are depicted as defective males (both mentally and physically), as insatiable, as evil temptresses, as whores. Peter of Spain writes of insatiable females, citing Constantine the African as his authority (Peter *Viaticum B* 245). St. Thomas Aquinas wonders whether woman "ought to have been produced in that original production of things" since she is considered both "defective" and passive (ST Q.92.1.2). In the *Summa Theologiæ* he writes:

> Yet woman is by nature of lower capacity and quality than man; for the active cause is always more honorable than the passive, as Augustine says. So woman ought not to have been produced in the original production of things before sin. (ST Q.92.1.2)[12]

Aquinas considers women passive creatures—yet in the *Confessio* Gower's women are active, often transgressing their gender to perform the male, active role. In the *Mirour* Gower praises woman as the creature God formed to be man's friend and lover:

> ... in Genesis it can be found that when God saw that Adam was alone,
> He said it would not be good for man to be alone in this life, and therefore
> God, to aid him, made woman to be man's companion. (MO 17197)

The *Confessio* is not a misogynistic poem, and Gower continually makes an effort to be impartial when it comes to love and love suffering.

Figures of authority are often undermined in Gower: male authority is frequently inverted, Genius' authority is subverted, and the authority of Richard II is questioned. In some versions of the *Confessio* Gower praises Richard II, expressing obedience to the king.[13] Yet at the end of the poem, Gower praises God as the high authority and subjects himself willingly to that authority, not to Richard's. Traditionally the husband is the voice of authority in the home, but in the tales I examine the women's voices—the Four Wives and the five Forsaken Women's voices—often seem to be authoritative, and in their actions they perform the masculine role. Again and again Gower's women transgress their gender roles to either express and receive sexual satisfaction or to exact a painful revenge. Each Wife acts independently out of "honeste" love to rescue her husband: Penelope rescues Ulysses from Sloth, Alceone and Alcestis both release their husbands from death, and Lucrece salvages her husband's Roman reputation from dishonor. All Four Wives are rewarded by the poet, and in some cases, the gods, for her devotion and chaste love. The Forsaken Women all transgress their gender roles too: Medea controls whether or not Jason succeeds in winning the Fleece, Ariadne teaches Theseus how to escape from certain death in the Minotaur's maze, Phyllis repairs Demephon's ships, and both she and Dido welcome, feed, and shelter seafaring men. These are virtuous women, strong women, women who carry the royal scepter, and Gower emphasizes their positions of authority and power over men who prove to be dishonorable. Once the women fall under Love's rule, however, they relinquish their reason and lose their royal power. Each woman is then undone by the man she foolishly trusts, for she underestimates the importance of truth in love. If Love can put a wise man under, as Genius tells Amans it can, it can also topple a queen or heir to the throne, as Dido, Medea, Ariadne, and Phyllis know too well (CA VI.90–99). That Gower remains gender neutral in the *Confessio* is notable and enlightening.

Throughout the *Confessio* Gower emphasizes the benefits of mutual love and reciprocal affection as he celebrates sexual love in marriage, concurrent with God's plan for humankind.[14] He holds the bonds of marriage in high regard, and he punishes those who break marriage vows. In the *Mirour* Gower stresses that the adulterer will suffer for his misdeeds:

> Therefore, whoever corrupts marriage shall be brought to ruin unless he has the grace to make amends (MO 9073).

Genius tells Amans in no uncertain terms what the fate of an adulterer will be in several tales.[15] Gower's female characters are never reduced to a type, such as the passive female figure of Aquinas or the temptress in the *Roman*. To Gower, who views the bonds of marriage as sacred, adultery is the worst crime a man or woman can commit, and he makes it clear that the adulterer will be served severe punishment; in the tales Genius tells, it is often the woman in the role of avenger.[16] Through the tales Genuis tells Gower continually reminds us that if love is not carefully nurtured, infidelities and treason follow, and dissension is thus let loose into the world at large.[17]

Gower longs for an England engulfed in harmony, and this is apparent in all his works. His England was a time of strife, conflict, and uncertainty, from the war with France to the Peasant's Revolt to the concern in the late 1380s and early 1390s over the lack of an heir to the throne. Gower writes with an eye on politics—the first book of the *Vox* is devoted to the events which rocked London in 1381. Living in Southwark, it is possible to imagine that Gower observed the peasants running riotously into the City,[18] and this event fueled his already-strong passion about man's proper comportment. Gower was landowner and possibly a lawyer,[19] and he belonged to the rising middle class of London, yet he believed that the peasants should remain in their proper position, at the bottom of the three-tier estate system, and did not see the incongruity of this belief with his own status in a new class of men. Gower was thoroughly a man of conservative views, and in the *Vox* he seems particularly determined to educate man in the behavior proper to his social class; in the *Confessio* he focuses on the individual in order to teach Amans the importance of remaining responsible for his actions.

Genius' role is to teach Amans how to rein in his lusts and learn to love properly, but it is difficult at times to determine what lesson Amans learns from the tales. By the end of the *Confessio*, however, with help from Venus[20] and her "wonder mirour" (CA VIII.2821), Amans is able to recognize his true self and make adjustments to how he lives his life, turning towards prayer and study, proper behavior for his situation and age. To say that Amans is too old for passionate emotions is not enough; there is more to Gower's denouement than that.[21] If Gower's cure for the lovesick Amans is to simply retreat from love, then Amans has not learned how to love properly, despite Genius' efforts, and we as an audience have perhaps missed Genius' lessons too. It is Amans' type of loving—a debilitating and unrequited passion—combined with his age that makes him unsuitable for passionate love. Amans is an old man whose loving is unreasonable and one-sided, disqualifiers for which Venus removes him from her court. Had he been a young lover, his petition would have also failed—as Deianira, Dido, Medea, Phyllis, and Ariadne fail in Venus' court. Amans' type of loving, like the type of love embraced by the Forsaken Women, is not balanced or moderated by reason, and that is why their relationships fail. Reciprocal love ordered by wisdom is the ideal, and the ideal represents Gower's hope for mankind. Olsson's remark that there is "no question that Gower is skillful at introducing the problem of melancholy and obsessive passion, [yet] his success at solving it is less certain"[22] is only part true, for I believe that Gower has solved it in the exempla of the Marriage Tales of the Four Wives. By the end of the *Confessio* Gower concludes that *kinde* and reason can coexist in love if they are managed by proper law, the law of marriage. Nature is ruled by or at least is susceptible to lust, and in the world Gower draws, there is no room for this natural instinct to roam where it will, unchecked by reason.

Gower illuminates the importance of proper loving throughout his tales of love, and among lovers who rule it is enormously important for the couples to love wisely, for the success of their country—and the succession of their heirs—depends upon it. This is a subtle message to Richard II, who, by the early 1390s, when Gower is writing and revising the *Confessio*, had not yet produced an heir.[23] That there is no heir to Richard's crown is a concern of importance to all Londoners, and it underlies Gower's theme throughout the poem. If the *Confessio* is a book commissioned for Richard II, as Gower tells us it is in one version of the Prologue,[24] then these stories and the advice Genius gives to Amans are in reality for the king.[25]

The poet whom Chaucer called "moral" does not deny erotic love, nay, Gower promotes it in the tales he tells, but it is always within a marriage created of reciprocal and truthful, "honeste" love. If man governs all his actions reasonably, he will find great joy in life and in marriage, and the world that ensues from this well-governed individual state will be a peaceful one. Marriage offers man the means to placate his passion and satisfy his reason. Gower calls marriage "honeste" love:

> Bot thilke love is wel at ese,
> Which set is upon mariage;
> For that dar schewen the visage
> In alle places openly.
> (CA IV.1476–79)

To love in "alle places openly" is Gower's hope for mankind. By using his reason, Gower urges man and woman to "modefie" his passions to achieve this end (CA VII.5379). By telling the tales he does, and by continually illustrating how *kinde* battles with man's reason, Gower admits that the modifying is the difficult part. For Amans, Genius recommends leaving love completely; for the rest of us, perhaps behavioral modification will do.

Notes

Notes to the Introduction

¹ John Gower, *Confessio Amantis, The English Works of John Gower, Vols. I and II*, ed. G. C. Macaulay (1900; 1957; 1969; Oxford: Early English Text Society and Oxford UP, 1979). All quotations from the *Confessio Amantis* will come from Macaulay's edition and be indicated in the text by siglum (CA), book and line number. See also the Introduction to *John Gower Confessio Amantis, Volume I*, editor Russell A. Peck, with Latin translations by Andrew Galloway (Kalamazoo, Michigan: Consortium for the Teaching of the Middle Ages, Medieval Institute Publications, 2000) 1–43. In his introduction to this new multi-volume set, Peck writes "Gower first circulated the poem in 1390 with a dedication and concluding prayers addressed to King Richard. In 1392, he changed the dedication and conclusion to honor Henry of Derby (later king Henry IV) and to conclude with prayers for the state of England." See Peck's discussion on *Politics and Society* in the Introduction, 22–27. Also refer to Winthrop Wetherbee, "John Gower," *The Cambridge History of Medieval English Literature*, ed. David Wallace (Cambridge: Cambridge UP, 1999) 589–609.

² Collins 114.

³ G. C. Macaulay, *The Complete Works of John Gower, Vol. I* (Oxford: Clarendon Press, 1901) xliii. The *Mirour* "refers to the Great Schism of 1378 (ll.18814–40)" (Wetherbee, "John Gower" 590n).

⁴ G. C. Macaulay, *The Complete Works of John Gower, Vol. IV* (Oxford: Clarendon Press, 1901) xxx. Macaulay writes that "all we can say [about the date of the *Vox*] is that the work in its present form is later than the Peasant's rising in the summer of 1381, and yet it was evidently composed while the memory of that event was fresh, and also before the young king had grown beyond boyhood" (Vol. IV, xxx). The king married at the end of the year 1382, and because Gower addresses the king with regard to fidelity in marriage, "perhaps it is more natural to suppose that it was written after that event than before." (Vol. IV, xxx). Stockton dates the earliest part of the poem after 1378 (Stockton, Introduction 11–12). See also Fisher, "John Gower," 99–115. Wetherbee notes that the "final version of the *Vox*, like the *Mirour*, cites the Great Schism [1378] as an example

of the corruption of the clergy, but several manuscripts which include the post-1378 *Visio* make no reference to the divided papacy, and hence may preserve a text of the other books which pre-dates it. A further argument for an earlier version is that Books 2–7, even in their final form, make no reference to the Revolt which dominates the *Visio*" (Wetherbee, "John Gower" 594n).

⁵ G. C. Macaulay, *The Complete Works of John Gower, Vol. I* (Oxford: Clarendon Press, 1901) lxxxiii-lxxxiv. All three texts have been edited by Macaulay in *The Complete Works of John Gower, Vols. I-IV*, (Oxford: Clarendon Press, 1901): *Mirour de l'omme, Vol. III, Vox Clamantis, Vol. IV, Traitié pour essampler les amantz marietz, Vol. IV*. I rely upon the Wilson translation of the *Mirour*, and Stockton's translation of the *Vox*. John Gower, *Mirour de l'Omme*, trans. William Burton Wilson (East Lansing: Colleague's Press, 1992). John Gower, *Vox Clamantis, The Major Latin Works of John Gower: The Voice of One Crying and The Tripartite Chronicle, An Annotated Translation into English with an Introductory Essay on the Author's Non-English Works*, ed. and trans. Eric W. Stockton (Seattle: U of Washington P, 1962) 201. All quotations from the *Mirour* will come from Wilson's translation and will be indicated in the text by siglum (MO) and line number; all quotations from the *Vox* will come from Stockton's translation and will be indicated in the text by siglum (VC) and line number. All quotations from the *Traitié* will come from Macaulay's edition and will be indicated in the text by siglum (Tr) and verse and line number.

⁶ Little has been published on this tale: R. F. Yeager refers to it in his 1990 book-length study on Gower; Charles Runacres' 1983 article details the tale's destructive power; Arno Esch explores this tale along with two others; and G. C. Macaulay identifies Godfrey of Vitterbo as Gower's source.

⁷ The Pyramus and Thisbe Tale, and other tales told by Chaucer in the *Legend*, have recently come under scrutiny by Chaucerian scholars. The bibliography on the *Legend* is expanding. See Robert Worth Frank, Jr.'s pioneering study; Lisa J. Kiser; Carolyn Dinshaw's chapter on the *Legend* in *Chaucer's Sexual Politics*; Sheila Delany; A. J. Minnis's chapter on the *Legend* in his *Oxford Guide to Chaucer: The Shorter Poems*; and Ruth Morse. Gower critics focus on Gower's close examination of the Ovidian text, as well as compare it to Geoffrey Chaucer's rendition. Bruce Harbert examines the Ovidian passages which Gower either eliminates or improves upon. Delany points to another possible source, the Latin schooltext of Matthew of Vendôme, as a source for Chaucer only; I assert that Gower may have known this version too. I compare Matthew's and Chaucer's texts to Gower's tale. See Ian Thomson and Louis Perraud 219–20.

⁸ I rely upon *The Riverside Chaucer* for all Chaucer poems. Geoffrey Chaucer, *The Riverside Chaucer*, ed. Larry Benson, 3rd edition (Boston: Houghton Mifflin Company, 1987). All quotations from Chaucer's poems will come from Benson's edition and will be indicated in the text by siglum, and book and line number. I use the following sigla: (BD), Book of the Duchess; (HF), House of Fame; (PF), Parliament of Fowls; (TC), Troilus and Criseyde; (LGW), Legend of Good Women.

⁹ Treatments of the Four Wives, as I label them, tends to focus on the women as individuals, comparing Chaucer's depiction of them to Ovid's; some research has been published on Gower's women, notably Linda Barney Burke, "Women." See also Gotz Schmitz, *The Fall of Women*; Delany; Minnis, *The Shorter Poems*; Mainzer; Bennett,

Middle English Literature; Ann Mcmillan's introduction to *The Legend*.

[10] Macaulay and Burke both note Gower's unusual depiction of the mutual love between Jason and Medea, agreeing that it serves to enhance the magnitude of Jason's crime. Recently full-length book studies have appeared on both Medea and Dido, but none of the works focus solely on Gower's heroines. See Morse; Delany; Mary Louise Lord; Marilynn Desmond; Minnis, *The Shorter Poems*; Schmitz, *The Fall of Women*; Yeager, *Arion*; Mainzer; Burke, "Women"; Harbert, "Lessons"; Kiser.

[11] See Minnis, *The Shorter Poems*; Delany; Kiser; Mainzer.

[12] Mary Frances Wack, *Lovesickness in the Middle Ages*. Carol Falvo Heffernan published a work on melancholy in Chaucer and Shakespeare, and an article of Troilus' lovesickness, yet no published work has focused on the lovesick behavior of Amans in the *Confessio* until now. Heffernan, "Chaucer's 'Troilus and Criseyde'"; also, Heffernan, *The Melancholy Muse*. I presented an earlier version of this chapter as a paper entitled "Lovesickness in the Confessio Amantis" at the International Congress on Medieval Studies in Kalamazoo in May 1996.

[13] I rely upon the scholarship by Joan Cadden, and Danielle Jacquart and Claude Thomasett, works which shed light upon the prevalent thought on the physiology of male and female thought to exist by medical practitioners in the Middle Ages. Joan Cadden, *Meanings of Sex Differences*; Danielle Jacquart and Claude Thomasset.

[14] Burke points out that there is "an almost total absence of negative female stereotypes and antifeminist propaganda" in the *Confessio* (Burke, "Women," 239). See also Pearsall, "Gower's Narrative Art," 62–80.

[15] Scholarly research on John Gower has increased within the last ten to fifteen years, much of it led by the John Gower Society. The 1993 for 1990 issue of *Mediævalia* is dedicated to Gower studies and includes Burke's work on some of the women characters in Gower, one of the first articles to study his heroines. On rape, see Kathryn Gravdal; also Isabelle Mast. Kurt Olsson published a book on Gower in 1992, which focuses upon the interrelated concepts in the *Confessio*. Sian Echard and Clare Fanger published a useful book which translates the major Latin verses in the *Confessio* in 1991. Yeager published a full-length study on Gower in 1990, and served as the editor for another book in 1991. *Arion* sheds light on tales such as the Tale of Albinus and Rosemund which previously had little scholarly attention. In 1989 the John Gower Society published *John Gower: Recent Readings*, articles complied by Yeager which were originally presented at the International Congress of Medieval Studies in Kalamazoo, Michigan, between 1983 and 1989. One of the articles in this book, Hugh White's work on nature, was of particular help to my study. Also in 1989 Peter Nicholson published a very useful annotated index to the *Confessio*, and in 1991 he served as editor to an anthology which gathers together Gower scholarship that has informed the modern critical discussion of the *Confessio*. An earlier anthology, *Gower's Confessio Amantis*, published in 1983 with A. J. Minnis as the editor, gathered material on Gower. Among others, this anthology includes the work of Runacres, Christopher Ricks, and J. A. Burrow, all helpful articles. Gotz Schmitz's book on women in medieval literature includes some Gowerian heroines and therefore was very helpful to me, and Edwin Craun's book on deviant speakers in medieval literature includes a chapter on Gower's Genius (113–156). Michael Hanrahan's 1995 doctoral dissertation on Gower shared some parallel ideas with

my work, but for a different purpose. (Hanrahan's dissertation focuses on how the literary conventions of infidelity in poems by Chaucer, Gower, and Usk, figure as treason in Richard II's reign.) Another book with Yeager as the editor was published in 1998. Russell A. Peck's work on Gower is illuminating. He is currently serving as the editor of a new reprint of the *Confessio*; Volume 1 is now in print.

Notes to Chapter One

[1] Economou, *The Goddess Nature* 2.

[2] Economou, *The Goddess Nature* 53. Bernard's Nature in the *De Mundi Universitate* (1145–1156) suggests that the goddess "was conceived out of a wide and rich erudition. No single work has been discovered that adequately covers all of the features Bernard assigns to his figure" (Economou, *The Goddess Nature* 67–68). Economou writes that "the suggestions that parallels [between Bernard's Nature] can be found in Hugh of Saint Victor's *Didascalicon*, written in the late 1120s…was an actual source are reasonable" (Economou, *The Goddess Nature* 67–68).

[3] Economou dates *De Mundi Universitate* (*Cosmographia*) as 1145–1156, and his death in 1160. (*The Goddess Nature* 59). According to Wetherbee, however, "only two dates in . . . [Bernard's] career can be even tentatively established: the *Cosmographia* was read before Pope Eugene III in 1147, and the *Experimentarius* has been dated by its editor about thirty years later" (intro, *Cosmographia* 20). Wetherbee asserts that very little is known of Bernardus' life; most of what is known is "based on the evidence of his relations with others" (intro, *Cosmographia* 20). Wetherbee points out that in a 1934 work, A. L. Poole "manages to show only that Bernardus probably lived at Tours between 1130 and 1140, that his *Cosmographia* was presumably read to Pope Eugenius III during the latter's visit to France in 1147 or 1148, and that since the Pope did not visit Tours, Bernardus may by this time have been resident at Paris" (intro, *Cosmographia* 134n). Early scholarship incorrectly identified him with Bernard of Chartres (intro, *Cosmographia* 134n). Wetherbee cites A. L. Poole, *Studies in Chronology and History* (Oxford, 1934) 228–35; 246–47.

[4] James J. Sheridan, trans., *Alan of Lille, The Plaint of Nature (De Planctu Naturæ)* (Toronto: Pontifical Institute of Mediaeval Studies, 1980). All quotations from Alan of Lille's *De Planctu Naturæ* (hereafter *De Planctu*) are taken from Sheridan's translation and will be indicated in the text by siglum (DP) and line number. In his introduction to the *De Planctu*, Sheridan writes that details about Alan's life and schooling are few, but it is assumed that he was born at Lille in Flanders around 1116 (intro 8).

[5] Economou, *The Goddess Nature* 58.

[6] Economou, *The Goddess Nature* 58–60. Bernard's *De Mundi Universitate* (*Cosmographia*) "laid the foundations for subsequent poets to explore man's relation to nature and to God in a world shaken by the Fall," and his work "established a frame of reference to which every subsequent Natura poet—Alan, Jean de Meun, Chaucer, and even Spenser—was in one way or another indebted" (Economou, *The Goddess Nature* 59). Bernard's "extensive learning and the variety of his literary activities earned him the respect not only of his contemporaries but also of medieval intellectuals for at least the next two centuries" (Economou, *The Goddess Nature* 59).

Notes to Chapter One

⁷ Sheridan, *De Planctu* 58. See also Economou, *The Goddess Nature* 72.

⁸ Sheridan, *De Planctu* 60.

⁹ Wetherbee, "Genius." See also Wetherbee, "John Gower," 589–609. For more on Gower's Genius, see the Lovesickness chapter in this book.

¹⁰ Luscombe 705.

¹¹ Luscombe 705–706. Further Luscombe he writes that natural law is "the union of male and female, the procreation of offspring and their education which have been taught to animals by nature" (705). Luscombe notes that similarly, Isidore of Seville believed natural law to be common to all men in all nations, controlled by a natural instinct.

¹² Luscombe 706.

¹³ Sheridan introduction, *De Planctu* 62.

¹⁴ St. Thomas Aquinas, *Summa Theologiæ* Q.92.2.2, ed. and trans. Thomas Gilby, O.P., Vol. 28 (London and New York: Blackfriars and McGraw Hill Book Company, 1964) 81–83. All quotations from Aquinas are taken from this edition and will be indicated in the text by siglum (ST), question and response number.

¹⁵ Luscombe 708.

¹⁶ Alan's Nature is closely associated with reason and "like Boethius' nature, is identified as the giver of reason" (Economou, *The Goddess Nature* 110).

¹⁷ Sheridan, *De Planctu* 62. Sheridan writes that "Nature may well call Genius her other self. Genius gives the final form to the things of Nature" (62).

¹⁸ Sheridan, *De Planctu* 35. Ovid often depicted gods as "living in palaces . . . on the Milky Way"; furthermore, descriptions of gods and goddesses descending to earth in medieval literature are common" (73n).

¹⁹ Although the goddess Nature is distressed that man has turned to homosexuality and sexual transgressions, of "far greater significance to the work and to the subsequent history of the goddess Natura are her pronouncements on heterosexual love (Economou, *The Goddess Nature* 87).

²⁰ Nature abandoned her post on earth because she "decided to spend my time in the delightful palace of the ethereal region," preferring heaven, where "unadulterated calm" reigns, to earth (DP 146). Sheridan thinks this passage illuminates a fatal flaw in Alan's work (147n).

²¹ Wetherbee, *Platonism* 258.

²² Guillaume de Lorris and Jean de Meun, *The Romance de la Rose*, trans. Harry W. Robbins, ed. and intro., Charles W. Dunn (New York: E. P. Dutton and Co., 1962). All quotations are taken from this translation of the *Roman* and will be indicated in the text by siglum (RR) and line number.

²³ Economou, *The Goddess Nature* 123.

²⁴ Marital affection—holding and kissing each other—is visible in several tales, including the Tale of Alceone and in the Tale of Alcestis. An example of Gower's liberality towards controlled sensuality is in the Penelope/Ulysses tale, in which it is implied that this married couple enjoy their lovemaking. I examine these tales n the Four Wives chapter.

²⁵ Rowe 99.

²⁶ Bennett, "Gower's 'Honeste Love,'" 59.

27 Whether or not he will listen and follow her advice is another story.

28 Rowe 111.

29 Economou, "The Character of Genius" 112.

30 Jenny Rebecca Rytting suggests that it is possible to read the *Confessio* as "a marriage (or conduct) manual, similar to works such as *The Goodman of Paris, The Book of the Knight of La Tour-Landry*, and Christine de Pizan's *The Three Virtues*, in that it teaches proper behavior for spouses through the use of both direct advice and exempla" (114).

31 Wetherbee, "Genius and Interpretation" 241.

32 Wetherbee, "Genius and Interpretation" 241.

33 Olsson writes that for Gower, "natural law . . . governs or affects every aspect of sentient life, including sexual desire. It is, in medieval legal tradition, a natural instinct, or a *motus sensualitatis* which in its first impulses is not subject to free will" (Olsson, *Structures of Conversion* 78).

34 Fisher, *Moral Philosopher* 195.

35 *Dictionary of the Middle Ages* 365.

36 The work is not dated by Macaulay, Yeager, or Esch. For Gower's source, Macaulay and Yeager suggest that Gower many have also known a version of the tale related by Paulus Diaconus, (ca. 720–799), *Gesta Langobardorum*, ii.28. Macaulay, *English Works*, Vol.I 476. Yeager (*Arion* 145) agrees with Macaulay, but believes it more likely Gower's source was Godfrey's *Pantheon*. Esch ("John Gower's Narrative Art" 90), writes that Godfrey, who followed Paulus, is the source.

37 Esch 96. Esch follows Fisher and calls the tale a "tragedy of love."

38 One particular exception is Gower's very detailed description of the old hag's ugliness in the Tale of Florent. Gower also describes Lucrece's beauty.

39 Yeager, *Arion* 151. He notes that Gower "positions the wheel at the two turning-points of the exemplum," 151. Also, at this point, Albinus has moved "beyond his depth," 151.

40 Rytting 120.

41 Olsson, *Structures of Conversion* 85.

42 Esch 93.

43 Esch writes that the "precision, severity, and directness of these words, which make no reference at all to the imminent disaster, are extremely impressive" and "dramatize the incident with the utmost suspense" (93).

44 In both his verse and his prose versions, Godfrey writes that Rosemund is unaware that Albinus killed her father, and that the cup was her father's head. Yeager, *Arion* 148n. He translates two short passages, one from the prose version and the other from the verse. Yeager, discussing the corresponding verse and prose passages from Godfrey, makes the point that Gower alters the source to focus on the sin of Pride; Godfrey does not "offer pride as the force driving" Albinus, (148n).

45 Ricks 29.

46 Yeager, *Arion* 149.

47 Esch 94.

48 Rytting notes that "the two of them raid the king's treasury on their way out of town caps off their treachery (since robbery is yet another form of dishonesty), and one

can only speculate as to whether Rosemund's maid had intended to place her lover on permanent loan with her mistress or whether she was also deceived" (120).

[49] Jill Mann writes about Chaucer's women and states that harmony between man and woman is "achieved through a chain of surrender," (124). In the Franklin's Tale and the Wife of Bath's Tale, she writes that "the surrender of power…creates power" (Mann 124).

[50] Yeager, *Arion* 145.

[51] On Venus not Fortune spinning the wheel, Yeager notes that this is not an original idea in Gower: "its analogues are myriad—but his combined addition of them to his source is the structural masterstroke of the piece" (Yeager, *Arion* 151). Yeager refers the reader to Howard R. Patch, *The Goddess Fortuna in Medieval Literature* (Cambridge, MA: Harvard UP, 1927) 90–98, for many examples of Venus in combination with Fortune. As a lover Albinus is under Venus' care, and as king he falls under Fortune's rule. By sinning against Venus he loses his love, but he also loses his life and his kingdom, things which are controlled by the whim of Fortune (Yeager, *Arion* 151–52).

[52] Alan of Lille writes that everything man does, specifically regarding his sexual passion, must be controlled by moderation, so that "the flesh will thus become the handmaiden of the spirit" (DP 194).

[53] Mainzer 217.

[54] Delany remarks that from Thisbe's fate Boccaccio draws "the enlightened moral that parents ought not to interfere too rashly in their children's love" (Delany 124).

[55] Kiser writes that it is unusual for Chaucer to include the Thisbe tale because it concerns the tragic deaths of two faithful lovers instead of just one, both of whom die for love (118).

[56] Kiser, *Telling Classical Tales* 118.

[57] Macaulay thought that Chaucer followed Ovid closely while Gower paraphrases the tale. He lists the changes Gower makes to the Ovidian text. Macaulay, *English Works*, Vol.I 497–98.

[58] See the *Dictionary of the Middle Ages* Vol. 2.194–195 on Bernard Silvester.

[59] Matthew's text reduces the lovers to "types, not individuals," and eliminates their thoughts and feelings, which, according to Ian Thomson and Louis Perraud, "serves to emphasize his own distinctive purpose, the shaping and ornamenting of the tale in accord with the canons of his rhetorical art (Thomson and Perraud, 219–20). Thomson and Perraud write that Matthew shows little interest in "plot and characterization," and since all his works are associated with the classroom, his main concern is constructing a rhetorical verse composition (218–219). Matthew precedes the tale of *Piramus et Tisbe* with a *sententia* "on the folly of passion, especially suicidal passion" (220). Gower emphasizes the lovers' foolish passion, as does Matthew, but does not specifically condemn their suicide. All quotations are from this translation will be indicated in the text by the siglum (PT) and page number.

[60] Bennett, *Middle English Literature* 424.

[61] Harbert 92.

[62] She notes that Chaucer "dwells gently" on it "with considerably more restraint" (Delany 128–132).

[63] Delany 127–28.

[64] MED, Vol. L 1087.

[65] Medieval medical authorities prescribed sexual therapy for their lovesick patients, as I will explore in chapter four.

[66] Harbert 92.

[67] The lion in both Ovid's and Chaucer's rendition has already eaten its prey, and Thisbe watches it approach the spring to drink. It too tears and bloodies her wimple.

[68] Runacres 133.

[69] Harbert 93.

[70] Kiser suggests that in Chaucer's rendition of the tale neither Pyramus or Thisbe can be blamed for the misfortunes that befall them. She asserts that "simple accidents, such as Thisbe's loss of her veil" and "Pyramus' belief that blood on a wimple" signifies her death, "are often prime cause of earthly tragedy in love" (120).

[71] Harbert notes that this speech is "entirely independent of that in Ovid, on the cruel power of love as personified by Venus and Cupid" (93).

[72] I am thinking specifically of Cresseid's blasphemy in Henryson's *The Testament of Cresseid*.

[73] Writing on Chaucer, Jane Chance argues that it is the "destructive blindness of the separated lovers . . . which leads to their mutual deaths" (242).

[74] Bennett, *Selections* ix.

[75] Thomson and Perraud 221. In his rendition Matthew states generally that amongst the young there is a predisposition to love which he intimates is not found in older people, utilizing it as a notion of cause and effect.

[76] Minnis, *The Shorter Poems* 409. The lines Minnis refers to seem to have more to do with promising to meet at Ninus' tomb than a promise of marriage, but it is clear they plan to consummate their love at this meeting.

[77] Minnis, *The Shorter Poems* 417.

[78] Often when "the woman plays the active role in gaining her husband, [the poet] alters traditional sexual images by entrusting women with male responsibilities"; however, the woman always "speedily returns to her role as obedient wife" (Hotchkiss 212).

[79] Hotchkiss 218.

[80] Hotchkiss 218.

[81] In Chaucer Thisbe specifically states that she can kill herself for love, just as Pyramus, a man, has done (LGW II. 910–11); it is as if she wants to prove her female masculinity, her physical strength.

[82] Referring to Chaucer's Thisbe only, Mann writes that Thisbe passionately identifies with her lover and realizes her "own virile qualities: imbued with 'strengthe and hardyness' by her love," and she kills herself with his sword, still warm with his blood (42).

[83] Mann 42.

[84] Esch writes that the metamorphosis is eliminated because it "could contribute nothing more to his theme of 'rashness in love'" (95).

[85] White 1.

[86] White 1.

Notes to Chapter Two

¹ Minnis "John Gower," 207. Minnis writes: "Various scholars have pointed out that . . . [Gower] took from the *Ovide moralisé* details for his stories of Pyramus and Thisbe, Phoebus and Coronis, and Seys and Alcione. . . . Gower was probably indebted to the 'Medieaval Ovid' for details in fifteen stories from the *Metamorphoses*; he may have used Pierre Bersuire's *Ovidius moralizatus* in his sections on the pantheon in the fifth book of the *Confessio*. Moreover, he seems also to have made use of a commentary on Ovid's *Heroides*" ("John Gower," 207, 226n). Delany (110) also cites Bersuire as a source, writing that his tale of Ametus and Alcestis includes a Christian moral. The story is glossed as "an allegory of the good wife, whose perfect love of her husband causes Jesus to lead her out of purgatory into heaven, and also as an allegory of the virgin martyrs who preferred to die for their God rather than to live physically but perish spiritually" (Delany 110). It is possible that both Gower and Chaucer were familiar with this compendium. Christian overtones of self-sacrifice are visible in Gower's version of the tale, regardless of whether or not he knew Bersuire: Alcestis dies to give Ametus life, as Christ dies for mankind.

² Olsson, *Structures of Conversion* 32.

³ Minnis, *The Shorter Poems* 259.

⁴ Bennett, *Middle English Literature* 417. Bennett notes that the psychology of love inherent in the *Confessio*, as well as in the *Roman*, owes much indirectly to this "amorous" Ovid (*Middle English Literature* 417).

⁵ Minnis, "John Gower, *Sapiens*" 208. Bennett points out that "handbooks for priests and penitents had for a century been recommending the use and study of *exempla* that would bring home the evils of the capital sins. [For Gower] to fit religious practice to the general relish for tales and love-doctrine was a brilliant stroke" (Bennett, *Selections* vii-xvii).

⁶ Behind Gower's "love-doctrine, as behind that of most medieval poets, lies the Ovid of the *Ars Amatoria*," yet Gower's "presentation of Amans the lover is as distant from the cynicism of that work as it is from the naturalism of Jean de Meun's" (Bennett, *Selections* xiii).

⁷ Minnis, *The Shorter Poems* 259.

⁸ Bennett, *Middle English Literature* 417.

⁹ Minnis, "John Gower, *Sapiens*" 211.

¹⁰ Delany asserts that because Chaucer did not tell Penelope's tale in the *Legend* "perhaps [it is] a clue to . . . [his] ironic intention . . . , for the figure of Penelope reached the Middle Ages as the most unambiguous example of female virtue that a genuine vindicator of the sex would use" (105). She recognizes that "silence is not a strong argument in the case of an unfinished work, and we do not know how Chaucer might have ironized even Penelope" (Delany 105).

¹¹ MED, Vol. L 615.

¹² Margaret Paston is an example of a fifteenth century woman who managed a large estate and raised her children alone while her husband was away either collecting rent from his other estates, or fighting legal battles. For squire families like the Pastons, maintaining the family property was a time-consuming job that took every ounce of energy

they had, and having a two-partner marriage in which the wife is thoroughly involved in the business affairs of the family seems to be the Pastons' way of both maintaining and increasing their wealth.

[13] McMillan 13.

[14] MED, Vol. A 348.

[15] On November 1, 1396, Richard II married the young Isabella, a French princess too immature to bear children. Londoners, especially those politically-minded folk like Gower, were very concerned about the lack of an heir to the English throne, for Richard's marriage to Anne of Bohemia did not produce any heirs, and neither did his union with Isabella.

[16] Minnis writes that "Ulysses' sloth is all the more reprehensible because he is slow in returning to so good a wife" ("John Gower, *Sapiens*" 211).

[17] Hotchkiss 218.

[18] Stanford 188.

[19] Minnis, *The Shorter Poems* 360. The medieval commentaries on the *Heroides* "regularly insisted that these poems affirmed the value of married love, as exemplified by the story of Penelope, and reprehended foolish passion of the type to which Phyllis succumbed" (360).

[20] Gower can describe private thoughts: in the Tale of Rosemund he tells us with great empathy but few words how Rosemund feels when her husband brazenly and foolishly announces that she is holding a cup made of her father's skull: she ". . . was softe" (I.2564).

[21] Yeager, *Arion* 123.

[22] Penelope refers to this mutual passion in the letter episode when she reminds her slothful husband that once he returns home, they can enjoy reciprocal, passionate love-making as often as he desires (CA IV.193,195).

[23] MED, W-Z 262–263. The OED translates the verb "to weld" as "to unite intimately or inseparably; to join closely together" (OED, XX 107). The OED further notes that the form of the word which Gower used, "welde," is an obsolete form of the verb, "wield," which is defined as "control, possession, to have command or control of" (XX 322–323).

[24] Stanford 142.

[25] I will explore the "maladie / Of lovedrunke" in the final chapter of this book (VI. 108–111).

[26] Bennett notes that Gower's rendition of this Ovidian tale demonstrates that Gower is much more than a "mere translator"(Bennett, *Selections* xii). Although Gower follows the Ovidian text, he "greatly abbreviates the story, yet deletes almost nothing completely" (Bennett, *Selections* 42). See also Gaston 42.

[27] Pearsall, "Gower's Narrative Art" 71.

[28] Gower "makes . . . use of the transformations to suggest human values in poeticized forms" (Pearsall, "Gower's Narrative Art" 71).

[29] Ovid, *The Metamorphoses of Ovid*, trans. Mary M. Innes (London: Penguin Books, 1955) 257. All quotations are taken from this translation of the *Metamorphoses* will be indicated in the text by siglum (Met.) and book and line number.

³⁰ In the Tale of Penelope, Penelope has been running the household alone for ten years, but once her husband returns, she accepts his authority, and he is the head of the castle once again. Penelope welcomes him home, never questioning his tardiness or his reasons for being so slothful in his return.

³¹ Minnis, *The Shorter Poems* 59. He writes: Chaucer's Blanche "is not only the 'fairest' but also the 'beste,' a woman in the mold of those virtuous wives of antiquity, the 'good' Penelope and the 'noble' and 'trewe' Lucrece (1079–87). Only the latter is identified as a 'wyf' here, the term having the technical sense of 'married woman,' but the reputation of both figures as illustrative of *bona matrimonii* was widespread, and the clear implication is that White is also 'good wife' material" (Minnis, *The Shorter Poems* 59).

³² This is an intriguing concept, which I am exploring elsewhere. I presented a paper on this topic for the John Gower Society "Gower and Speech Acts" session at the 33rd International Congress on Medieval Studies, Western Michigan University, Kalamazoo, Michigan, in May 1998.

³³ The Alcestis tale is a tale-within-a-tale, and the two tales are closely related. Burrow writes both Chaucer and Gower "produce stories-within-stories" (Burrow, *Ricardian Poetry* 63).

³⁴ Ovid mentions her briefly in the *Ars*, Euripides wrote a play entitled *Alcestis*, Plato mentions her in the *Symposium*, and there are several classical glosses, quotations, florilegium which either or both of the poets could have known. Delany, writing on Chaucer's possible sources, notes that Ovid mentions the Alcestis story in the *AA* 3.17–20 "and such a reference would certainly have been glossed in medieval commentaries on the *Ars*" (Delany 109).

³⁵ Burke, "Sources" 11n. It is unusual to find the Alcestis tale squeezed within the Tale of King, Wine, Woman and Truth. Burke notes that the "fullest medieval version of the story is Boccaccio's "*De Genealogia Deorum*," and that Gower's rendition of the tale is "selective and independent with relation to its probable sources" (Burke, "Sources" 11n).

³⁶ Nicholson, *Annotated Index* 449.

³⁷ It is impossible, of course, to know whether Chaucer influenced Gower, or Gower Chaucer.

³⁸ As the royal mistress, Perrers "disgusted many of her contemporaries by putting the aging but frivolous monarch completely under her thumb" (Stillwell 456).

³⁹ Stillwell 458. Stillwell writes that both "Tatlock and Macaulay are agreed in thinking that Gower refers to the inglorious last phase of Edward's reign when he inveighs against flatterers" in the *Mirour* (456). See MO 22801, quoted in text. William' Burton Wilson, the translator of the *Mirour*, concurs with the earlier scholars that this passage refers to Alice Perrers' control of Edward III during the last years of his reign. See Wilson, *Mirour* 407.

⁴⁰ Burke, "Sources and Significance" 3.

⁴¹ Gower emphasizes the conjugal tenderness and loving relationship in this tale, and in each of the other Four Wives' Marriage Tales.

⁴² See Delany 107–114. She writes that Alcestis' kindness is limited by her loyalty to the angry God of Love (Delany 107).

⁴³ Olsson calls this example an "inverted tribute to the power of woman," but I think he misses Gower's point—that a woman, especially a Good Wife, can be an accomplished helpmeet to a man (Olsson, *Structures of Conversion* 207).

⁴⁴ Burke writes that in choosing Minerva, Alcestis appropriately chooses a deity "in keeping with her virtues of courage, initiative, and wifely self-sacrifice" (Burke, "Sources" 12). Mainzer notes that in most versions of the tale, and in the *Ovidius moralizatus*, Alcestis prays to Apollo, not Minerva for help (222).

⁴⁵ Burke, "Sources and Significance" 12.

⁴⁶ Gower is often curiously silent, even though he is quite capable of meticulously illustrating small love scenes. Gower excludes all physical descriptions and dramatic speech from this tale. Alcestis is never described; of the Four Wives, Lucrece is the only one who is described, and even her description is rather slim. We do not know what she prays to Minerva, nor what she tells her husband of Minerva's decree. See the Tale of Penelope where Gower's silence is also discussed.

⁴⁷ Medea, whose tale is detailed in chapter three, is devoted to Jason, and her acts towards him are benevolent, but her love is a misplaced love, and their relationship is not one of mutual concern and harmony.

⁴⁸ Troilus continues his praise for Alcestis:

'For whan hire housbonde was in jupertye
To dye hymself but if she wolde dye,
She ches for hym to dye and gon to helle,
And starf anon, as us the bokes telle.'
(TC V.1530–33)

This is all Chaucer tells us of the Alcestis tale in the *Troilus*.

⁴⁹ MED, Vol. T, 123.

⁵⁰ Burke, "Sources and Significance" 13. She writes that "Gower's exemplum highlights the topological parallels with the Virgin Mary and Christ in Alcestis' intercession and death on another's behalf (VII.1944–49)."

⁵¹ Burke, "Women" 239. In *The Fall of Women* Schmitz notes "tenderness" is what "distinguishes" Gower from other medieval writers (Schmitz 80).

⁵² Boccaccio tells the Lucrece story in *Concerning Famous Women*, and Lydgate treats her twice in his *Fall of Princes*; two hundred years later, Shakespeare tells her tale too.

⁵³ James George Frazer, trans. and introd., *Fasti*, by Ovid, ed. G. P. Goold (1931; Cambridge, MA: Harvard UP, 1989) xxi. Frazer praises *Fasti* as ranking "next to the *Metamorphoses* as the most elaborate and important of Ovid's works"(xxi). He notes that Ovid "expressly says that he has written the *Fasti* in twelve books," but only six books are extant. If the last six books were written, they "have disappeared without a trace; for no ancient writer cites or refers to them" (xxi).

⁵⁴ See Gravdal.

⁵⁵ Schmitz, *The Fall of Women* 77. In "his history of Rome, *Ab urbe condita* (I.lvii-lx), Livy places the rape of Lucrece firmly in the military and political context" (Schmitz, *The Fall of Women* 77).

⁵⁶ In a new work Louise Sylvester points out that "It is clear that the testing of wives is the reification of what Arrons has set up, and that the competition over wives' chastity is a way of enacting the male homosocial bonding implicit in the relationships" (129).

[57] Ovid and Chaucer both use "Tarquin" for Gower's "Arrons"; to simplify, I use the name "Arrons" throughout.

[58] MED, Vol. A 7.

[59] Rytting notes—as I do—that there is a lot of kissing in the *Confessio*. Rytting 122.

[60] Facial expressions often reflect inward emotion in Middle English literature. Curry 78.

[61] Gower also describes Rosemund's beauty, and the ugly appearance of the hag in the Tale of Florent.

[62] As C. S. Lewis notes, "Gower does not dwell on shapes and colors; but this does not mean that he keeps his eyes shut" (Lewis, "Gower" 22).

[63] I presented a paper on Gower's women and their silent actions in May, 1998. See note above.

[64] Pearsall, "Gower's Narrative Art" 74.

[65] MED, Vol. S 326.

[66] Schmitz, *The Fall of Women* 79.

[67] Concerning animal imagery, Louise Sylvester writes that it "would seem self-evident that we should feel pity for this lamb caught by the wolf, and yet the simile compels the reader to recognize that wolves by their nature seize lambs, in the same way, presumably, as male desire, by its nature, exercises coercion upon female resistance. As in the romance paradigm, the woman is represented as the focus of male thought and active preparation, and is shown to be powerless to prevent this natural force" (Sylvester 124). I point out that Gower, in the *Mirour*, which I quote two lines hence, writes that the "rapacious man"—even when he is described as a beast— acts against reason," and this is something Gower believes is most certainly not (to quote Sylvester) a "natural force" (MO 6841). Arrons is not acting with a natural force but with an irrational one.

[68] Minnis, *The Shorter Poems* 438.

[69] Other tales of rape in the *Confessio* include the rapes of Philomela, Pauline, Virginia, and the rape at the Marriage of Pirithous.

[70] Hillman 263.

[71] Pearsall, "Gower's Narrative Art" 74.

[72] Chaucer also employs bestial imagery to describe Arrons. In Chaucer Lucretia is awakened as Arrons, who has slipped into her house like a thief, climbs into her bed, and she wonders aloud "'What beste is that?'" (LGW V.1788).

[73] Donaldson 70. Donaldson characterizes Clarissa's swoon to be "like the swoon of Chaucer's and Gower's Lucrece, . . . as a kind of death, prefiguring the final death" scene (70).

[74] Bland 289.

[75] Pearsall writes that Lucrece's "actions on the morrow have the momentous, preordained quality of one who has . . . already passed beyond suffering into a different world" (Pearsall, "Gower's Narrative Art" 74).

[76] Hussey 219. Hussey points out that Lucrece "tells all her friends" (219).

[77] Schmitz, *The Fall of Women* 80.

[78] Schmitz, *The Fall of Women* 80.

[79] Minnis notes that "decorous arrangements of garments while dying can be regarded as a saint's life motif" (Minnis, *The Shorter Poems* 364). Delany points out that cov-

ering oneself is a classical topos, and points to Polyxena in the *Metamorphoses* and Julius Caesar in the Monk's Tale who both cover themselves while dying (146). For Polyxena, see Met. 13.479–80; for Julius Caesar, see MkT (2715).

[80] Saint Augustine, *Concerning the City of God Against the Pagans*, trans. Henry Bettenson (London: Penguin Books, 1972). All quotations are taken from this translation of *The City of God* and will be indicated in the text by siglum (CG), book and chapter number.

[81] Schmitz, *The Fall of Women* 86.

[82] Schmitz, *The Fall of Women* 86.

[83] Hotchkiss 214.

[84] Bland 289.

[85] For discussions on Chaucer's ironic technique in the *Legend*, see McMillan; Overbeck; Hansen; Frank; and Kiser 95–98.

[86] McMillan 39.

[87] McMillan 39, and Overbeck 84.

[88] Schmitz, *The Fall of Women* 82.

[89] Schmitz, *The Fall of Women* 77.

[90] St. Jerome, *Against Jovinianus* I.46, *A Select Library of Nicene and Post-Nicene Fathers of the Christian Church: Volume VI, The Principal Works of St. Jerome*, trans. W. H. Fremantle, G. Lewis, W. G. Martley (1892; Grand Rapids, MI: Wm. B. Eerdmans Publishing Company, 1983) 382. All quotations will come from Fremantle's translation of Jerome and be indicated in the text by the siglum (AJ) followed by book, line number, and page number.

[91] It may seem surprising to find Dido on Jerome's list but she is also known as the woman who swore to remain unmarried and chaste when her husband Sychaeus was murdered by her brother Pygmalion, king of Tyre. In this version of her story, she killed herself before she was forced to marry Iarbus, a neighboring king. Dido is most famous for her sexual liaison with Aeneas. In this myth she disavowed her pledge of chastity to sleep with Aeneas.

[92] Minnis, *The Shorter Poems* 405. He writes that the "'shadowy perfection' of these women of the past is . . . quite apparent. Lucrece prefers death to forgiveness," and Phyllis dies for a man who is false (Minnis, *The Shorter Poems* 405). Schmitz acknowledges that "most medieval commentators follow Jerome rather than Augustine and set Lucretia first among Roman matrons" (Schmitz, *The Fall of Women* 77).

[93] Minnis, *The Shorter Poems* 405.

[94] Mast casts a hopeful note that "Within the didactic framework of the *Confessio*, Gower's rethinking and reworking of rape, provides an alternative paradigm of women and female sexuality, which the audience, as well as Amans, may have found instructive"(Mast 125).

[95] See Schmitz, *The Fall of Women* 79–104. Schmitz cites Gower, Chaucer, Shakespeare, and Middleton as among the poets who treat Lucrece's tale with a sensitive hand.

[96] Delany remarks that Chaucer's personal experience with *raptus* in 1380 may have given him "a particular awareness of the subject" (77). She refers, of course, to the discovery of the formal documents in the Court of Chancery in which Cecily Champain

unconditionally releases Chaucer "from all actions concerning her rape or anything else," documents which have proved to be problematic for Chaucer biographers since Furnivall uncovered them in 1873 (Delany 77). Pearsall seems loath to accuse Chaucer of rape, but writes that "the more obvious conclusion seems the more likely one: the charge referred to in the document of release is indeed one of rape" (Pearsall, *Life* 137). Having said this, Pearsall seems to hedge: "That Chaucer was guilty of *something* is clear from the care he took to secure immunity from prosecution, but it need not have been rape. The charge, after all, was neither brought nor its truth tested" (Pearsall, *Life* 137).

[97] Delany 77. For rape in medieval literature see Gravdal; also Mast.

[98] Orr 122. Orr writes that "the author of the treatise attributed to Glanvill, writing in 1179, thought the punishment for rape should be the same as for any felony, presumably including capital punishment. The treatise called by the name of Bracton specified a fierce corporal punishment, blinding and castration, in the case of rape of virgins" (Orr 122).

[99] Orr 122.

[100] Orr 121.

[101] Orr 124.

[102] Power 86–88.

[103] Orr 151.

[104] Orr 152.

[105] I agree with Hillman that the "engagingly human" emotions found in Gower's tale of Lucrece make it a "more complex and more powerful narrative" than the versions written by Ovid and Chaucer (Hillman 268). Hillman writes that "... her resolution [to kill herself] is immediate and strong, full of dignity, yet poignantly superimposed on her palpable agony" (268).

[106] Schmitz, *The Fall of Women* 83.

[107] Hillman 269. He compares Gower's version of the tale to Shakespeare's poem, determining that Shakespeare's main source was Gower. The "emotional tension [found in the tale] . . . raises both Shakespeare's and Gower's heroines to a tragic stature which has no equivalent in the cognate texts [by Livy, Ovid, and Chaucer]" (Hillman 269).

[108] Bennett, *Middle English Literature* 411–12.

[109] In the Tale of Rosemund, another tale of a ruinous marriage, Gower illustrates a moment which, although it is not a private one, conjures up an image of a couple who have shared many intimate intervals. Albinus and Rosemund, described as loving "ech other wonder wel," enjoy themselves at a spectacularly lavish feast which resembles a banquet Edward III might have given for his Order of the Garter Knights (I.2488–89). Moments later, boasting leads to infidelity and murder, and soon after their marriage and kingdom crumble.

[110] Peck, introduction, *Confessio* xv.

[111] As readers we are aware of Ulysses' infidelity, but in Gower's Tale of Penelope his transgressions are never mentioned.

Notes to Chapter Three

[1] Joan Cadden, whose study of medieval medical theories of reproduction, refers to Saint Albertus Magnus, the Dominican scholar and patron of the natural sciences, who often wrote on reproduction and sexuality. In *Quaestiones de animalibus*, XV, Q.11, a treatise on whether males or females are more suitable for learning good behavior, Cadden notes that "in an extraordinary burst of misogyny," he concludes that women's humid natures made them "unconstant" and in search of something new (Cadden, *Meanings of Sex* 185). She translates Albertus: "Hence when she is engaged in the act under one man, if it were possible, she would like at the same time to be under another.... In short I would say, every woman is to be avoided as much as a poisonous snake and a horned devil" (Cadden, *Meanings of Sex Difference* 185 and 185n).

[2] Desmond 58. Cadden, coming at the discussion from the wider perspective of medicine and science, writes that in the Middle Ages there existed an "impetus to control female sexuality in the interests of the family in particular and society in general" (Cadden, *Meanings of Sex* 224).

[3] In a recent article Diane Watt notes that "Hercules' act of cross-dressing is itself a form of 'Falssemblant.' The image of Hercules wearing a woman's coat is symbolic of his self-emasculation and loss of identity" (Watt 537).

[4] In the *Traitié* we are told that Hercules wins Deianira as a wife in a battle with Achelous (Tr VII.1–7). Soon after, however, Hercules falls in love with Iole and marries her. He becomes her fool and she had of him all that she wanted (Tr VII.8–12).

[5] Deianira and Medea are the only two Forsaken Women who are married. In The Monk's Tale Deianira is Hercules' "lemman," his paramour, and if Hercules has a wife, she is not mentioned in Chaucer's brief account (MkT 3309).

[6] There seems to be no other explanation for this restraint. Kelly stresses that "it must not be thought that Gower deliberately suppressed the fact that Hercules and Deianira were married, out of some thematic purpose" (133). He cites the Hercules-Achelous myth in Book IV as proof that they were married.

[7] Isbell 76. Isbell writes that in the *Heroides*, "Deianira is not so much cognizant of an injury to love as she is of an injury to her wifely status" (76).

[8] Isbell 83.

[9] Madness is a symptom of melancholy, from which lovesickness derives. The Latin sidenote alludes to Achelous, as if he had something to do with Hercules' death, although no explanation is given here or in the *Confessio* (Tr VII.1.1).

[10] Doob 7–8.

[11] Peck, *Kingship* 61.

[12] Macaulay, *The English Works*, Vol.I xiii.

[13] Burke, "Women" 243.

[14] Morse's new and thorough work on Medea traces her full story from the legends and the myths available to us in the various renditions of the tale. She writes that the Medea story is one filled with "incoherences and incompatabilities, of invention and its limits, of the ways that writers could believe and play with belief" (Morse xiii).

[15] Yeager, *Arion* 118–123. He points out that "Benoit, and Guido who followed him, stop their narratives when Jason leaves Colchis" (Yeager, *Arion* 122n).

[16] Mainzer 219. He points out that the major events which Gower details in the Tale of Medea, such as the mantle which Medea made and sent to Creusa, and how she killed both their sons before Jason's eyes, are "only alluded to in the *Metamorphoses*" (Mainzer 219). In *Arion*, Yeager notes that "Ovid tells of Medea's restoration of Aeson's youth, and of the killing of Peleus [which is not in Gower] in the *Metamorphoses*, Book VII" (Yeager, *Arion* 122n).

[17] Morse writes that "traditional critical misogyny and ethnocentricity [read Medea as] . . . one of Euripides' 'bad women' who, although provoked, undoubtedly goes 'too far'" (Morse 26). Gower more than likely did not know Euripides' *Medea*, although it is one of the most famous as well as most interpreted Greek tragedies; elements of this play could have appeared in medieval commentaries with which Gower was familiar.

[18] Morse 26.

[19] Guido delle Colonne, *Historia Destructionis Troiae*, trans. Mary Elizabeth Meek (Bloomington, IN: Indiana UP, 1974) 13–32. All quotations will be from this translation and will be indicated in the text by siglum (Troy), book and line number.

[20] Minnis, *The Shorter Poems* 375. Minnis writes that Gower "presents her sympathetically throughout the narrative" (*The Shorter Poems* 375).

[21] In a recent article on Medea, Natalie Grinnell points out the similarities between "the flaming shirt and the poisoned robe designed by Medea" (80).

[22] Peck, *Kingship* 111.

[23] Harbert 94.

[24] Chaucer's version of the Medea myth lacks the romance of Gower's, and his hero and heroine are not drawn as fully as they are in the *Confessio*.

[25] Burke, "Women" 244–245. She writes "In Benoit and Guido, the go-between sent by the princess to summon Jason is an old woman servant. Elderly chaperones had, of course, a most unsavory reputation in the Middle Ages. They not only permitted young men access to their charges, but were known to give amatory advice based on their extensive experience. In Benoit's more detailed account, . . . this passage . . . constitutes a very pejorative description of feminine scheming. . . . By contrast, Medea's companion and go-between in the *Confessio* is called simply a 'Mayden,' and she gives no advice at all" (Burke, "Women" 244–245). To Burke's comments I add that Medea treats her maid as a trusted friend; the maid is also the witness to their marriage vows.

[26] Grinnell thinks that "Hercules' role in bringing together Jason and Medea is suspect," due to the similarities between "the flaming shirt and the poisoned robe designed by Medea, combined with the identical faithlessness of the two heroes" (80). Furthermore, "because the structure of the *Confessio* is filled with such interlaced motifs, the irony of Jason whispering his plans to sleep with Medea in Hercules' ear is evident to the reader" (Grinnell 80). I am not sure I agree; Gower uses young people to bring young people together, something I think is a sweet addition to the tale.

[27] Yeager, *Arion* 120n. Guido's couple swears upon a Jupiter idol, too (Troy III.50–65).

[28] Having a witness ensures that their marriage might have been declared a legal one by the English ecclesiastical courts. See Hornsby 52–68. All the Forsaken Women exact some sort of a promise of fidelity from their lovers before they sleep with them, but unless there is a witness to the event, Gower does not recognize the pledge as a legal mar-

ital bond. Often, as Minnis notes, "where marriage is neither proclaimed nor implied through deliberate obfuscation," there is a "firm plighting of troth, a solemn undertaking to marry in the future, what was technically known as *desponsatio* by *verba de futuro*. Dido, Medea, Ariadne, and Phyllis all seem to enter into such contracts with their men before they sleep with them" (Minnis, *The Shorter Poems* 417). Minnis' comments refer to Chaucer's *Legend*, but they are applicable to Gower too (*The Shorter Poems* 417). Richard Firth Green agrees with Minnis, pointing out that "fourteenth-century canon lawyers would probably have seen . . . [their pledges] as quite sufficient to constitute legal matrimony even without ecclesiastical blessings" (Green 14). In another context V. A. Kolve argues that "pagan marriage does not normally carry sacramental value for a medieval poet," but in the tales of the Forsaken Women, Gower seems to accept the validity of the marriages, focusing instead upon the manner in which the couple behaves once married (Kolve 173).

[29] Peck, *Kingship* 112.

[30] Peck, *Kingship* 113.

[31] Morse 168. Morse's book includes plates from illustrated romances of the legend. See Plate Two (following p. 176), from the Bibliothéque Nationale MS. fonds français, 331, fol. 132, which shows Medea gathering herbs.

[32] Jason's "unjust refusal to complete his bargain with Medea—and to exchange fairly what she has so clearly earned—is affirmed and condemned by the legalistic phrasing" of Medea's curse as she kills their sons (Yeager *Arion* 121n).

[33] Isbell 103.

[34] Guido writes that Medea meets an obscure death, and Jason goes off to battle with Hercules, but he does not tell us anything more. Jason's remarriage is not in the myth (Troy III. 377–85).

[35] Morse 15.

[36] Morse 15.

[37] Morse 190.

[38] Morse xiii-xiv.

[39] Morse xiv. She notes that there exists "iconographic representations [of Medea] which correspond to no known literary treatment [which] is a further reminder of the variety of possible episodes and of the choices open to writers and artists in periods before the legend 'set'" (Morse 2n).

[40] Morse xv.

[41] Delany writes that "they were thought to have lived three centuries apart" (Delany194).

[42] Lord 216. Delany writes that the chaste-Dido tradition was "sustained by various grammarians, Virgil commentators, and medieval authors including Servius, Macrobius, Priscian, Petrarch, and early Dante commentators; indeed, the question seems to have attained the status of a fairly significant debate in fourteenth-century Italian letters (Delany 194–95). A contemporary text readily available to Chaucer was Boccaccio's *De mulieribus claris*, which Chaucer used for his Monk's account of Zenobia. Boccaccio's extended version of the Dido material argues that although Dido's death took place during Aeneas' visit, its occurrence had already been determined as a gesture of fidelity to her dead husband Sychaeus" (Delany 194–95).

Notes to Chapter Three

⁴³ St. Jerome praises Dido for remaining chaste and therefore loyal to her first husband Sychaeus; in his version of the story, she kills herself on Sychaeus' funeral pyre rather than subject herself to a second marriage.

⁴⁴ Schmitz, *The Fall of Women* 30.

⁴⁵ Jacobson 62–63.

⁴⁶ Schmitz, "Classics" 103. He writes that it is possible that Gower worked from "an annotated Latin manuscript of Ovid's *Letter of Dido* when writing his short exemplum of Dido and Aeneas. There is no reference to his source in the *Heroides* and no sign that he knew Virgil's epic version of the story at all. With Chaucer, the situation appears to be exactly the reverse. He used and named both authorities in his Legend of Dido" (Schmitz, "Classics" 103).

⁴⁷ Schmitz, *The Fall of Women* 17.

⁴⁸ In *The Riverside Chaucer* notes to the HF, the editors write that Chaucer "complicates Virgil's account of Dido and Aeneas by adopting Ovid's perspective [Her 7] which wholeheartedly takes Dido's view of the affair" (*The Riverside Chaucer* 980).

⁴⁹ Ovid, *Ars Amatoria*, trans. and intro., Peter Green, *Ovid: The Erotic Poems: Amores, The Art of Love, Cures for Love, On Facial Treatment for Ladies* (London: Penguin Books, 1982). All quotations will be taken from this translation of the *Ars Amatoria* and will be indicated in the text by siglum (AA) and line number.

⁵⁰ Desmond 50.

⁵¹ Green10. See *Roman* 13187–94.

⁵² Schmitz, "Classics" 101.

⁵³ I examine this illness in the following chapter.

⁵⁴ Desmond 58. Desmond notes that Dido is characterized "either by her ability to resist sexual temptation in the historical version or by her tendency to succumb to sexual desire in the Virgilian tradition" (Desmond 58). Gower more than likely did not know Virgil.

⁵⁵ In Chaucer's *House of Fame* Dido complains of wicked Fame, who will never allow her reputation to recover from the shame, and she blames her sister Anne for her heartache, because Anne convinced her to love Aeneas (HF I.368–70). In the *Legend* Chaucer writes that Anne cautions Dido against loving Aeneas (LGW III.1185). In Ovid's *Heroides*, Dido writes that her sister Anne knows of her "shameful guilt," and that she is now Aeneas' "abandoned bride," but she does not blame her (Her. 7.273,100).

⁵⁶ Chaucer's Dreamer in the *Book of the Duchess* tries to dissuade the Black Knight from despair by reminding him that if he kills himself, he will be damned along with Dido and Phyllis, who suffer in purgatory for their sins of suicide (BD 721–34).

⁵⁷ Unlike the Tale of Lucrece, in which we are made to understand early that Lucrece is a pagan Roman who seeks and secures an honorable death in her suicide, in this tale there is no reassurance that Dido's suicide is acceptable.

⁵⁸ Green 15. The Narrator's sincerity has been questioned, but I have not found any reference that questions Chaucer's use of the word "traitor."

⁵⁹ Gawain Poet, *Sir Gawain and the Green Knight*, trans. and editor William Vantuono (Notre Dame, Indiana: University of Notre Dame Press, 1999) 54. Book II.927.

⁶⁰ Mainzer 223, and Bennett *Selections*, xiii.

⁶¹ Curry 77.

⁶² Minnis, *The Shorter Poems* 438.

⁶³ Minnis, *The Shorter Poems* 381.

⁶⁴ Ovid implies that Demephon is the son of Theseus, and Chaucer emphasizes this link twice: the second time is at the close of her letter, when Phyllis curses Demephon, saying that when men talk of how he abandoned her, they will remember his father, too:

> But sothly, of oo poynt yit may they rede,
> That ye ben lyk youre fader as in this,
> For he beguiled Adriane, ywis,
> With swich an art and with swich subtilte
> As thow thyselven hast begyled me.
> (LGW VIII.2543–47)

⁶⁵
> Ye han wel herd of Theseus devyse
> In the betraysynge of fayre Adryane
> That of hire pite kepte him from his bane.
> At shorte wordes, ryght so Demophon
> The same wey, the same path hath gon,
> That dide his false fader Theseus.
> (LGW VIII.2459–64)

⁶⁶ The word "enchantement" appears in the Tale of Nectanabus (VI.1977), in the Prudence of the Serpent Tale (I.477); twice in the Tale of Medea; in the Tale of Canace and Machiere (III.169 -78); and in the Tale of Geta and Amphitrion (II. 2492).

⁶⁷ Olsson, *Structures of Conversion* 114n. Olsson argues that "moral blame for an enchantment is often transferred to an external agent, to an enchanter who beguiles the innocent."

⁶⁸ In Ovid she stands on the shoreline, searching the horizon for sails, too.

⁶⁹ Chaucer, by contrast, follows Ovid and allows Phyllis' voice to dominate the tale.

⁷⁰ Mainzer 223. Mainzer acknowledges that this transformation is not in the *Heroides* itself, but may have been found in a commentary to Ovid's epistles.

⁷¹ Bennett, "Gower's 'Honeste Love'" 59. Bennett writes that "this lover's malady [assoted love; infatuation] destroys Reason (which in Gower connotes 'measure' and restraint)" ("Gower's 'Honeste Love'" 59).

⁷² In the *Legend* Phyllis is said to commit suicide out of despair (LGW VIII.2557), which in a Christian context is a terrible sin for it implies that there is no hope of salvation.

⁷³ Minnis, *The Shorter Poems* 437.

⁷⁴ Jason honors Medea for a short time—and then he casts her aside to wed Creusa.

⁷⁵ Mainzer 21. Euripides and Sophocles both wrote plays entitled *Theseus*, and the Ariadne myth was available in numerous versions in prose and probably poetry also, although there is no way of knowing what sources Gower knew.

⁷⁶ Chaucer's sources for his Ariadne tale in the *Legend* may include Machaut's *Jugement dou Roy de Navarre*, 2741–69. See *The Riverside Chaucer* 981.

⁷⁷ Kelly argues that the use of the word "for" in the line "for he so faire tho behihte" (V.5383), "shows that his promise of marriage came before" they slept together (212).

78 In Medieval England, witnesses were necessary for clandestine marriages—private wedding ceremonies, secret or private—to be considered lawful. See Hornsby 58.

79 Chaucer's Narrator often interjects editorial comments, most notably in *Troilus and Criseyde*. Whether it is Chaucer's voice or the character of the Narrator speaking is a debatable subject, and not one for this paper. The topic of Gower's Genius as a character or as the poet's voice, is also a lively scholarly debate, which deserves further research.

80 In Gower Ariadne brings her Phaedra along on the journey for "For Sosterhode and compainie / Of love, which was hem betuene" (V.5398–99).

81 The MED defines "pallen" as "to impair, weaken, diminish," and refers to the passage I quote.

82 Dionysus does not rescue Ariadne in the *Heroides* or in the *Legend*.

83 In the Latin sidenote to the tale, Gower writes that the ungrateful Theseus promised marriage to Ariadne, but marries her sister Phaedra once he arrives in Athens. See Kelly 213.

84 Echard and Fanger 63.

85 In writing about the *Heroides*, Schmitz notes that from the point of view of women such as Ariadne, Penelope and Dido, "whose only claim to heroism is their involvement with a hero, these are phantom fields, subterfuges of sluggish or of faithless men" (Schmitz, *The Fall of Women* 24).

86 Burke, "Women" 239.

Notes to Chapter Four

1 Bland 289.
2 Wack, *Lovesickness in the Middle Ages* xiii.
3 Wack, *Lovesickness in the Middle Ages* xiii and 35.
4 Wack, *Lovesickness in the Middle Ages* 149.
5 Wack, "Lovesickness in Troilus," *Pacific Coast Philology* 19.1–2 (1984): 55.
6 Wack, "Lovesickness in Troilus" 56.

7 Heffernan, *The Melancholy Muse* 63. Heffernan suggests that Chaucer's portrayal of the lovesick Troilus "tempts one to think that Chaucer's knowledge may have included Galen or Constantine the African, Bernard of Gordon or Avicenna" (*The Melancholy Muse* 3).

8 Heffernan 63. In this connection she notes that Rossell Hope Robbins has demonstrated that "ten of Chaucer's authorities were among the 230 medical works in St. Augustine's Abbey at Canterbury" in the fourteenth century (*The Melancholy Muse* 63).

9 Heffernan 67.
10 Echard and Fanger 15.
11 See *Vox*, chapter 5.2 in which he describes the inconstancies of love.
12 Wack, *Lovesickness in the Middle Ages* 102.

13 Peter of Spain, *Questions on the Viaticum*, B., trans. Wack, *Lovesickness in the Middle Ages* 247. All quotations will be taken from this translation of Peter of Spain's work and will be indicated in the text by the abbreviation (Peter *Viaticum B*) and page number.

14 Wack, "The *Liber de heros morbo*" 328. All quotations will be taken from this translation of Johannes' work and will be indicated in the text by the abbreviation (Johannes *Liber*) and page number.

15 Wack writes that "the origins of and motives for that convergence remain obscure" (324). Wack, "The *Liber de heros morbo*" 324.

16 Jacquart and Thomasset 82–83.

17 Cadden, *Meanings of Sex Difference* 139.

18 Jacquart and Thomasset 83.

19 Jacquart and Thomasset 83.

20 Book I is also a departure from the *Mirour* and the *Vox*, works which treat similar material as does the Prologue to the *Confessio*.

21 Later in the poem Genius tells Amans that the "jolif wo" is strong enough to overcome wise Solomon, strong Sampson, the Knight David, Virgil, and even Aristotle, who "was put under" (CA VI.93–95,99).

22 MED, Vol. C 10. "Caitif" is defined as "1. A captive, prisoner; a slave; 2. A miserable or unfortunate person, a wretch." The editors cite Gower's *Confessio* I.171, in the second definition.

23 Nicholson, *Annotated Index* 11. See notes on the character Genius below.

24 Nicholson, *Annotated Index* 11. Genius sounds like a Christian priest, especially when he answers Amans' affirmatively when he asks whether or not killing infidels in the name of the Faith is murder (CA III.2490ff).

25 Genius can be a problematic figure because of this dual nature, and several scholars have focused upon Gower's Genius in recent years. See Economou, "The Character of Genius"; Baker; Wetherbee, "Genius and Interpretation"; Simpson 134–66; Schueler, "Gower's Characterization of Genius"; Minnis "'Moral Gower.'" As Nicholson points out in his *Annotated Index*, some scholars view Genius "as the poet's device to bridge different realms of value or the gap between the human and the divine," while others claim Genius' complexity make him "an effective spokesman for the multifacetedness of Gower's perspective on human love" (*Annotated Index* 11).

26 Bennett, *Selections* xviin.

27 Minnis, "'Moral Gower'" 61.

28 Minnis, "'Moral Gower'" 61.

29 Craun 116. See also Wetherbee, *John Gower* 600–01. Wetherbee notes that Genius "speaks directly to human lovers like an Ovidian *praeceptor amoris*, and participates in the impulses and aspirations of courtly poetry. He has, in short, become a spokesman for cultural, as well as natural, values; and while this greatly enhances his role as teacher, he also preserves the elusive status of the traditional Genius in his new cultural role" (*John Gower* 600–01).

30 See Economou, "The Character of Genius"; Baker; Wetherbee, "Genius"; Wetherbee, "John Gower"; Simpson; Schueler, "Gower's Characterization of Genius"; Craun; Peck, "Introduction," *John Gower Confessio Amantis, Volume 1*.

31 Gerard of Berry, *Glosses on the Viaticum*, trans. Wack, *Lovesickness in the Middle Ages* 203. All quotations are taken from this translation of Gerard of Berry's work will be indicated in the text by the abbreviation (Gerard *Glosses*) and page number.

32 Heffernan, *The Melancholy Muse* 45.

[33] Heffernan, *The Melancholy Muse* 44–55.
[34] Heffernan, *The Melancholy Muse* 45.
[35] Heffernan, *The Melancholy Muse* 45.

[36] The God of Sleep's house is situated with all the accoutrements needed for a good night's sleep, something Amans needs. Had Genius been interested in curing Amans of sleeplessness, all he had to do was to suggest the Lover try some of the sleeping cures found in Sleep's house, the birthplace of sleep, and no better place for a sleepless lover. Chaucer's Narrator in the *Book of the Duchess* is so delighted to read that there such is a god as the God of Sleep that he offers up a feather bed and a black and gold sleeping room as a sacrifice (BD 251–53). This offering must please the god, for the Narrator soon falls fast asleep and dreams his dream of the Black Knight who is grieving for his beloved, Fair White.

[37] Troilus worries that other lovers will deride him for joining the "daunce / of hem that Love list febly for to avaunce" (TC I.517–18).

[38] Danger typically guards the lady in medieval poetry, as he does in the *Roman*, a text from which Gower and Chaucer both borrowed liberally.

[39] Ovid, *Amores*, trans. and intro., Peter Green, *Ovid: The Erotic Poems: Amores, The Art of Love, Cures for Love, On Facial Treatment for Ladies* (London: Penguin Books, 1982) 106. All quotations will be taken from this translation of the *Amores* and will be indicated in the text by the abbreviation (Amores) and line number. All quotations will be taken from this translation of the *Remedia* and will be indicated in the text by siglum (RA) and line number.

[40]
>   Busie old foole, unruly Sunne,
>   Why dost thou thus,
>   Through windowes, and through curtaines call on us?
>   Must to thy motions lovers seasons run?
>   Sawcy pedantique wretch, goe chide
>   Late schoole boyes and sowre prentices,
>   Goe tell Court-huntsmen, that the King will ride,
>   Call countrey ants to harvest offices;
>   Love, all alike, no season knowes, nor clyme,
>   Nor houres, dayes, monoths, which are the rags of time.
>   (1–10)

John Donne, "The Sunne Rising," *The Complete English Poems of John Donne*, ed. C. A. Patrides (London and Melbourne: J. M. Dent and Sons, Ltd., 1985) 53–54.

[41] Wack, *Lovesickness in the Middle Ages* xii.

[42] Wack, *Lovesickness in the Middle Ages* 127. Wack writes that "evidence is lacking for this author's identity, career, and place of teaching," but notes that textual evidence possibly places him as "a Montpellier master who taught a course on the *Viaticum* sometime between 1300–1320," (*Lovesickness in the Middle Ages* 127).

[43] Wack, *Lovesickness in the Middle Ages* 255.

[44] Constantine the African, *Viaticum*, trans. Wack, *Lovesickness in the Middle Ages* 187. All quotations will be taken from this translation of the *Viaticum* and will be indicated in the text by abbreviation (*Viaticum*) and page number.

[45] Lowes 515.

⁴⁶ Heffernan, *The Melancholy Muse* 68.
⁴⁷ Heffernan, *The Melancholy Muse* 81.
⁴⁸ Wack, *Lovesickness in the Middle Ages* 61.
⁴⁹ Heffernan, *The Melancholy Muse* 79.
⁵⁰ MED, Vol. E-F 959.
⁵¹ Simpson 146.
⁵² Simpson writes that "solidarities between the lover and all with whom he consorts are dissolved in both texts" (Simpson 146).
⁵³ Yeager, "Allusion" 201. Yeager points out that "Gower is particularly skillful here in linking the sin of gluttonous intoxication with the "sin" of love-drunkenness" ("Allusion" 202). He also argues that Gower takes the allusion to drunkenness and subtly applies Christian overtones to it, thus underscoring his final message of proper living at the poem's end. He notes that the allusion is "relatively simple, employing as it does but a single sub-text," that of a Christian man needing to cleanse his soul by drinking Christ's blood (Yeager, "Allusion" 202, 205).
⁵⁴ Yeager applies an intriguing and engaging Christian meaning to his line by seeing a parallel between Amans' behavior and the Good Samaritan woman who misunderstands Christ's command that she drink from the well of everlasting life ("Allusion" 205). According to Yeager's reading, the well Amans seeks is the one where the Good Samaritan woman meets Christ. Christ tells her to drink from him and receive everlasting life, but she of course misunderstands. Amans' thirst for Love increases as he drinks more, and "his need for grace and for God's help to find peace," are all recognizable "against the understructure of Biblical allusion. Acting with it, they define the poetry's 'moral edge' quite clearly" (Yeager, "Allusion" 205). Yeager argues that Amans will die if he does not leave his foolish loving and remove himself from Venus's court to embrace Christ, the true source of Love.
⁵⁵ Macaulay notes that Gower assigns Cupid to the role of butler; in the *Roman* the butler is Fortune. See *English Works*, Vol.II 512.
⁵⁶ Heffernan, *The Melancholy Muse* 77-78.
⁵⁷ Wack, *Lovesickness in the Middle Ages* 66-67.
⁵⁸ Wack, *Lovesickness in the Middle Ages* 41.
⁵⁹ Wack, "Lovesickness in Troilus" 57.
⁶⁰ Jacquart and Thomasset 102.
⁶¹ Cadden, *Meanings of Sex Difference* 276-77.
⁶² The Church generally agreed that "chastity remained the preferred state" (McGlynn and Moll 104).
⁶³ The passage, translated by Cadden, states that "no one who does not have intercourse will be healthy" (*Meanings of Sex Difference* 273). Wack writes that this work describes the "circumstances in which intercourse is healthful or harmful and describes how it best may be accomplished" (Wack, *Lovesickness in the Middle Ages* 41).
⁶⁴ Cadden, *Meanings of Sex Difference* 273.
⁶⁵ Cadden, *Meanings of Sex Difference* 273.
⁶⁶ Wack, *Lovesickness in the Middle Ages* 68. See also Brundage. Brundage notes that by the middle of the thirteenth century, after over two hundred years of wrangling over

the issue, clerical celibacy remained a controversial matter, but married clergymen were rare (37).

[67] Jacquart and Thomasset 85.

[68] Wack, *Lovesickness in the Middle Ages* 68.

[69] Wack, "The *Liber de heros morbo*" 343.

[70] 'Troilus comes very close to "adopting Pandarus' attitude towards Criseyde, that is, viewing her primarily as a remedy for his lovesickness, [but] Troilus finally transcends a material view of love through memory, dematerializing it and transferring it to a realm beyond time and change" (Wack, "Lovesickness in Troilus" 59).

[71] Wack, *Lovesickness in the Middle Ages* 41.

[72] Giles, *Gloss on the Viaticum*, trans. Wack, *Lovesickness in the Middle Ages* 211.

[73] Peter of Spain, *Questions on the Viaticum*, A., trans. Wack, *Lovesickness in the Middle Ages* 225. All quotations will be taken from this translation of Peter of Spain's work and will be indicated in the text by abbreviation (Peter *Viaticum A*) and page number.

[74] In her recent work, Andrea Schutz writes on the mirror of self-awareness and Gower's theory of gaze. See Schutz.

[75] Cadden, "Western Medicine" 65.

[76] Heffernan, *The Melancholy Muse* 60.

[77] Heffernan, *The Melancholy Muse* 56–65. Whereas Heffernan characterizes Chaucer's Narrator as tactfully eavesdropping upon the Black Knight's complaint, in the *Confessio* it is the reader who eavesdrops upon Amans' complaints.

[78] In the introduction to Volume 1 of the *Confessio*, Peck notes that Amans "is not an adept reader any more than he is an adept listener. The tales provide him with information, but, given his preoccupation, their significance often passes him by. Like all readers, he is obliged to be inventive—to find a personal means of framing the ideas of the tales within his unique consciousness" (Peck, *Confessio Amantis Volume 1*, 8).

[79] Simpson 135.

[80] Peck, introduction, *Confessio Amantis* xvi.

[81] Peck, *Confessio Amantis* 520.

[82] Bland considers this "one of the most surprising denouements in medieval literature" (289). Burrow points out that "our sense of the folly of his love is moderated by the fact that for the greater part of the poem we have seen the affair from his own point of view—which excludes, of course naturally enough, the fact of his age" (15). Simpson argues that the ultimate deception in both Gower and Ovid's *Amores* is the one the Lovers practice "not only against others, but more especially against themselves: . . . we are only gradually made to realize that the lover is impotent" in both works (Simpson 146). Simpson's work devotes a portion of his chapter entitled "Ovidian disunity in Gower's *Confessio Amantis*" to the similarities between the *Amores* and the *Confessio* (134–166). Bennett agrees that the lover's age is a surprise, but suggests that if the reader keeps the meaning of the name Genius in mind, that of a sponsor of reproduction, one can recognize "why the priest's attitude towards Amans' chances of personal success in his love-affair is throughout so non-committal. Being face to face with his penitent Genius knows from the outset what we as readers sense but slowly and do not clearly learn until the denouement—that Amans is being shadowed by Elde" (Bennett,

"Gower's 'Honeste Love'" 59). Schueler, on the other hand, argues that the Lover's age is expressed explicitly and implicitly throughout the *Confessio*, not just at its conclusion. Schueler points out that Amans refers to himself as no longer youthful several times in the poem: in VI.1365–69, Amans says "in my lusti youth," and earlier in Book I, when he says "in my youth" (I.730), pointing to the fact that he is no longer young (Schueler 153).

83 As Olsson notes, "with the lover's discovery and admission that he is old comes a sense of possible wholeness and redemption." Olsson, "Love, Intimacy," 95.

84 McCarthy 486.

85 Macaulay, *English Works*, Vol.II, sidenote 453.

86 Macaulay, *English Works*, Vol.II 547.

87 Macaulay wonders if Thisbe is still "unable to pardon ... [Pyramus'] lateness" (*English Works*, Vol.II 547).

88 Genius is, perhaps, partly to blame for this hope, for he has sustained Amans' delusion by holding out the possibility of love to him by telling him such tales as the Tale of Pygmalion, a story of a man who is granted love against incredible and unbelievable odds.

89 Gower recognizes his true self in the mirror. See Schmitz, "Rhetoric and Fiction" 121. See also Schutz.

90 Similarly, the Black Knight in the *Book of the Duchess* is also given the chance to reflect before he is brought back into the world of the present. Once the Black Knight states that his lady is dead, he is able to re-enter the real world. See Heffernan, *The Melancholy Muse* 58.

91 Gower suggests that man blindly accepts love—he cannot fight it—but when he calls his wits home and is thus cured of his desire, he is unable to recognize love.

Notes to the Conclusion

1 Simpson 164.

2 In the Tale of Rosiphelee, one of Gower's most beautiful tales, the Armenian princess Rosiphelee overcomes her slothfulness towards and unwillingness to love by using her reasoning capabilities.

3 McCarthy 494. McCarthy writes that "Augustine's formulation of the three goods of marriage, '*fides, proles et sacramentum*,' was enormously influential: authoritative legal and theological texts such as Gratian's *Decretum* and Peter Lombard's *Sentences* quote Augustine's assertation that these three goods were present in the marriage of Christ's parents. In Augustine's formulation, however, *sacramentum* refers not to the conferring of grace, but to indissolubility" (McCarthy 494).

4 St. Augustine, "Sermo LI: Advent; Matrimonial Agreements and Arrangements, *Sermons to the People: Advent, Christmas, New Year's, Epiphany*, trans. and ed. William Griffin (New York: Doubleday, 2002) 33. Augustine cites St. Paul as his authority, in his First to the Corinthians: 'I say this with compassion, not with command, in my voice'" (7:6).

5 McCarthy 494. See also Goody.

⁶ Hornsby 58. The word "clandestine" was used whether or not the marriage was contracted in secret. Christopher Brooke asserts that in Medieval England there was often great confusion as to whether or not a couple who had had a clandestine marriage were legally married. Brooke 252. Hornsby points out that English ecclesiastical courts dealt with espousal and marriage agreements, and quite often the disputes centered upon "the validity of an existent but secretly formed marriage" (56). Hornsby notes that the courts' jurisdiction focused upon the agreement itself: "the fact that promises to marry now or in the future had been exchanged, rather than just that pledges of faith or oaths had been given to secure the promises" (56).

⁷ Hornsby 58. Although the clandestine marriages were considered legitimate, Hornsby notes that "those who chose to . . . [marry] in this fashion were assigned penance and threatened with excommunication if the marriage was not sanctified by church ritual" (58).

⁸ Jean LeClercq translates a twelfth-century text by Robert of Melun as stating: "Union in the flesh between a man and a woman would be a sin were they not married" (LeClercq 21).

⁹ McCarthy states that in the *Confessio* "even marital intercourse is presented as something potentially sinful," but I disagree with this statement (494). Gower presents several happily married couples enjoyed a healthy sex life: all Four Wives and their husbands, and Jason and Medea.

¹⁰ Ames 58–59.

¹¹ Ames 58–59.

¹² Aquinas does concede that it was good that God made woman from man "in order to make the man love the woman more and stick to her more inseparably, knowing that she had been brought forth from himself" (ST Q.92.2.3).

¹³ Eberle 117. Eberle writes on the ascending and descending views of authority which are applicable to Richard II and the Wonderful Parliament of 1386, but some of her comments center upon the issue of authority in the *Confessio*. In some versions of the *Confessio* Gower dedicates the poem to Henry Lancaster, the future king. See also Fisher, "John Gower," and notes below on Fisher.

¹⁴ Burke, "Sources and Significance" 14.

¹⁵ I am thinking of Medea's Tale and the Tale of Deianira, but also of The Tale of Philomela.

¹⁶ In the *Confessio* Deianira and Medea (and Progne) manage to avenge—and remain unpunished.

¹⁷ Esch argues and I agree that "in the final analysis, the breakdown of love is only a symptom of the deeper *discordia* of a world threatened with dissension and anarchy, and is thus a variation on a basic theme of Gower's writing" (Esch 95).

¹⁸ In Book I of the *Vox* Gower likens the rioting peasants to animals.

¹⁹ Although Macaulay concluded that Gower could not have been a lawyer, due to the vicious attacks he makes upon lawyers in the *Mirour* (MO 24535, 24584, 24592, 24940), Fisher argues that by Gower's "own statement it would appear that he held some legal or civil office" (Fisher, *John Gower* 55). Also, "the data in hand are sufficient to indicate that Gower had some sort of legal connection" (Fisher, *John Gower* 58; see 45–58). See also Wetherbee, "John Gower" (589–590).

²⁰ Venus guides the lover back to his senses with reason's help: it is unusual that she works in conjunction with reason.

²¹ Benson writes that when Amans realizes he is too old for passionate emotions, he abandons them, but there is more to it than that, as I state in the text (Benson 108). See also Olsson and Yeager, who provide insight into the ending of the poem (Olsson, *Structures of Conversion* 34–37; Yeager, *Arion* 275–79).

²² Olsson, *Structures of Conversion* 34.

²³ Anne died in 1394, and Richard married Isabella in March 1396.

²⁴ There are three versions of the *Confessio*, but Fisher notes that in 11 of the 49 extant MS, and in presumably another twenty MS, the poem is attributed "to the meeting with Richard" (Fisher 116). Gower revised the Prologue after 1392, ("in the winter after Richard's [1392] quarrel with the Londoners" (Fisher 123). When Henry returned to London in the summer of 1393 Gower presented him with a revised copy of the *Confessio* which contained a new dedication (Fisher 123). "The new dedication cannot in itself be considered an act of disloyalty to Richard since Henry had shared with Richard the dedication of the first version by being named in the explicit of at least eight manuscripts" (Fisher 123). Double dedications are not "uncommon in literary history," but this one, Fisher contends, is notable because Henry succeeded to Richard's throne and thus "the partisan emotions surrounding the deposition of Richard" has brought the double dedication into question (Fisher 123).

²⁵ Yeager asserts that it matters not if the advice is for Richard II, the Estates, or Henry IV, "the salient point . . . [is that] no harmony might be achieved without the king's enlightenment," for he is the "head and 'reason' of the body politic" in the Middle Ages (Yeager, *Arion* 267).

Bibliography

Primary Sources

Alan of Lille. *The Plaint of Nature (De Planctu Naturae)*. Trans. James J. Sheridan. Toronto: Pontifical Institute of Mediaeval Studies, 1980.

———. *Anticlaudianus*. Trans. James J. Sheridan. Toronto: Pontifical Institute of Mediaeval Studies, 1973.

Aquinas, St. Thomas. *Summa Theologiæ*, 61 vols. London and New York: Blackfriars and McGraw Hill Book Company, 1964.

Augustine, St. *Concerning the City of God against the Pagans*. Trans. Henry Bettenson. London: Penguin Books, 1972.

———. "Sermo LI: Advent; Matrimonial Agreements and Arrangements." *Sermons to the People: Advent, Christmas, New Year's, Epiphany*. Trans. and ed. William Griffin. New York: Doubleday, 2002.

Bernardus Silvestris. *The Cosmographia of Bernardus Silvestris*. Trans. Winthrop Wetherbee. New York and London: Columbia UP, 1973. 1–62.

Boethius, Anicius Manlius Severinus. *The Consolation of Philosophy*. Trans. V. E. Watts. London: Penguin Books, 1969.

Chaucer, Geoffrey. *The Riverside Chaucer*. Ed. Larry Benson. 3rd. ed. Boston: Houghton Mifflin Company, 1987.

delle Colonne, Guido. *Historia Destructionis Troiae*. Trans. Mary Elizabeth Meek. Bloomington, IN: Indiana UP, 1974.

Donne, John. "The Sunne Rising." In *The Complete English Poems of John Donne*. Ed. C. A. Patrides. London and Melbourne: J. M. Dent and Sons, Ltd., 1985. 53–54.

Gawain Poet. *Sir Gawain and the Green Knight*. Trans. and ed. William Vantuono. Notre Dame, IN: University of Notre Dame Press, 1999.

Geoffrey of Vinsauf. *Poetria Nova*. Trans. Margaret F. Nims. Toronto: Pontifical Institute of Mediaeval Studies, 1967.

Gower, John. *The Complete Works of John Gower*, 4 vols. Ed. G. C. Macaulay. Oxford: Clarendon Press, 1901.

———. *The English Works of John Gower*, 2 vols. Ed. G. C. Macaulay. Oxford: Early English Text Society and Oxford UP, 1900; 1957, 1969, 1979.

———. *Confessio Amantis*. Trans. Terence Tiller. Baltimore: Penguin Books, 1963.

———. *Vox Clamantis. Major Latin Works of John Gower*. Ed. Eric W. Stockton. Seattle: U of Washington P, 1962. 3–289.

———. *Confessio Amantis*. Ed. Russell A. Peck. New York: Medieval Academy of America, 1980.

———. *Mirour de l'Omme*. Trans. William Burton Wilson. East Lansing: Colleague's Press, 1992.

———. *Confessio Amantis*. Ed. Russell A. Peck. 1980 Toronto: U of Toronto P, 1994.

———. *John Gower Confessio Amantis, Volume I*. Ed. Russell A. Peck. Trans. Andrew Galloway. Kalamazoo, MI: Medieval Institute, The Consortium for the Teaching of the Middles Ages, 2000.

de Lorris, Guillaume and Jean de Meun. *The Romance of the Rose*. 3rd ed. Trans. Charles Dahlberg. Princeton: Princeton UP, 1971.

———. *The Romance of the Rose by Guillaume de Lorris and Jean de Meun*. Trans. Harry W. Robbins. New York: E. P. Dutton and Company, 1962.

Ovid. *The Metamorphoses of Ovid*. Trans. Mary M. Innes. London: Penguin Books, 1955.

———. *Heroides*. Trans. Harold Isbell. London: Penguin Books, 1990.

———. *Ovid's Fasti: Roman Holidays*. Trans. and ed. Betty Rose Nagle. Bloomington: Indiana UP, 1995.

———. *Ovid: The Erotic Poems: Amores, The Art of Love, Cures for Love, On Facial Treatment for Ladies*. Trans. Peter Green. London: Penguin Books, 1982.

———. *Ovid, Fasti*. Trans. James George Frazer, ed. G. P. Goold. Cambridge: Harvard UP, 1989.

St. Thomas Aquinas, *Summa Theologiæ*. Ed. and trans. Thomas Gilby, O.P., Vol. 28. London and New York: Blackfriars and McGraw Hill Book Company, 1964.

Virgil, *The Aeneid*. Trans. Rolfe Humphries. New York: Charles Scribner and Sons, 1951.

Secondary Sources

Ames, Ruth. "The Feminist Connection of Chaucer's LGW." In *Chaucer in the Eighties*, eds. Julian N. Wasserman and Robert J. Blanch. Syracuse: Syracuse UP, 1986. 57–74.

Baker, Denise. "The Priesthood of Genius: A Study of the Medieval Tradition." *Speculum* 44 (1969): 568–584.

Bennett, J. A. W. "Gower's 'Honeste Love.'" In *Gower's "Confessio Amantis": A Critical Anthology*, ed. Peter Nicholson. Cambridge: D. S. Brewer, 1991. 49–61.

———. Ed. and intro. *Selections from John Gower.* Oxford: Clarendon Press, 1968.
———. *Middle English Literature. The Oxford History of English Literature.* Vol. I, part II. Ed. and compiled by Douglas Grey. Oxford: Clarendon Press, 1986. 407–429.
Benson, C. David. "Incest and Moral Poetry in Gower's *Confessio Amantis.*" *The Chaucer Review* 19.2 (1984): 100–108.
Bland, D. S. "The Poetry of John Gower." *English* 6–7 (1947–48): 286–290.
Brooke, Christopher N. L. *The Medieval Idea of Marriage.* Oxford: Oxford UP, 1989.
Brundage, James A. "Sex and Canon Law." In *Handbook of Medieval Sexuality,* eds. Vern L. Bullough and James A. Brundage. New York and London: Garland Publishing, Inc., 1996. 33–50.
Burke, Linda Barney. "Women in John Gower's 'Confessio Amantis.'" *Mediævalia* 3 (1977): 239–259.
———. "Sources and Significance of the Tale of King, Wine, Women, and Truth." *Greyfriar* 21 (1980): 3–15.
Burrow, John Anthony. "The Portrayal of Amans in Confessio Amantis." In *Gower's Confessio Amantis: Responses and Reassessments,* ed. A. J. Minnis. Cambridge: D. S. Brewer, 1983. 5–24.
Cadden, Joan. *Meanings of Sex Difference in the Middle Ages: Medicine, Science, and Culture.* Cambridge: Cambridge UP, 1993.
———. "Western Medicine and Natural Philosophy." In *Handbook of Medieval Sexuality,* eds. Vern L. Bullough and James A. Brundage. New York and London: Garland Publishing, Inc., 1996. 51–80.
Chance, Jane. *The Mythographic Chaucer: The Fabulation of Sexual Politics.* Minneapolis, MN: U of Minneapolis P, 1995.
Collins, Marie. "Love, Nature, and Law in the Poetry of Gower and Chaucer." In *Court and Poet: Selected Proceedings of the Third Congress of the International Courtly Literature Society,* ed. Glyn S. Burgess. Liverpool: ARCA, 1980. 113–128.
Craun, Edwin D. *Lies, Slander, and Obscenity in Medieval English Literature: Pastoral Rhetoric and the Deviant Speaker.* Cambridge: Cambridge UP 1997. 113–156.
Curry, Walter Clyde. *The Middle English Ideal of Personal Beauty as Found in the Metrical Romances, Chronicles, and Legends of the Thirteenth, Fourteenth, and Fifteenth Centuries.* Baltimore: J. H. Furst Company, 1916.
Delany, Sheila. *The Naked Text: Chaucer's Legend of Good Women.* Berkeley: U of California P, 1994. 202–208.
Desmond, Marilynn. *Reading Dido: Gender, Textuality, and the Medieval Aeneid.* Minneapolis and London: U of Minnesota P, 1994.
Dinshaw, Carolyn. *Chaucer's Sexual Politics.* Madison: U of Wisconsin P, 1989. 3–27; 65–87.
Donaldson, Ian. *The Rapes of Lucretia: A Myth and Its Transformations.* Oxford: Clarendon Press, 1982.

Doob, Penelope Reed. *Nebuchadnezzar's Children: Conventions of Madness in Middle English Literature*. New Haven, CT, and London: Yale UP, 1974.

Eberle, Patricia J. "The Question of Authority and The Man of Law's Tale." In *The Centre and Its Compass: Studies in Medieval Literature in Honor of Professor John Leyerle*. Kalamazoo: Medieval Institute Publications and Western Michigan UP, 1993. 111–127.

Echard, Sian, and Clare Fanger. *The Latin Verses in the "Confessio Amantis": An Annotated Translation*. East Lansing: Colleagues Press, 1991.

Economou, George D. *The Goddess Natura in Medieval Literature*. Cambridge: Harvard UP, 1972.

———. "The Character of Genius in Alan de Lille, Jean de Meun, and John Gower." In *Gower's Confessio Amantis: A Critical Anthology*, ed. Peter Nicholson. Cambridge: D. S. Brewer, 1991. 109–116.

Esch, Arno. "John Gower's Narrative Art." In *Gower's Confessio Amantis: A Critical Anthology*, ed. Peter Nicholson. Trans. Linda Barney Burke. Cambridge: D. S. Brewer, 1991. 81–108.

Fisher, John H. *John Gower: Moral Philosopher and Friend of Gower*. New York: New York UP, 1964.

Frank, Robert Worth, Jr. *Chaucer and* The Legend of Good Women. Cambridge, MA: Harvard UP, 1972.

Gaston, John B. "The Tale of Ceyx and Alceone." In *John Gower's Literary Transformations in the* Confessio Amantis, ed. Peter Beidler. Washington, DC: UP of America 1982. 41–43.

Goody, Jack. *The Development of the Family and Marriage in Europe*. Cambridge: Cambridge UP, 1983.

Gravdal, Kathryn. *Ravishing Maidens: Writing Rape in Medieval French Literature and Law*. Philadelphia: U of Pennsylvania P, 1991.

Green, Richard Firth. "Chaucer's Victimized Women." *Studies in the Age of Chaucer* 10 (1988): 3–21.

Grinnell, Natalie. "Medea's Humanity and John Gower's Romance." *Medieval Perspective* 14 (1999): 70–83.

Hanrahan, Michael. "'Legend of Good Women,' Gower's 'Confessio Amantis,' and Usk's 'Testament of Love.'" Diss. Indiana University, 1995.

Hansen, Elaine Tuttle. "Irony and the Antifeminist Narrator in Chaucer's *Legend of Good Women*." *Journal of English and Germanic Philology* 82 (1983) 11–31.

Harbert, Bruce. "Lessons from the Great Clerk: Ovid and John Gower." In *Ovid Renewed: Ovidian Influences on Literature and Art from the Middle Ages to the Twentieth Century*, ed. Charles Martindale. Cambridge: Cambridge UP, 1988. 83–97.

Heffernan, Carol F. "Chaucer's 'Troilus and Criseyde': The Disease of Love and Courtly Love." *Neophilologus*. 74:2 (1990) 294–309.

———. *The Melancholy Muse: Chaucer, Shakespeare, and Early Medicine*. Pittsburgh: Duquesne UP, 1995.

Hillman, Richard. "Gower's Lucrece: A New Old Source for The Rape of Lucrece." *The Chaucer Review* 24.3 (1990): 263–70.

Hornsby, Joseph Allen. *Chaucer and the Law.* Norman, OK: Pilgrim Books, 1988. 52–68.

Hotchkiss, Valerie R. "Gender Transgression and the Abandoned Wife in Medieval Literature." In *Gender Rhetorics: Postures of Dominance and Submission in History*, ed. Richard C. Trexler. Binghamton, NY: Center for Medieval and Renaissance Texts and Studies, 1994. 207–218.

Hussey, S. S. *Chaucer: An Introduction.* London: Methuen and Co., Ltd, 1971. 195–222.

Isbell, Harold, trans. and ed. *Heroides.* London: Penguin Books, 1990.

Jacobson, Howard. *Ovid's Heroides.* Princeton: Princeton UP, 1974.

Jacquart, Danielle and Claude Thomasset. *Sexuality and Medicine in the Middle Ages.* Trans. Matthew Adamson. Princeton: Princeton UP, 1988.

Kelly, Henry Ansgar. *Love and Marriage in the Age of Chaucer.* Ithaca: Cornell UP, 1975.

Kiser, Lisa J. *Telling Classical Tales.* Ithaca: Cornell UP, 1983. 95–98.

Kolve, V. A. "From Cleopatra to Alceste: An Iconographic Study of the *Legend of Good Women.*" In *Signs and Symbols in Chaucer's Poetry*, eds. John P. Hermann and John J. Burke. University, AL: U of Alabama P, 1981. 130–178.

LeClercq, Jean. *Monks on Marriage: A Twelfth-Century View.* New York: Seabury Press, 1982.

Lewis, C. S. "Gower." In *Gower's Confessio Amantis: A Critical Anthology*, ed. Peter Nicholson. Cambridge: D. S. Brewer, 1991. 15–39.

Middle English Dictionary. Gen. ed. Robert E. Lewis. Ann Arbor: U of Michigan P, 1952–1996.

Lord, Mary Louise. "Dido as an Example of Chastity: The Influence of Example Literature." *Harvard Library Bulletin* 17.2 (1969): 216–232.

Lowes, John Livingston. "The Loveres Maladye of Hereos." *Modern Philology* 11 (1914): 491–546.

Luscombe, D. E. "Natural Morality and Natural Law." In *Cambridge History of Later Medieval Philosophy: From the Rediscovery of Aristotle to the Disintegration of Scholasticism, 1100–1600*, eds. Norman Kretzman, Anthony Kenny, and Jan Pinborg. Cambridge: Cambridge UP, 1982. 705–719.

Mainzer, Conrad. "Gower's Use of the Mediaeval Ovid." *Medium Ævum* 41 (1972): 215–229.

Mast, Isabelle. "Rape in John Gower's *Confessio Amantis* and Other Related Works." In *Young Medieval Women*, eds. Katherine J. Lewis, Noel James Menuge, and Kim M. Phillips. New York: St. Martin's Press, 1999. 103–132.

Mann, Jill. *Geoffrey Chaucer.* Atlantic Highlands, NJ: Humanities Press International Inc., 1991.

McCarthy, Conor. "Love and Marriage in the *Confessio Amantis.*" *Neophilologus* 84 (2000): 485–499.

McGlynn, Margaret and Richard J. Moll. "Chaste Marriage in the Middle Ages: 'It were to hire a greet merite.'" In *Handbook of Medieval Sexuality*, eds. Vern L. Bullough and James A. Brundage. New York and London: Garland Publishing, Inc., 1996. 103–122.

McMillan, Ann, trans. and introduction. *The Legend of Good Women by Geoffrey Chaucer.* Houston: Rice UP, 1987.

Minnis, A. J. "John Gower, *Sapiens* in Ethics and Politics." *Medium Ævum* 49.2 (1980): 207–29.

———. Ed. *Gower's Confessio Amantis: Responses and Reassessments.* Cambridge: D. S. Brewer, 1983.

———. "'Moral Gower' and Medieval Literary Theory." *Gower's* Confessio Amantis*: Responses and Reassessments.* Ed. A. J. Minnis. Cambridge: D. S. Brewer, 1983. 50–78

———. *Oxford Guides to Chaucer: The Shorter Poems.* Oxford: Clarendon Press, 1995. 322–443.

Morse, Ruth. *The Medieval Medea.* Cambridge: D. S. Brewer, 1996.

Nicholson, Peter. *An Annotated Index to the Commentary on Gower's* Confessio Amantis. Binghamton: Medieval and Renaissance Texts and Studies, 1989.

———. *Gower's "Confessio Amantis": A Critical Anthology.* Cambridge: D. S. Brewer, 1991.

Olsson, Kurt. "Natural Law and John Gower's 'Confessio Amantis.'" *Medievalia et Humanistica* 11(1977): 229–61.

———. *John Gower and the Structures of Conversion: A Reading of the* Confessio Amantis. Cambridge: D. S. Brewer, 1992.

———. "Love, Intimacy and Gower." *The Chaucer Review* 30.1 (1995): 71–100.

Orr, Patricia. "Men's Theory and Women's Reality: Rape Prosecutions in the English Royal Courts of Justice, 1194–1222." In *The Rusted Hauberk: Feudal Ideals of Order and Their Decline.* Gainesville: UP of Florida, 1994. 121–61.

Overbeck, Pat Trefzger. "Chaucer's Good Women." *The Chaucer Review* 2.1 (1967): 75–94.

The Oxford English Dictionary, eds. J. A. Simpson and E. S. C. Weiner. Oxford: Clarendon Press, 1989.

Pearsall, Derek. "Gower's Narrative Art." In *Gower's* Confessio Amantis*: A Critical Anthology*, ed. Peter Nicholson. Cambridge: D. S. Brewer, 1991. 62–80.

———. *The Life of Geoffrey Chaucer: A Critical Biography.* Oxford: Blackwell, 1992.

Peck, Russell A. *Kingship and Common Profit in Gower's "Confessio Amantis."* Carbondale, IL: Southern Illinois UP, 1978.

———. Introduction. *Confessio Amantis.* By John Gower. New York: Medieval Academy of America, 1980.

———, ed. *John Gower: Confessio Amantis, Volume 1.* Latin translations by Andrew Galloway. Kalamazoo, Michigan: Medieval Institute Publications, 2000.

Pickles, J. D. and J. L. Dawson, eds. *A Concordance to John Gower's "Confessio Amantis."* Woodbridge, Suffolk: D. S. Brewer, 1987.

Power, Eileen. *Medieval Woman.* Ed. M. M. Postan. Cambridge: Cambridge UP, 1975.

Ricks, Christopher. "Metamorphosis in Other Words." In *Gower's* Confessio Amantis: *Responses and Reassessments,* ed. A. J. Minnis. Cambridge: D. S. Brewer, 1983. 25–49.

Rowe, Donald W. "Reson in Jean's Roman de la Rose: Modes of Characterization and Dimensions of Meaning." *Mediævalia* 10 (1984): 97–126.

Runacres, Charles. "Art and Ethics in the Exempla of *Confessio Amantis.*" In *Gower's* Confessio Amantis: *Responses and Reassessments,* ed. A. J. Minnis. Cambridge: D. S. Brewer, 1983. 106–134.

Rytting, Jenny Rebecca. "In Search of the Perfect Spouse: John Gower's *Confessio Amantis* as a Marriage Manual." *Dalhousie Review* 82.1 (2002): 113–126.

Schmitz, Gotz. "Gower, Chaucer, and the Classics: Back to the Textual Evidence." In *John Gower: Recent Readings,* ed. R. F. Yeager. Kalamazoo: Medieval Institute Publication, 1989. 21–38.

———. *The Fall of Women in Early English Narrative Verse.* Cambridge: Cambridge UP, 1990.

———. "Rhetoric and Fiction: Gower's Comments on Eloquence and Courtly Poetry." In *Gower's* Confessio Amantis: *A Critical Anthology,* ed. Peter Nicholson. Cambridge: D. S. Brewer, 1991. 117–142.

Schueler, Donald. "The Age of the Lover in Gower's *Confessio Amantis.*" *Medium Ævum* 36.2 (1967): 152–158.

———. "Gower's Characterization of Genius in the *Confessio Amantis.*" *Modern Language Quarterly* 33 (1972): 240–56.

Schutz, Andrea. "Absent and Present Images: Mirrors and Mirroring in John Gower's *Confessio Amantis.*" *Chaucer Review* 34:1 (1999): 107–124.

Simpson, James. *Sciences and the Self in Medieval Poetry: Alan of Lille's Anticlaudianus and John Gower's Confessio Amantis.* Cambridge: Cambridge UP, 1995.

Stanford, W. B. *The Ulysses Theme: A Study in the Adaptability of a Traditional Hero.* Oxford: Basil Blackwell, 1963. 43–65.

Stillwell, Gardiner. "John Gower and the Last Years of Edward III." *Studies in Philology* 45 (1948): 454–71.

Stockton, Eric W. *The Major Latin Works of John Gower: The Voice of One Crying and The Tripartite Chronicle, An Annotated Translation into English with an Introductory Essay on the Author's Non-English Works.* Seattle: U of Washington P, 1962.

Sylvester, Louise. "Reading Narratives of Rape: The Story of Lucretia in Chaucer, Gower, and Christine de Pizan." *Leeds Studies in English* 31 (2000): 115–141.

Thomson, Ian, and Louis Perraud, eds. and trans. *Pyramus and Thisbe, Ten Latin Schooltexts of the Later Middle Ages: Translated Selections.* Lewiston, NY: The Edwin Mellen Press, 1990. 219–20.

Wack, Mary F. "Lovesickness in Troilus." *Pacific Coast Philology* 19.1–2 (1984): 55–61.

———. "The *Liber de heros morbo* of Johannes Afflacius and Its Implications for Medieval Love Conventions." *Speculum* 62.2 (1987): 324–344.

———. *Lovesickness in the Middle Ages: The Viaticum and Its Commentaries.* Philadelphia: U of Pennsylvania P, 1990.

Watt, Diane. "Sins of Omission: Transgressive Genders, Subversive Sexualities, and Confessional Silences in John Gower's *Confessio Amantis.*" *Exemplaria* 13 (2001): 529–551.

Wetherbee, Winthrop. *Platonism and Poetry in the Twelfth Century: The Literary Influence of the School of Chartres.* Princeton: Princeton UP, 1972.

———, trans. and introd. *The Cosmographia of Bernardus Silvestris.* New York and London: Columbia UP, 1973. 1–62.

———. "Genius and Interpretation in the *Confessio Amantis.*" In *Magister Regis: Studies in Honor of Robert Earl Kaske*, ed. Arthur Gross et al. New York: Fordham UP, 1986. 241–60.

———. "John Gower." *The Cambridge History of Medieval English Literature*, ed. David Wallace. Cambridge: Cambridge UP, 1999. 589–609.

White, Hugh. "Nature and the Good in Gower's *Confessio Amantis.*" In *John Gower: Recent Readings*, ed. R. F. Yeager. Kalamazoo: Medieval Institute Publications, 1989. 1–20.

Yeager, Robert F. *John Gower Materials: A Bibliography Through 1979.* Garland Publishing, Inc., New York, 1981.

———. "John Gower and the Uses of Allusion." *Res Publica Litterarum* 7 (1984): 201–13.

———. ed. *John Gower: Recent Readings.* Kalamazoo: Medieval Institute Publications, 1989.

———. *John Gower's Poetic: The Search For a New Arion.* Cambridge: D. S. Brewer, 1990.

———, Mark West, and Robin L. Hinson, eds. *A Concordance to the French Poetry and Prose of John Gower.* East Lansing: Michigan State UP, 1997.

———, ed. *Re-Visioning Gower.* Asheville, NC: Pegasus Press, 1998.

Index

Abandonment, in Tale of Ariadne, 116–17
Abstinence, 141
Aeneas, as faithless, 100
Alan of Lille, DP, 3–12, 3n, 5n, 6n, 19, 19n
Alceone
    Chaucer, 47–48
    Ovid, 46–47
    loss of reason in, 50
    Tale of, 45–52
    sources for Gower, 45, 45n
Alcestis
    Chaucer's Troilus and, 56n
    Chaucer, 52n
    Medea, 100
    self-sacrifice and Christ, 57
    sources for Gower, 52, 52n
    Virgin Mary, 57
Amans
    age 147n, 147–148, 150–151, 150n, 151n, 158
    confession, 146
    cured of lovesickness, 151n
    parallels to lover in *Amores*, 137
    selfish love, 151n
Ames, Ruth, 156n
Amor hereos, 123
Anti-feminism (see also Women, Gower's treatment of)
    ST, 156
    lack of in CA, 153, 155–156
Ariadne
    beautiful, 114
    Dionysus, 118n
    Heriodes 121n
    Medea, 119
    Phaedra, 11, 119n
    sources for Gower, 113, 113n
    Tale of 113–120
Armenian princess (Rosiphelee), 154n
Augustine, Saint, 12, 68n, 71n, 154, 154n

Baker, Denise, 129n, 130n
Bennett, J. A. W., xviiin, 8n, 21n, 27n, 34n, 36n, 45n, 73n, 106n, 112n, 129, 129n, 147n
Benoit de Sainte-Maure, 20, 26, 86n, 91n
Benson, Larry, xviiin, 158n
Bernard Silvestris, 3–12, 3n, 21n
Bestial imagery
    rape, 64
    LGW, 64
    MO
    Tale of Ariadne, 116
    Tale of Lucrece, 63–64
    Tale of Philomela, 63
    VC, 157n
Bland, D. S., 65n, 69n, 124n, 147n
Blasphemy in medieval literature, 25–26, 25n, 72n
Boccaccio, 20, 20n, 52n, 58n, 100
Burke, Linda Barney, xviiin, xixn, 52n, 53n, 54n, 55n, 57n, 85n, 91n, 121, 121n, 157n

Burrow, J. A., xixn, 52n
Brundage, James A., 141n

Cadden, Joan, xixn, 77n, 127n, 141n, 144n
Cephalus and Aurora, 132–33
Chance, Jane, 26n
Chaperone (or go-between), 91n
Chaucer, Geoffrey (see individual tales)
    Black Knight, 104n, 125n, 131n, 150n
    Cecily Champain, 71n
    Constantine the African, 125n
    BD, 36
    Dreamer in BD, 104n
    FranT, 18n, 36
    irony, 70n
    LGW, 3n, 20, 20n, 36
    MLT, 36
    MerT, 21
    Narrator, 115n
    TC, 36
    Wife of Bath's Tale, 18n
    Virtuous wives (Lucrece and Penelope), 47n
Christ/Christian, 34n, 57n, 138n
Christine de Pizan, 11n, 64
Cicero, 4, 15
Clarissa, 65n
Clerical celibacy, 141n
Collins, Marie, xviin
Company of Lovers, 33, 78
    Four Wives, 148–150
Confessio Amantis
    advice to King, 158–59, 159n
    Amans' age, 147n
    double dedications, 159n
    end as surprise, 147n
    three versions, 159n
Confession, Amans', as frame of CA, 123–24, 129–130, 146
Constantine the African, 124, 125n, *eros*, 134–35
Contraries of love (oxymorons), 1, 10, 125
Craun, Edwin, xixn, 129n, 130n
Criseyde, as independent woman, 39
Cupid
    arrow, dart, 38, 62, 102
    CA, 128, 139, 150
    Tale of Thisbe 21

Curry, Walter Clyde, 61n, 106n

Dares Phryguis and Dictys Cretensis, 20, 100
Deadly Sin
    Avantance, boasting, in Tale of Rosemund, 12–13
    Avarice in Tale of Medea, 93, 97, 113
    Covoitisel covetousness, greed in Tale of Medea, 85
    Envy, damaging Reason, 84–85
    Hyprocrisy
        Tale of Deianira, 80–82
        VC, 82
    Falssemblant, in Tale of Deianira, 80–83, 83n
    Forgetfulness
        Amans, 105–06, 111
        CA, 105
        Tale of Phyllis, 105
    Gluttony (and Drunkenness), 137–138
    Hyprocrisy
        Tale of Deianira, 80–82
        Forsaken Women's lovers, 82
        MO, 82, 102
    Ingratitude (*unkindeschipe*), 118
        MO, 95, 116–119
        Tale of Ariadne, 95, 113, 119, 119n
        Tale of Medea, 95
    Jealousy in MO, 81
    Lust (carnal love)
        Tale of Lucrece, 63
        VC, 63
    Perjury, in Tale of Medea, 97
    Pride (and vainglory)
        MO, 15
        ST, 15
        Tale of Rosemund 14–16, 18–20, 31
    Sloth, slackness
        CA, Book IV, 100
        MO, 103
        Tale of Penelope, 35, 38–9
        Tale of Phyllis, 105
        Tale of Rosiphelee, 154n
            Lachescel procrastination
            Tale of Dido, 101
            Tale of Penelope, 36

Index

Sompnolence, in Amans, 45
Wantonness
   Tale of Dido, 103
   MO, 103, 112
Wrath, 27
   Tale of Thisbe, 21, 27
   Contek/contention
      CA, 29
      MED, 29–30
      MO, 29, 20
         Anger in Tale of Rosemund, 30
         Foolhaste in MO, 30
         Homicide in Tale of Thisbe, 30
Deianira
   Medea, 100
   MkT, 83n
   sources for Gower, 80
   Tale of, 80–85
   Wife of Hercules, 83–84
Delany, Sheila, xviiin, 20n, 23n, 34n, 36n, 52n, 53n, 67n, 71n, 72n, 100n
Demephon
   scoundrel, 107
   schemer, 107
   Theseus' son, 107, 107n
   Tale of Phyllis, 105–113
Desmond, Marilynn, xviiin, 77, 77n, 101n, 103n
Despair
   Black Knight, 104n
   Tale of Ariadne, 118
   Tale of Phyllis, 110–12, 112n
Dido
   chaste or insatiable, 100, 100n, 103n
   Ovid, 100n, 104n, 121n
   Saint Jerome, 71, 71n, 100
   Sychaeus, 71n, 100n
   sources for Gower, 100
   Tale of Dido, 100–105
   Virgil, 102,103n,104n
Dinshaw, Carolyn, xviiin
Disguise, 23–24, 28
Donaldson, Ian, 65n
Donne, John, 133n
Doob, Penelope Reed, 84n

Eberle, Patricia J., 156n
Echard, Sean and Clare Fanger, xixn, 119n, 125n
Economou, George D., 3n, 6n, 7n, 11n, 129n, 130n
Edward III, 52–54, 52n, 74n
Enchantment, 108, 108n
Esch, Arno, xviiin, 13n, 15n, 16n, 17n, 28n, 157n
Euripides, 52n, 86n, 113n

Faithless/deceiptful lovers or heros, 78, 91n (see Forsaken Women's Tales)
Female masculinity
   Alceone, 50
   Alcestis, 55
   Penelope, 40
   Lucrece, 62, 69
   Medea, 88
   Rosemund, 18
   Thisbe, 28, 28n
Feminine beauty in Gower, 13, 13n, 37, 61–2, 61n, 106
Fisher, John, xviiin, 11n, 156n, 157n, 159n
Forsaken Women, 78 (and see Chapter 3)
Fortune and her Wheel, 18, 18n, 50n
Four Wives, xviiin, 6, 8n, 53n, 86 (*and see* Chapter 2)
Frank, Robert Worth Jr., xviiin
Frazer, James G., 58n

Gaston, John B., 45n
Gawain Poet, 106n
Genius, 3, 11, 115n, 129–130, 129n, 150n
Godfrey of Vitterbo, 12–13, 13n, 16n
Gravdal, Kathryn, xixn, 58n, 72n
Green, Richard Firth, 91n, 101n, 104n
Grinnell, Natalie, 87n, 91n
Guido delle Colonne, 36, 86n, 91n, 97n

Hanrahan, Michael, xixn
Hansen, Elaine Tuttle, 70n
Harbert, Bruce, xviiin, 22n, 24n, 25n, 88n
Heffernan, Carol Falvo, xixn, 125n, 131n, 135n, 140n, 145n, 150n
Hercules
   Cross-dressing, 83n

Jason, 91, 91n, 97n
  Tale of Deianira, 80–85
  Traitié, 84
Hereos, 135, 135n
Hillman, Richard, 64n, 72n
Honeste love / truth in marriage in CA, 8, 158–59
  definition, 151
  Marriage Tales of the Four Wives, 78–9, 118 (see individual tales)
  Tale of Alceone, 50–52
  Tale of Alcestis 53, 57
  Tale of Lucrece, 60, 72–73
  Tale of Penelope, 35
Hornsby, Joseph Allen, 91n, 115n
Hotchkiss, Valerie R., 28n, 40n, 69n
Hugh of Saint Victor, 3n
Hussey, S. S., 66n

Idleness in RR, 8
Imperial destiny, 101–103, 108–109, 121
Infidelity / adultery, 41, 42, 69, 70–71, 75n, 85, 95–96, 157, 157n (see individual Forsaken Women tales and Tale of Penelope)
  MO, 42, 69, 157
Innes, Mary M., 46n
Intimacy / intimate moments, 47, 55, 66–68, 74n, 73–74, 92–93
Irony, and lack of in CA, 71
Irrational behavior (intolerance for) in Gower, 29, 121
Isbell, Harold, 84n, 97n

Jacobson, Howard, 100n
Jacquet, Danielle, and Claude Thomasett, xixn, 127n, 141n
Jason
  Creusa, 113n
  Hercules, 91n, 97n
  scoundrel, 95
  Tale of Medea, 85–100
Jerome, Saint, 12, 71n
John Gower Society, and Kalamazoo, xixn, 50n, 62n
Jupiter, 138–139

Kelly, Henry Ansgar, 83n, 115n, 119n
Kiser, Lisa, xviiin, 20n, 21n, 25n, 70n

Kolve, V. A., 91n

LeClercq, Jean, 155n
Lewis, C. S., 62n
Lord, Mary Louise, xviiin, 100n
Love
  blind in VC, 125–126
  entering through the eyes, 62, 87, 126–127
  forbidden, 22
  incurable sickness, 127–128
  power of, 43–44, 54
  reckless, 21, 42n, 159
Lovedrunke, 45n, 138n
Lovesickness, 123–152
  cures
    conversation, 145–146
    sexual intercourse, 140–141
    travel, 143–144
    wine drinking, 142–143
  death, 134
  definition, 124–125
  despair, 104n, 140
  leisure, in RA, 135
  nobles, 135
  reason, and loss of, 11n, 138, 144–145, 151
  solitude, 136
  madness, 84, 84n, 133
  thirst, 138–139
  MO, 112
  Sompnolence / sleeplessness, 45, 62, 88, 109–110, 130–133,
Lowes, John Livingston, 135, 135n
Lucrece
  Augustine, Saint, 70
  beauty, 61–62, 61n
  Chaucer, 47n, 60, 65, 70
  guiltless, innocent, 65, 71
  Jerome, Saint, 71
  lack of anti-feminist tone in CA, 57
  loss of reason, 62, 63, 70
  RR, 58, 71
  rape, 62–73
  suicide (and seeking an honorable death), 104n
  sources for Gower, 58, 58n
  Tale of, 57–73
Luscombe, D. E., 4n

Index

Lydgate, John, 58n

Macaulay, G. C., xviiin, xviiin, 13n, 21n, 52n, 85n, 139n, 148n, 149n, 157n
Maînzer, Conrad, xviiin, 20n, 54n, 86n, 106n, 111n, 113n
Magic, 92–96
Mann, Jill, 18n, 28, 28n
Marriage, 6, 8n, 34, 46, 61, 74, 154, 154n
   Tale of Medea, 91–92, 96
   Traitié, 74–75, 77–78, 117
Marriage ceremony, 91n
   fourteenth century canon law, 91n
   legal bond, 91n, 96, 155, 155n
   medieval England, 154, 154n, 156
   secretive, clandestine, 115, 115n, 155n
   troth-pledging, 91n
   witness, 91, 91n
Matrimony
MO, 35, 46
Matthew of Vendôme, xviiin, 21, 21n, 27n
Mast, Isabelle, xixn, 71n, 72n
Medea
   Alcestis, 100
   Chaucer, 89–90, 90n
   devoted to Jason, 56n
   Deianira, 100
   Guido (as educated woman in), 86, 90
   Gower's unusual depiction of, 85, 90
   infanticide, 96–97, 99
   maid, 91, 91n
   Ovid, 90
   powerful woman and sorceress, 94
   sources for Gower, 86, 86n
   Tale of, 85–100
   Traitié, 98
Meek, Mary Elizabeth, 86n
Metamorphosis, 28n, 45, 50, 111
Mirror, 144, 144n, 150n
Misogyny, 46, 77, 77n, 84, 98
Minerva, 54, 54n
Minnis, A. J., xviiin, xixn, 27n, 34n, 35n, 36n, 38n, 42n, 47n, 64n, 67n, 71n, 87n, 91n, 106n, 107n, 113n, 129n
Moderation, and love, 134
Morpheus, God of Sleep, 48–49, 131, 131n
Morse, Ruth, xviiin, 86n, 93n, 97, 97n, 98n, 100n

Murder, 96–97, 99
McCarthy, Conor, 154n, 155n
McGlynn, Margaret and Richard J. Moll, 141n, 148n
McMillan, Ann, xviiin, 37, 37n, 70n

Nature, 3–4, 8, 31 (see Chapter 1)
Nicholson, Peter, xixn, 52n, 129n

Olsson, Kurt, xixn, 12n, 15n, 34n, 53n, 108n, 148n, 158n
Orr, Patricia, 72, 72n
Overbeck, Pat Trefzger, 70n
Ovid (see individual tales), 20, 21, 21n, 24n, 28, 28n, 34, 34n, 42n, 52n, 54n, 58n, 84n, 147n

Passion, 7
   excessive passion, 29, 83–84, 86, 105, 111–112, 114–115, 119
   sexual passion, 27, 155, 155n (see Chapter 2 and Tale of Medea)
   mutual passion, 17, 33, 35, 37, 43–46, 43n, 51, 85, 91–93, 153–154
   (see *Honeste* love)
Paston, Margaret, 37n
Patch, Howard R. 18n
Paul, Saint, 4
Pearsall, Derek, xixn, 45n, 62n, 64n, 65n, 71n
Peck, Russell A., xviiin, xixn, 74n, 85n, 87n, 92n, 130n, 146n, 147n
Penelope
   Chaucer, 36n, 47n
   Heroides, 39, 121n
   independent woman, 39
   Jerome, Saint, 71
   RR, 58
   Tale of, 35–44
   voice of, 37
   woman running household, 47n
Philomela, 74
Phyllis
   beautiful, 106
   Chaucer, 107, 109, 110n
   Ovid, 109, 100n
   sources for Gower, 106
   suicide, 103–105, 104n, 112n
   Tale of Dido, 112–113

Tale of, 105–113
use of voice, 110
Poisoned clothing, 83, 87, 87n
Power, Eileen, 72, 72n
Progne, 157n

Rape, 62–73, 64n,
   bestial imagery, 64–65
   Chaucer, 71, 71n
   fourteenth century England, 71, 72, 96n-104n
Reason, 3, 8, 12, 26–27, 29–30, 38, 44, 93, 99, 105, 119–122, 151, 154
Revenge, 17, 97–98
Richard II, 38n, 158–159, 158n
Ricks, Christopher, xixn, 16, 16n
Robbins, Harry, 7n
Robbins, Rossell Hope, 125n
Rosemund
   beauty, 62n
   revenge, 17
   sources for Gower, 12–13
   Tale of, 12–20
   Traitié, 19
Rowe, Donald W. 8n, 10n
Runacres, Charles, xviiin, xixn, 24n
Rytting, Jenny Rebecca, 11n, 14n, 17n, 61n

Schmitz, Gotz, xviiin, xixn, 57n, 63n, 66n, 68n, 70n, 71n, 72n, 100, 100n, 101n, 121n, 150n
Schueler, Donald, 129n, 130n, 147n
Schutz, Andrea, 144n, 150n
Shakespeare, William, 58n, 71n, 72n
Sheridan, James J., 3n–6n
Silence, private thoughts, in Gower, 16, 16n, 42, 42n, 54n
Simpson, James, 129n, 130n, 137n, 146n, 147n, 153n
Slander/Talebearer, 80–81
Speech acts, speaking through actions, 39, 41, 50, 50n, 61, 65, 62n, 69, 74n, 88 104, 117, 156–157
Stanford, W. B., 41n, 44n
Stillwell, Gardiner, 52n
Stockton, Eric, xviiin
Suicide, 68, 70, 104n

Tale of Dido, 100, 100n, 103–104, 104n
Tale of Lucrece, 67–68, 104n
Tale of Phyllis, 104n, 111–113
Tale of Thisbe, 21n, 25
Sylvester, Louise, 59n, 63n

Theseus
   father to Demephon, 107n
   fiend, 118
   scoundrel, 118
Thisbe
   Chaucer, 23n–26n, 28n
   DP, 23
   Ovid, 20–23
   sources for Gower, 21, 21n
   Tale of, 20–35
Thomas, Ian and Louis Perraud, xviiin, 21n, 27n
Thomas Aquinas, Saint, 4, 4n, 15, 156, 156n
Transgressing gender roles, 62, 156–157
   men as women, 67
   Tale of Alceone, 49–50
   Tale of Alcestis, 55, 62
   Tale of Lucrece, 62, 68–69
   Tale of Medea, 97–98
   Tale of Penelope, 40
   Tale of Thisbe, 28, 28n
Troilus
   blasphemy and Cupid, 131–132
   Criseyde as lovesickness remedy, 141n
   lovesick, 125n, 131n, 134

Unkynde behavior, 20

Virgin Mary, 57, 57n
Virtues, 17, 92, 112, 116
Venus, 5, 18n, 128–129, 158n

Wack, Mary Francis, xixn, 124, 124n, 125n, 126n, 127n, 133n, 134n, 135n, 140n, 141n, 142n, 143n
Watt, Diane, 83n
Wetherbee, Winthrop, xviin, xviiin, 3n, 4n, 7n, 11n, 129n, 130n, 157n
White, Hugh, xixn, 31n
Wife, 28, 28n, 34n, 37, 51, 54–57, 54n, 59n, 60–61, 64, 73, 77, 83–84, 86,

Index

87, 92, 113
Wilson, William Burton, xviiin, 52
Women
  bad, and Medea, 86n
  Gower's treatment of
    CA, 18, 34, 53–54, 56, 79, 108–109, 153, 155–156,
    lack of anti-feminist tone, 121, 121n
    MO, 77
    sympathy towards, 121–122
      (and throughout individual tales)
    Tale of Lucrece, 57–58
    VC, 56–58
  insatiable, 77n
  revenge, 17, 97–98, 157n (*see* Tale of Deianira, Tale of Medea, Tale of Philomela)

Yeager, R. F., xviiin, xixn, 13n, 14n 16n, 17n, 18n, 42, 43n, 86n, 91n, 96n, 138n, 158n, 159n

For Product Safety Concerns and Information please contact our EU representative GPSR@taylorandfrancis.com
Taylor & Francis Verlag GmbH, Kaufingerstraße 24, 80331 München, Germany

www.ingramcontent.com/pod-product-compliance
Lightning Source LLC
Chambersburg PA
CBHW070606300426
44113CB00010B/1421